"The ant sets an example to us all, but it is not a good one."

— MAX BEERBOHM

Antæus is published semiannually by The Ecco Press, 18 West 30th Street,
New York, N.Y. 10001
Distributed to bookstores in the United States by
W. W. Norton & Company, Inc., 500 Fifth Avenue, New York, N.Y. 10110
Distributed to newsstands in the United States by
B. DeBoer, Inc., 113 East Centre St., Nutley, New Jersey 07110
Distributed in England & Europe by
W. W. Norton & Company, Inc.

Contributions and Communications: Antæus
American address: 18 West 30th Street, New York, N.Y. 10001
European address: 42A Hay's Mews, London, W. 1, England
Four-issue Subscriptions: $20.00 Back issues available.
Second-Class Postage paid at New York, N.Y.,
and at additional mailing offices.

ISSN 0003-5319
Printed by Wickersham Printing Co., Inc.
ISBN 0-88001-080-0
Library of Congress Number: 70-612646
Copyright © 1985 by Antæus, *New York, N.Y.*

Publication of this magazine has been made possible in part by grants from the
National Endowment for the Arts
Logo: Ahmed Yacoubi / Cover drawing: DANCING FIGURE, Auguste Rodin
National Gallery of Art, Washington
Gift of Mrs. John W. Simpson

Antæus

EDITED BY

DANIEL HALPERN

TANGIER / LONDON / NEW YORK

NO. 55, AUTUMN, 1985

CONTENTS

FICTION

POETRY

ESSAY

DOCUMENTS

Effective April 15, 1985, *Antæus'* subscription rates are $20.00
for four issues (two years); eight issues will run $37.00; and a
twelve-issue subscription will be $53.00. *Antæus* subscribers
will continue to be entitled to a 20% discount on all Ecco
Press books. (Please write for the current catalogue.)

Paul Bowles

Autobiography

ONE

I think that my father would have preferred not to have been burdened with a child. Quite possibly my coming into existence was the result of an accident. He was nervous and hypochondriacal, having become a dentist only after his goal of a career as violinist had been thwarted by his parents. He was easily upset, as I learned very early; he did not let it be seen that anything ever pleased him. At the beginning of his dental practice he met my mother, who was teaching a subject called Domestic Science at a training school for student teachers. They married, and I was born three years later.

The material of a piece of autobiographical writing ought to be restricted to that which the author remembers; everything else is hearsay. The documents state that I was born on December thirtieth, 1910. My first shadowy memories date probably from 1913. I learned to read and print from a set of wooden blocks carved with the letters of the alphabet. There was nothing else to do, since I was shut in all day with my mother. I had an extraordinarily uneventful early childhood; only my imagination made it bearable, substituting fantasy for reality. Being entered in school changed the elements of reality, if not those of fantasy.

This enforced isolation resulted in a total ignorance of the nature of children. I thought of myself as a small adult, and assumed that other children were like me, and that the inevitable concomitant of childhood was being obliged to sit motionless and silent in the presence of adults until given specific permission to move or speak. Therefore one never ran or made a noise. In school I discovered with amazement that children were neither silent nor motionless. Their world was chaotic, insane, without any relationship to the true — that is, the adult — world. The irrationality and violence of children have never ceased to fascinate and disturb me. (The same qualities evinced in the behavior of grown people, while far more reprehensible, are somehow less striking, because adults generally feel called upon to offer excuses for their behavior.)

As I grew, it became clear to me that happiness, which was made up of freedom, adventure and mystery, was to be found only in the country, where I was surrounded by inexplicable natural forces. True, I never spent a winter on a farm or in a cabin; my impressions were formed during the summers, when katydids and owls called outside the window. Each year the months of July and August brought forth the supreme pleasure of going to stay with my grandparents at a place called The Boat House, which was built into a cliff on Seneca Lake. Here there were motorboat rides and picnics, and I was allowed to go by myself in a rowboat to fetch the mail.

Labor Day put an end to the magic of summer. Not only did I have to begin studying again, I also went twice a week for music lessons. These consisted of theory, solfeggio and ear-training. This schedule continued for ten years, as did weekly visits to an orthodontist who was attempting to broaden my jaw. Living through those years seemed to take an endless length of time. In retrospect I can see that this was because there were so few diversions; everything had to do with reading and writing. The radio had not yet appeared, and although we had a phonograph for which I bought one record each week, I was not allowed to play the instrument if my father was in the house. It would be impossible to pretend that the years spent going to school were anything more than profoundly boring. I took the monotony for granted; discipline was the purpose of education. From 1917 through 1927 when I finished high school, relaxation meant writing what I wanted to write. When I sat in my room working, I could impose my own discipline on a fictitious cosmos. In the seventh grade I wrote (and read to the students) a chapter each day in an endless murder mystery. This was not a captive audience; the readings took place after class had been dismissed.

As soon as I got into high school I began to buy books. I would find them remaindered at lending libraries, generally for less than a dollar. Knowing nothing about literature, I bought the books whose bindings and typography I thought the most attractive, and these were published by Knopf. (Borzoi books were exceptionally handsome in the twenties.) This meant that I read more British novels and translations than I did works by American writers. Indeed, when I was thirteen and fourteen my favorite writers were Francis Brett Young, Arthur Machen and Walter de la Mare. A year later I moved on to Mann and Gide. The point is that they were all published by Knopf. Surely if the Knopf list of authors had been different from what it was, my tastes would have varied correspondingly.

High school was more enjoyable than grammar school. There was a monthly magazine in which I published continuously: stories, poems, book reviews and even a department called "Humor," which I edited. And then I headed a school literary society which met every Friday night; there were as many girls as there were boys. When they met at my house and my father came into the room for a minute, he would greet us by saying: "Good evening, kidlets." I found this embarrassing, and imagined the others saying afterward: "What'd he call us?"

My four grandparents, each one born in a different New England state, had one characteristic in common: while they considered religion a good thing for those who needed it, personally they kept themselves clear of it. Thus I was spared all religious instruction. I understood that God was a mythical figure, and that some people chose to believe that it was a person who actually existed. Agnosticism may be deplorable, but it seems to me that anything is preferable to new, synthetic religions, or to attempts to revive failing orthodoxies. I must confess that as a child, although I kept quiet about it ("It's not nice to hurt people's feelings"), I felt superior to anyone who thought that God was alive and lived in the sky.

My pleasantest memories of high school are of the small office I was allowed to use, ostensibly for the typing up of material for the school magazine, but which I used as well each day for writing my own verse. My discovery of the Paris review *transition* in 1927 altered my style and increased my output, and the publication of a long poem in *transition 12* left me in a state of euphoria: I had reached what I considered the summit of distinction.

After high school I enrolled at the School of Design and Liberal Arts, where I learned that I had no talent for painting. That autumn I started my freshman year at the University of Virginia. Now in retrospect I have the impression that it was at this point when existence began to move and gather impetus. There in Charlottesville I discovered that life could be a consistently pleasant experience once one was free from parental discipline. I developed an appetite, ate what I pleased, put on weight, and was suddenly persuaded that the future consisted of infinite possibilities. I had the unaccustomed sensation of taking part in living, which might sound absurd to someone who has not suffered from excessive restraint during childhood and adolescence. The future suddenly seemed close enough to touch, and I lost my head, and tossed a coin to see whether I should take an overdose of sleeping pills or set out for Paris. (I doubt now that I should have taken the pills even if the coin had fallen the other side up.)

I sent a telegram to a woman in New York who I thought would be willing to perjure herself to get me a passport. She agreed to swear to the authorities that she was my guardian (although my parents were not a mile distant). This woman was a follower of Gurdjieff, with whom the Bowles family was on terms of permanent enmity; thus I knew that any action on her part would be motivated not by the desire to help me, but rather by the wish to vex my family. I got my illegally obtained passport and went confidently off to Paris with twenty-five dollars in my pocket. But along with the passport the woman had given me several letters of introduction, and through one of these I found work at the rue du Louvre office of the *Herald-Tribune*. Subsequently her daughter, who was amused by the members of my family and held no animus against them, suddenly gave me what seemed to me an enormous sum of money so that I could travel for a while around Europe.

I went down to the Côte d'Azur and made walking tours in Switzerland and in the Black Forest. In Paris I was taken to dinner at Tristan Tzara's; he was the only literary celebrity I met in Europe that year. I did not have the courage to present myself at the office of *transition*, much as I wanted to. Before returning to New York (which I knew was inevitable but which I tried to put off as long as I could) I was taken by a friend of my father's to Saint Moritz.

After recriminations, my father told me that I should work in New York as I had done in Paris. I found a job at Dutton's bookshop. It may have lasted two months. In the meantime I had met Aaron Copland. (I had been to some of the Copland-Sessions concerts.)

It was Copland's encouragement which made me decide to become a composer. To my parents I suggested that I return to Virginia and finish out my freshman year there. The spring term was a pleasure.

During the autumn and winter I studied with Copland. When February came and he prepared to leave for Berlin, I saw that if my returning to Europe were presented as a means of continuing my studies with him, my parents would not oppose my going. There were reminders that I would not be "of age" until the following year, but I managed to take a freighter to Le Havre.

TWO

In Paris this time I was less shy. I presented myself to Gertrude Stein at 27 rue de Fleurus, and was welcomed. Thus when Copland arrived in Paris, I was able to introduce them to one another. Both Stein and Toklas liked him, and they invited us both to visit them at Bilignin the coming summer.

I did not feel at home in Berlin. I smelled chaos beneath the ordered surface of things. Everything seemed excessive: the display of wealth in the West End and the nightmarish poverty of the East End. There were little swastika stickers decorating walls and lamp posts, but no one paid them any attention.

In July I went to visit Gertrude Stein at Bilignin in the country. After ten days Copland arrived from England. Somewhat later he and I set out, not for Villefranche, where we had been bound, but for Tangier, because Stein and Toklas recommended it. As a result of this arbitrary action my life was permanently altered. If Morocco had been then as it is now, I should have spent the summer and gone away, probably not to return. But Morocco in 1931 provided an inexhaustible succession of fantastic spectacles. The richness and diversity of the scenes were overwhelming; I had the feeling that no amount of time spent studying the phenomenon would suffice to provide the key to understanding it. (Westermarck's *Ritual and Belief in Morocco* had been published in 1926, but I did not hear of it until much later.)

At the end of summer Copland returned to Berlin and I moved around Morocco until Christmas time, when I went to London to hear a performance of the piece I had been writing in Tangier. By March I was back in Morocco. This time I went down the coast to Agadir, a jerry-built town which the French were just beginning to construct. (The city was entirely destroyed by earthquake thirty years later.) Sanitation was nonexistent and I contracted typhoid, not diagnosed as such until I got back to Paris. A month in the American Hospital there got me over the fever, and I went down to a place near Grenoble to recuperate. My mother joined me to see for herself the state of my health. We went to Mallorca and ended the summer in Monte Carlo.

When I was alone once more I took a ship across to Algiers and traveled south to the M'Zab, where I found a house in the desert just outside Ghardaia. I furnished it with mats and rugs and the barest kitchen necessities, but I was a neophyte in practical matters. It was an experiment which did not work. I spent the rest of the cold season (it freezes at night) at a hotel in Laghouat. Nearby was the chapel of the White Fathers, who kindly gave me permission to use the organ. Working conditions were ideal, the food at the hotel was excellent, and I wrote a cantata, *Par le Detroit*. The text, in French, I had written earlier.

I returned later to Ghardaia, although not to stay in my house out in the *reg*. At the hotel, which was operated for the drivers of the produce trucks that came through, I met an American who was taking a year off from his courses at Northwestern in order to travel. He did not write or paint or photograph; he merely wanted to see the world. Together we took a trip by camel across the northern tip of the Grand Erg Oriental, out of Algeria into southern Tunisia. The camels had no saddles; we sat on the cartons that contained our food and water, their tops covered over with blankets. The motion of the camel's gait became well-nigh unendurable after a few hours. I found it better to walk most of the time, and mounted my beast only when I could no longer go on trudging through the sand. Nights we slept at bordjes established by the French military at roughly a day's journey apart. A bordj was a large courtyard enclosed by a high wall with stalls along its sides. In one of these open cubicles you were given a hot meal, and you could sleep on the sand, rolled in your blankets, with your camels and your driver in the courtyard in front of you.

The American and I arrived in Tunis the week that Franklin Roosevelt closed the banks. We had next to no francs and no one would accept American Express checks, so we spent what few francs remained sending urgent messages to friends in Europe. The college student went on to Italy; I was wired enough francs to pay for a railway ticket to Algiers, where I'd left a great amount of luggage. I collected it all, and being able by that time to cash some checks, set out for Morocco.

That summer I was obliged to return to the United States. I never had enough money at my disposal, and I had exhausted the small legacy left me by an aunt. There was nothing for it but to go to New York. I discovered a roundabout way of going, however, which removed some of the sting. From Cadiz I took a ship to San Juan in Puerto Rico and went up into the hills for a while before boarding another ship for New York.

During the following winter, through friends in the A.S.P.C.A., I managed to get what seemed to me a very desirable job, working for the American Fondouk of Fez. This meant that when summer arrived I went once again to Morocco and took up residence in Fez, typing correspondence and writing anti-bullfight propaganda for a Casablanca newspaper. It was understood that my services would be required for only three months, after which I would be free. At that point I decided to take a peek at South America; I took passage to Barranquilla. I came down with a fever which left me only after I'd spent a week in the relative coolness of a coffee plantation in the mountains.

When I got back to New York several months later, my father asked me why I moved around so much. What was I looking for? Nothing, I said, unless it was an opportunity to observe the differences between one place and another. "This, that, and the other thing," he fumed. "What's it all supposed to be leading to?" But I noticed that when I was earning my living his complaints were more restrained. I discovered, too, that he was considerably mollified by my having spent a month with his brother in Hollywood and another month with a cousin of his in San Francisco on my way up the Pacific coast from South America.

Eugene Berman, the Russian painter, whom I had known in Paris, was now in New York, and he had an idea for a ballet. I had written about a third of the score before we both discovered that we had lost interest in the argument of the ballet. At the same time Lincoln Kirstein commissioned a different ballet score from me, to be produced by the Ballet Theatre. This was *Yankee Clipper*; it was first presented in Robin Hood Dell with the Philadelphia Orchestra.

Now, Virgil Thomson, who always had given me sound musical advice when I showed him my work in Paris, suggested that I write a score for the Federal Theatre. It would contain an enormous amount of music, and the score had to be ready in two months. Parts of the abandoned material for the Berman ballet came in handy, and Thomson not only helped me orchestrate much of the music, but taught me exactly how a theatre score should be conceived and correlated with the cue-sheet, and also how to have the necessary patience during the weeks of rehearsal, something I found difficult. The play was an adaptation by Orson Welles and Edwin Denby of Labiche's *Un Chapeau de Paille d'Italie*, whose title became *Horse Eats Hat*. This was one of the great services performed for me by Virgil Thomson: I became a composer of theatre music and made my living at it for the next two decades. The same season I wrote another score for Welles: Marlowe's *Doctor Faustus*.

The first time I had gone to Tangier I had met the Dutch Surrealist painter Kristians Tonny; Gertrude Stein had mentioned his presence there. Now he arrived in New York with his wife, Marie Claire, and wanted to go to Mexico. I had never been there and was curious about the country, so we decided to go together. At that point a girl named Jane Auer, whom I had only recently met, announced her desire to accompany us. This seemed like a good idea, but it wasn't, as Jane flew back to the States after three days in Mexico City. The remaining three of us traveled around Mexico, going down to Chiapas, and finally to Guatemala. After four months I went back to New York, determined to pay another, longer visit to those parts at a later date.

What happened next was that I began to see a good deal of Jane Auer, and the following winter we were married. I had not expected to see Latin America again quite so soon, but we took a Japanese ship to Panama, and later went on to a ranch in Costa Rica, and eventually to Guatemala. Then we thought it would be good to be back in Europe, which Jane liked as much as I. We went to Paris. Later we rented a house on the Côte d'Azur, but stayed in it only a month or so. A cable arrived from John Houseman, who with Orson Welles had founded the Mercury Theatre, asking me to return to New York to write a score. Jane and I had a stupendous amount of luggage with us, including two wardrobe trunks, but we got it all aboard the *Europa* and headed for New York.

At the Hotel Chelsea I had no piano, and I needed one. The architect Kiesler provided me with a key to his flat; he and his wife were away in the country. After finishing the score and extracting the parts, I took it to Houseman, who sadly informed me that Welles had decided to produce a different play. This was very bad news, as it meant that I would get no down payment and no royalties. And I had no money. Fortunately the government was distributing large quantities of edibles free of charge. Each week Jane and I carried home great sacks of food. When my father learned of it he was incensed. "Good Americans are paying their taxes so that a lot of parasites like you can live without working. And you don't see anything wrong with accepting that food. What's happened to America's moral sense?"

It's true that I saw nothing unethical about carrying home the food. I was only glad that this period of official largesse happened to coincide with my lean season. Being more or less in the milieu and having numerous acquaintances who were members of the Communist Party, I made up my mind to join. I had always found the idea of adhering officially to any kind of organization repugnant, but the Party at that time seemed strong enough to make trouble. I thought it would be interesting to see from the inside. I stayed long enough to see that it wasn't, and that the only trouble it made was for those who had been ingenuous enough to join it using their true names.

I had been in touch with William Saroyan, whose play *My Heart's in the Highlands* was to be produced by the Group Theatre. He came from California and I agreed to write the score. This time I had the keys to Clifford Odets's apartment, where there was a Hammond organ. When the play had opened, Jane and I went out to a remote section of Staten Island and lived in an old farmhouse. I had joined the Federal Music Project as composer, and delivered a batch of music once a week to headquarters in Manhattan. This came to an abrupt end when a Relief investigator paid a visit to my parents' house, and pronounced me "Not in Present Need."

On Staten Island Jane was drinking too much because the generous girl who had given me money ten years before in Paris so I could travel had arrived from England to stay with us. Life became insupportable, and I took a room in Brooklyn Heights overlooking the harbor. I had no piano and wrote no music, but I did write the first short story of my adult years, "Tea on the Mountain." It was not immediately followed by others.

In the winter Jane and I were back at the Chelsea. The Theatre Guild asked me to provide music for Saroyan's *Love's Old Sweet Song*. Then the U.S. Department of Agriculture suggested that I go to New Mexico and write a score for a documentary film on the Rio Grande Valley. When that was done, the natural move seemed to be for us to go down from Albuquerque to El Paso and across the border. There was trouble brewing between the rival candidates in the coming election for the Mexican presidency, and I was in a hurry to get down there before events occurred which might hold us up on the way. The shooting began only two days after our arrival in Mexico City. When the atmosphere had cleared and General Almazan's threatened march from the Pacific had failed to materialize, we found a finca high up in the mountains above Mexico City, across the valley from the Volcano of Toluca, and settled into it as well as we could.

I soon found that the prolonged sojourn at eleven thousand feet disagreed violently with the functioning of my liver. We went down to Acapulco and stayed there for two months. The town was fairly empty in 1940, and Jane wanted to be where there were people. She decided we must move to Taxco, an arty town full of Americans. Before we did, a young man called at our door introducing himself as Tennessee Williams and presenting a letter from the Theatre Guild. He left in a day or so, but I was impressed to hear that Miriam Hopkins was to play the lead in his play *Battle of Angels*. (I never saw the play, because it closed in Boston.)

Within two weeks I had to fly to New York to write music for Helen Hayes's *Twelfth Night*. (In those days I did not mind taking planes.) That winter I was kept busy. The Theatre Guild asked for an elaborate score for Philip Barry's *Liberty Jones,* Lincoln Kirstein commissioned a new ballet, *Pastorelas*, and Lillian Hellman needed some music for *Watch on the Rhine*.

Jane came from Mexico, and we moved into a strange house in Brooklyn Heights, a kind of artists' commune. The poet Auden managed it. Oliver Smith lived there, as did Benjamin Britten. Since all expenses were shared, living costs were very low. The food was good and I got a lot of work done. At that moment I received a Guggenheim Fellowship to write an opera.

Before leaving Taxco, Jane had taken a house. In the spring we went back there and furnished it. Katharine Hepburn's brother had written a play with songs, and wanted music. I finished that by summer, and we went down to Acapulco. This was a mistake, for I fell ill with jaundice and had to be taken to the British Hospital in Mexico City. Later I recuperated for six weeks in a Cuernavaca sanatorium. While I was there two things happened: Jane completed *Two Serious Ladies* and Pearl Harbor was attacked.

I worked hard on the Guggenheim project. Originally Saroyan was to be the librettist; he sent me his text, which I felt I could not possibly use. Then I decided to make a zarzuela out of García Lorca's *Así que Pasen Cinco Años*, using only sections of it. For a while I had a house in Tehuantepec, and then I went to Lake Chapala.

My grandmother had died, leaving me a modest bequest; my Aunt Mary also had died, leaving her house, Holden Hall, to my father. It was Jane's idea that we should spend the summer and autumn in Holden Hall. While I was still in Mexico, she and Helvetia Perkins, a friend we had known in Taxco, found a cook in New York and transported her to Watkins Glen, where they installed themselves and her at Holden Hall. It was the summer of 1942, and Americans seemed to be in the grip of war hysteria. There were frequent blackouts, and vigilantes wandered over the grounds with flashlights, crying: "Put out those lights!" (It's not easy to observe a complete blackout in a big house that has no electricity, and where the only person who can manage oil lamps is the cook, who has retired for the night.)

The following winter I completed the zarzuela. Leonard Bernstein conducted at the Museum of Modern Art in New York, with Merce Cunningham as solo dancer. In the meantime Virgil Thomson, then Music Editor of the *New York Herald-Tribune*, had come up with the suggestion that I join the staff of the newspaper as a music critic. It was a constructive step, inasmuch as it obliged me to remain in New York for the next several years and thus to lead a life which was largely musical.

At the outset I was dubious about my ability to function as musical reporter. I feared that the maximum of forty-five minutes was too little time in which to turn out a literate review. For a few weeks I suffered; then, like most things, it became merely a matter of habituation. During the years I worked on the paper I was continuously engaged in writing incidental music for Broadway plays. My only excursions outside New York occurred when I accompanied the shows on the road, and in the summers when I would fly to Latin America for a few weeks of vacation.

The Marquis de Cuevas was organizing a ballet company. He had the peculiar idea of commissioning Dali to devise a ballet using Verlaine's famous poem *Colloque Sentimental* as its subject. Then he had an equally peculiar idea of asking me to write the music. The prospect of collaboration with Dali attracted me. I should have realized, however, that the very concept of collaboration was anathema to him. He provided the set, the costumes, and the onstage devices which he seemed to have invented solely to interfere with the choreography. The dancers had underarm hair which reached to the floor and got in the way of their footwork; they also had to beware of bicyclists riding across the stage in both directions at inopportune moments. An additional hazard was provided by a large mechanical tortoise whose course was unpredictable. It circled, backed up, and ran straight at the dancers' feet, the lights in its shell flashing on and off. Hisses and catcalls were more or less constant on opening night; I was unable to hear the orchestra, and left the theatre in a bad mood. The marquis was pleased that the work had enjoyed a *succès de scandale*.

That year I wrote a score for a film produced by the Belgian government-in-exile; it was called *Congo*, and was meant as a justification of the Belgian presence in that part of Africa. I was surprised that Paul Robeson agreed to be the commentator. I expected him to refuse, considering his alignment with the Left. Perhaps, like me, he felt that a job is a job.

During these years while I was confined to New York I managed, in the middle of all the music I was writing, to slip quietly into writing words. Jean-Paul Sartre was in the United States. With Oliver Smith, who wanted to produce the play, we worked out an agreement whereby my translation of *Huis Clos* as *No Exit* should be the standard version for American performances in English.

After Sartre returned to Paris, our friendship was soured by the insistence of John Huston, who directed the play, upon altering its meaning here and there, in such a manner that its purely existential argument occasionally became a political one. I was not in a position to do more than voice my personal discontent. Sartre considered that I had betrayed him. Possibly in France a translator's opinion carries some weight.

I had not a single specific idea in my head with regard to writing fiction, nevertheless I yearned for the experience of losing myself in a fictional world at the moment of creating it. Back in 1942, when Jane and I had gone over the manuscript of *Two Serious Ladies* prior to its publication, I had felt a strong urge to write some fiction myself. I suspected, first of all, that I had nothing to write about; furthermore, I had a fear that I had lost the power to translate thought into words. The practice involved in turning out daily reviews for the newspaper, however, had given me more confidence in my ability to manage the language.

I had been doing translations from the French and Spanish for *View*, a Surrealist review published in New York; thus it was natural that *View* should have printed the first stories I wrote at that time. At the end of 1945 I resigned my post as a music critic. Since I was continuing to provide theatre scores, sometimes writing two simultaneously, I no longer had the time for reviewing. The stories kept coming, and they were published in fashion magazines. But the people who I hoped would see them rarely read *Mademoiselle* and *Harper's Bazaar*; they read *Partisan Review*. I considered it a triumph when *Partisan* published my tale "A Distant Episode."

I had enough stories to make up a volume. I put them together and took them to a publisher, hoping somehow to bypass the unwritten law which makes it impossible for a writer to publish a book of short stories until after he has published a novel. Of course I did not succeed, but the publisher sent my stories to an agent, who lost no time in getting Doubleday to commission a novel. Thanks to the extraordinary vividness of a dream, I realized that I wanted to return to Tangier. I left within a month after signing the contract with Doubleday. I had a vague idea of what I wanted to write about, but I was not at all sure that I was capable of constructing a novel.

THREE

On the Norwegian freighter taking me to Casablanca I wrote a fairly long tale, "Pages from Cold Point." (My sojourn in Jamaica the previous winter suggested the locale.) From then on I turned out no more stories until I had completed *The Sheltering Sky*.

In Fez, to the sound of the stream rushing by under my window, I began to write. I had no plan, made no notes. I intended to take three Americans across the Sahara, but the events had to appear of their own accord as I accompanied them from oasis to oasis. I went to Tangier and worked for several months. I also bought a little house at the top of the Medina. Then with my parrot I began a long voyage into the Algerian desert, traveling by produce truck. When I came to a place I liked I stayed a week or two, and then continued. The novel made progress. A letter from Jane was forwarded to me, saying that she was about to leave for Tangier. This meant that she was already there. I flew from Adrar to Bechar, and from there to Algiers, but it took me a long time to get to Tangier.

Jane was there, accompanied by a friend with her leg in a cast. This made things difficult, as I was in a hurry to get back to Fez and finish the novel. We did go, but the alleys of the Medina were muddy, and the friend was on crutches, so we spent most of our time inside the Palais Jamai. When the friend had returned to New York, we both got down to work. Jane finished *Camp Cataract* and I finished *The Sheltering Sky*, eight months after I had begun it. (Doubleday rejected it, asserting that it was not a novel. I had to return the advance they had given me.)

I went to New York and wrote a score for Tennessee Williams's *Summer and Smoke*. When the show had opened, Tennessee decided to accompany me to Tangier. It was a rainy winter, and he was busy much of the time trying to make out his federal income tax; I recall being appalled when I saw that he was having to pay $111,000 tax that year. "Baby, they take everything," he said.

Jane and I traveled around the Algerian Sahara after he had left; then I made a hurried trip to Paris to hear a performance of my Concerto for Two Pianos, Winds and Percussion. Truman Capote spent the summer in Tangier at the Farhar, where we lived; we did not lack entertainment at mealtimes.

John Lehmann had published *The Sheltering Sky* in London. Jane and I went there, she with the intention of spending the winter there and in Paris, and I with the project of continuing to anywhere in Asia, depending upon what transportation was available. Ceylon came up first, so I set out for Colombo. On the trip eastward I started a new novel and worked steadily at it as I traveled around Ceylon and South India. (The British had great fun with the place names of Ceylon, just as they did in India. First they changed the pronunciation, and then they changed the spelling. So Sri Lanka became Ceylon, Kurunagala became Kornegalle, Tiruchirappalli became Trichinopoly, and so on; the Sinhalese and Tamils responded by pronouncing Ceylon Sloan.)

I joined Jane in Paris in the late spring, and then, since she wanted to stay on there, I left her and met Libby Holman in Málaga for a month in Andalucía while we discussed a project for an opera using García Lorca's *Yerma* as text. (She had visited Morocco two years earlier, and I had already translated the play and written some of the music.) During all these years the pattern of my work life was rather like that of a periodic dipsomaniac: intense preoccupation with music for a few weeks or months, and then a shift into the world of words for a while.

I spent most of the winter in the Sahara, and in the spring drove up to the French border to pick up Jane. By now the little house in the Medina which I'd bought several years earlier had been made livable, so we moved into it for a while. But soon Jane had to go to the States for a production of her play.

As soon as I had finished *Let It Come Down*, the novel I had been at work on, I became curious to see more of India. A ship took me from Gibraltar to Bombay. I spent a few months going from place to place there, and went on down to Sri Lanka until the southwest monsoons arrived. In the summer I went to Italy: the Lago di Orta in the north for a month and then to visit Peggy Guggenheim in Venice. I was in Madrid when I received a wire from Sri Lanka telling me that I could buy a little island called Taprobane, off the southern coast of Ceylon, at an advantageous price. (I had already examined the place.) I wired the money to Colombo the same day.

Now I was forced to go to New York to write a score for Jane's play *In the Summer House*, about to be produced on Broadway. This constant moving around was not a hindrance to work, and in retrospect that rather surprises me. Travel took a great deal of time and energy, but it also stimulated my imagination. It never became monotonous, which any recounting of it must necessarily be. I was addicted to movement; freedom meant the freedom to travel. My life consists of the places where I have lived and the work I have accomplished in those places.

The duo-pianists Gold and Fizdale had commissioned me to write a cantata on a text of the poet James Schuyler. I returned to Tangier and composed the work. Then at Tennessee Williams's suggestion I went to Rome to work with Lucchino Visconti on a film called *Senso*. I was a neophyte. I scarcely knew what I was doing. Nevertheless I was well paid and shared screen credits with Tennessee.

I had to go to Istanbul at that point, to do an article for *Holiday*, a travel magazine to which I contributed with some regularity. When I got back to Rome, Tennessee said he thought he'd drive to Tangier, too, so we set off in two identical Jaguars, through Italy and France and Spain. It took us a long time: we traveled only during the afternoons. Tennessee would spend each morning in his hotel room writing.

Now that I had my island in Sri Lanka, I was in a hurry to go there. I managed to persuade Jane to come along and see it; she was not eager to leave Tangier. The experiment was not successful. After two months she insisted on going back to Morocco. In spite of Peggy Guggenheim, who came to visit and who bubbled with enthusiasm over the beauty of the place, Jane did not agree. I finished writing my novel *The Spider's House* and sent it off to the publisher. Then, because I did not want to get back to Tangier before the summer, I took a ship that went to places I'd never been: Penang, Singapore, Hong Kong, Kobe, the Inland Sea. There seemed to be people everywhere in Japan, but here this ubiquitous humanity did not give me the feeling of claustrophobia that I got in India.

Morocco was in the throes of its war for independence. As despised Nazarenes, Jane and I found the atmosphere of our strictly Moslem neighborhood suddenly unfriendly. Jane went to California to visit Oliver Smith, and I spent an entire year in Tangier (although not in the Medina house) working on the opera *Yerma*, which I had recently been neglecting in spite of Libby Holman's repeated pleas for a finished piano score. In the midst of my work my parents appeared for a six-week visit. At the same time Jane arrived with Tennessee Williams.

I knew I should never be able to entice Jane back to Sri Lanka. A man in Bombay had offered to buy the island, and I decided to sell it.

So, after sending Libby Holman her completed piano score, at the beginning of winter I set out on my last voyage to Taprobane. The Suez Canal was blocked; I had to go via South Africa.

I had several weeks of complex negotiations with the Ceylon Finance Control in Colombo before it was agreed that the rupees I should receive for the island could be converted into dollars and remitted to me after my departure. The Sinhalese did not keep their word. Twenty-six years have passed, and I have yet to see a penny of the proceeds.

Now I took a ship to Mombasa, to see the wild life in Kenya. Later I got a ship going via Zanzibar and Moçambique to Cape Town. Upon my arrival at Las Palmas I was handed a telegram from Tangier, stating that Jane had suffered a "slight stroke."

FOUR

The "slight stroke" had resulted in the definitive impairment of Jane's sight; her field of vision was now divided into four stripes; sight, darkness, sight, darkness. She suffered as well from acute aphasia, which people in Tangier found amusing, although it depressed and terrified her, for she felt that she was no longer in command of her brain. A series of visits to hospitals began; she had to go twice to London that summer.

Allen Ginsberg came to visit William Burroughs. Jane never forgave him for describing the effects of William Carlos Williams's stroke, and then suggesting that she learn braille.

When I went again to England to fetch Jane from the hospital in Nottingham, I came down with pneumonia and spent a month hospitalized in London. We returned to Tangier, where Jane seemed to be in slightly better health. This proved to be ephemeral, for when we got to Madeira in March she fell into a serious depression. She had never been an epileptic, but now pressure on the cortex of the brain was causing frequent seizures. We returned to Lisbon, where the American embassy refused to renew her expired passport after having communicated with the F.B.I. She was given a slip of paper and shipped to New York; Tennessee met her at the airport. Her mother was not to know that she was in the United States.

I was still in Portugal when Libby Holman telephoned saying I was needed immediately for *Yerma*, which she was about to produce. By that time I had the opera orchestrated, and was able to carry the score with me. Rehearsals already had started when I arrived. We tried it out for two weeks in Denver, and then in Ithaca, New York, and that was the end of it.

Shortly after getting back to New York I was summoned to Hollywood to write a score for José Ferrer. I had provided music several seasons earlier for his *Cyrano de Bergerac*, which enjoyed a great success. The new play, however, was a flop when it came in to New York.

I took Jane out of the hospital and we set sail for Tangier. We had scarcely arrived when I heard from Tennessee, who wanted me in New York the following month to set *Sweet Bird of Youth*. With the script before me, I composed most of the music before I left Tangier, finishing it up and orchestrating it in the ship's ballroom late each night. Kazan was rehearsing in Philadelphia; I went directly there. He persuaded me to have the music recorded, rather than having musicians playing backstage. I had always held out against this procedure, but I was pleasantly surprised by the results.

While I was in New York that season I received a Rockefeller Grant to record Moroccan music for the Library of Congress. This was something I had been hoping for many years to accomplish. Upon my arrival in Tangier, I found that Jane's condition had improved somewhat. Although she could not read or write, she seemed to be able to carry on with her social life, so I did not hesitate to leave her again. We kept in touch by telephone, and I visited Tangier every six or seven weeks. At the end of the year I deposited the tapes at the American embassy in Rabat, and they were sent to Washington. I was more than satisfied with the results of the taping sessions. Records were to be pressed, but because of the growing trouble in Southeast Asia, thirteen years went by before sufficient funds for this were made available.

The following year I remained in Morocco, making recording trips of my own into the Pre-Sahara and the Djebel Bani, regions I had not been able to visit on the Rockefeller field trips. I was obsessed by what I felt was the necessity of getting the folk music on tape while it was still extant. Visitors arrived in Tangier: Allen Ginsberg, Gregory Corso and Tennessee. Afternoons Allen, Gregory and Bill Burroughs could be found in the garden of Narayan and Sonya Kamalakar having nasturtium sandwiches and discussing the facets of mysticism; Tennessee and Jane spent their days at the beach. I generally stayed home, working.

It seemed to be about time for Jane and me to go to the States to see our respective parents, who were clamoring for a glimpse of us, so we went to New York. Jane never wanted to be with her mother for longer than was necessary, and since Tennessee needed an incidental score for *The Milk Train Doesn't Stop Here Any More*, I put her on a ship for Tangier, and wrote the music in Virgil Thomson's empty apartment. After the show had tried out on the road, I came home to Tangier.

Earlier I had been working on a translation from the Moghrebi of a novel spoken onto tape by Larbi Layachi. Being anxious about possible official reactions to the book, he used an assumed name. He called the novel *Al Aicha Medloula*, which I translated as *A Life Full of Holes*. This was the first of more than a dozen books I eventually translated from spoken texts. I took a six-months' lease on a house by the ocean in Asilah, where I could work in complete quiet. Jane came for weekends, but she preferred to live in her flat in Tangier.

I had started a novel, and I spent the next winter and summer writing it. Again I took a house for six months, this one on the Monte Viejo outside Tangier, at the edge of a cliff above the sea. Random House, the publishers of my previous four books, rejected it. I sold it to Simon and Schuster. It was my last attempt at writing a novel; I called it *Up Above the World*. Tennessee came again as I was finishing it; he was in a depressed state, and went away after two weeks or so.

With the novel out of the way, I was able to concentrate on writing short stories. This activity always provided a welcome relaxation after the rigors of writing a novel.

In the spring we went once more to America to see our parents. We did not remain there for more than two months. The time she had spent with her mother had made Jane extremely nervous, and the anguish she had experienced during the first two years after her initial stroke seemed to have started up again, even before we got back to Morocco. When Little, Brown suggested that I write a book on Cairo, I somewhat frivolously suggested Bangkok instead, certain that this would not meet with their approval. When they accepted, I realized that Jane was apprehensive about being left alone for the eight or nine months I should be away. I saw that given the state she was in it would be out of the question to go away leaving her in Tangier. She wanted to go to Bangkok with me, but I remembered the fiasco in the heat of Ceylon, and refused even to consider it. In the end it was agreed that she would stay with friends in New York, making visits to her mother, who now lived in Miami. I took her to New York and continued to Bangkok.

Thailand was not at all as I'd expected it to be; I was sorry I had suggested writing about Bangkok. Jane's regular letters stopped arriving. Then letters from friends in Tangier informed me that she had left the States and returned alone to Tangier, which was the very thing I had not wanted. I had been working only about four months when I received word from Dr. Roux saying that Jane was ill and advising me to return to Tangier.

I found Jane in a state of apathy. The doctors recommended hospitalization. I took her to Spain, where she spent several months. The routine of hospital life, plus the proper medication there, helped her considerably, so that she was in a different state when I brought her back to Tangier. Soon I was offered a teaching stint in California. Once again there arose the question of how Jane could be cared for in my absence. She had four Moroccans and a Spanish woman looking after her, but none of these could be relied upon to see that she got the correct dosages of her various medicines. This could be done only in a hospital, said Dr. Roux. It was arranged that she would go into a different hospital in Málaga where she would be free to come and go, and that her mother and stepfather would come and spend two months in a hotel there, so that they could be together each day. (Jane did not seem to mind being with her mother as long as they were not living in the same house together.)

I spent only one semester teaching in California, and returned to Morocco. When I saw Jane she begged to be taken back home to Tangier. Dr. Roux warned me not to remove her from the hospital, but in the end I found it impossible to refuse her pleas. I took her to Tangier; it was not the right thing to have done. Very quickly she fell into a profound depression, and since she refused to eat, she became alarmingly thin and feeble. After four months I returned her to the hospital in Málaga; after that she never came back to Tangier.

During the latter years of Jane's illness I had discovered that it was impossible for me to write fiction. The periods which I had to myself were of very short duration: fifteen or twenty minutes, instead of several hours. Frequent interruptions destroyed inventive impetus. Still, I had to work each day at something, and luckily I found that the act of translating did not suffer in any way from being stopped at short intervals. I translated several books by Mohammed Mrabet in those years, and went on to find other Moroccan tale-spinners. Certain critics, particularly in England, have affected to confuse these translations with my own tales about Morocco. But not all critics read.

One day in 1970 when Daniel Halpern was living in Tangier, I remarked to him that it had always been a desire of mine to publish a literary magazine. I said that if I had a review I'd call it *Antaeus*, and publish it in Tangier, where the legendary giant is said to be buried. Halpern was enthusiastic, and thought I should do it. He made inquiries at printers and we began to take the matter seriously. We found that it would cost no more to have the printing and binding done in England than it would here in Morocco. I furnished the money for the first issue, which I assumed would also be the last, since I could not pay for any more.

Both Halpern and I wrote to our friends asking for contributions. He sent off a great many letters to poets he knew. Gore Vidal happened to be staying at a hotel only three blocks away, so Halpern went to him for an interview. The first issue was not very impressive, but *Antaeus* did now exist. I asked Halpern to be the editor; he could accept whatever critical praise or blame accompanied the venture. It was fortunate that he had the magazine, for when he went back to the States he was able to raise money for a second issue. It has appeared regularly ever since.

I stayed on here in Tangier, writing an autobiography commissioned by Putnam, and going to Spain to see Jane every month or six weeks. The making of the book of memoirs was a nightmarish task. After a full year of work, I still had not written a word. I had no documents to consult, no letters, no diaries or journals. In order to remember my life in any detail I was obliged to construct an accurate chronology listing the events of each month of every year. Even so, I had to hurry through the latter part of the book to meet the deadline. I was greatly relieved when I'd finished it, and consoled by the reflection that never would I need to repeat the experience. It seems to me that deadlines are all too likely to produce dead books.

Jane suffered more strokes, and was confined to bed. Each time I saw her she seemed to be a little farther away. One day when I arrived at the hospital the nurses told me she could no longer see. In spite of being partially paralyzed, she could still speak. Eventually even that faculty left her, and she merely lay without stirring.

In the spring Jane died; I had arrived at the hospital only a few hours earlier. She had been in a coma for several days. The nurses assured me that she had asked to be accepted into the Catholic church; accordingly she was buried the following day at the Cemeterio San Miguel in Málaga. I have not been out of Morocco in the ten years that have passed since that day.

Slowly I began to get back into the habit of writing fiction. Between 1974 and 1980 I wrote nineteen stories, which for me was a good many. One day a set of application forms arrived in the mail from the National Endowment for the Arts, an organization of which I had never heard. It appeared that they distributed grants of money, and that by filling out the forms I might possibly be the recipient of such a gift. There seemed to be no reason for not taking a chance. I was lucky: I got a grant. A year later I was given a further, larger grant called a Senior Fellowship Award. Since I was no longer earning any money, these sums were more than welcome; they also raised my flagging morale.

Sometimes I marvel at the absurdity of my present situation, one of my own making if not of my own choosing. Certainly I never expected that I would end my life holed up in a place like Tangier, a possibility which grows increasingly more likely. From the thirties through the sixties living in Tangier was predicated upon the ease with which one could sail to any part of the world. The precipitate disappearance of ships a decade ago meant that I would probably not go anywhere again, since I no longer enjoy flying. All accounts of present-day air travel make it sound much more like an ordeal than a joy. Boarding a ship, on the contrary, meant leaving all preoccupations behind one. The regular hours and prolonged periods of relaxation during the days or weeks one remained aboard made of travel an ideal rest cure. It's a matter of continuous astonishment to me that the human race should care so little for comfort and pleasure that it willingly exchanges a valid mode of travel for an unacceptable arrangement more suited to the transportation of animals. But I suspect that man, being the most adaptable animal of all, will reconcile himself to any situation as long as it is presented to him as something inevitable; he will even agree to the definitive extinction of all life on his planet.

Richard Ford

Communist

My mother once had a boyfriend named Glen Baxter. This was in
1961. We — my mother and I — were living in the little house my father
had left her up the Sun River, near Victory, Montana, west of Great
Falls. My mother was thirty-one at the time. I was sixteen. Glen Baxter
was somewhere in the middle, between us, though I cannot be exact
about it.

We were living then off the proceeds of my father's life insurance
policies, with my mother doing some part-time waitressing work up in
Great Falls and going to the bars in the evenings, which I know is
where she met Glen Baxter. Sometimes he would come back with her
and stay in her room at night, or she would call up from town and explain that she was staying with him in his little place on Lewis Street by
the GN yards. She gave me his number every time, but I never
called it. I think she probably thought that what she was doing was terrible, but simply couldn't help herself. I thought it was all right,
though. Regular life it seemed and still does. She was young, and I
knew that even then.

Glen Baxter was a Communist and liked hunting, which he talked
about a lot. Pheasants. Ducks. Deer. He killed all of them, he said. He
had been to Vietnam as far back as then, and when he was in our house
he often talked about shooting the animals over there — monkeys and
beautiful parrots — using military guns just for sport. We did not know
what Vietnam was then, and Glen, when he talked about that, referred
to it only as "the far east." I think now he must've been in the CIA and
been disillusioned by something he saw or found out about and had
been thrown out, but that kind of thing did not matter to us. He was a
tall, dark-eyed man with thick black hair, and was usually in a good
humor. He had gone halfway through college in Peoria, Illinois, he
said, where he grew up. But when he was around our life he worked
wheat farms as a ditcher, and stayed out of work winters and in the bars
drinking with women like my mother, who had work and some money.
It is not an uncommon life to lead in Montana.

What I want to explain happened in November. We had not been seeing Glen Baxter for some time. Two months had gone by. My mother knew other men, but she came home most days from work and stayed inside watching television in her bedroom and drinking beers. I asked about Glen once, and she said only that she didn't know where he was, and I assumed they had had a fight and that he was gone off on a flyer back to Illinois or Massachusetts, where he said he had relatives. I'll admit that I liked him. He had something on his mind always. He was a labor man as well as a Communist, and liked to say that the country was poisoned by the rich, and strong men would need to bring it to life again, and I liked that because my father had been a labor man, which was why we had a house to live in and money coming through. It was also true that I'd had a few boxing bouts by then — just with town boys and one with an Indian from Choteau — and there were some girlfriends I knew from that. I did not like my mother being around the house so much at night, and I wished Glen Baxter would come back, or that another man would come along and entertain her somewhere else.

At two o'clock on a Saturday, Glen drove up into our yard in a car. He had had a big brown Harley-Davidson that he rode most of the year, in his black-and-red irrigators and a baseball cap turned backwards. But this time he had a car, a blue Nash Ambassador. My mother and I went out on the porch when he stopped inside the olive trees my father had planted as a shelter belt, and my mother had a look on her face of not much pleasure. It was starting to be cold in earnest by then. Snow was down already onto the Fairfield Bench, though on this day a chinook was blowing, and it could as easily have been spring, though the sky above the Divide was turning over in silver and blue clouds of winter.

"We haven't seen you in a long time, I guess," my mother said coldly.

"My little retarded sister died," Glen said, standing at the door of his old car. He was wearing his orange VFW jacket and canvas shoes we called wino shoes, something I had never seen him wear before. He seemed to be in a good humor. "We buried her in Florida near the home."

"That's a good place," my mother said in a voice that meant she was a wronged party in something.

"I want to take this boy hunting today, Aileen," Glen said.

"There're snow geese down now. But we have to go right away or they'll be gone to Idaho by tomorrow."

"He doesn't care to go," my mother said.

"Yes I do," I said and looked at her.

My mother frowned at me. "Why do you?"

"Why does he need a reason?" Glen Baxter said and grinned.

"I want him to have one, that's why." She looked at me oddly. "I think Glen's drunk, Les."

"No, I'm not drinking," Glen said, which was hardly ever true. He looked at both of us, and my mother bit down on the side of her lower lip and stared at me in a way to make you think she thought something was being put over on her and she didn't like you for it. She was very pretty, though when she was mad her features were sharpened and less pretty by a long way. "All right then, I don't care," she said to no one in particular. "Hunt, kill, maim. Your father did that too." She turned to go back inside.

"Why don't you come with us, Aileen?" Glen was smiling still, pleased.

"To do what?" my mother said. She stopped and pulled a package of cigarettes out of her dress pocket and put one in her mouth.

"It's worth seeing."

"See dead animals?" my mother said.

"These geese are from Siberia, Aileen," Glen said. "They're not like a lot of geese. Maybe I'll buy us dinner later. What do you say?"

"Buy what with?" my mother said. To tell the truth, I didn't know why she was so mad at him. I would've thought she'd be glad to see him. But she just suddenly seemed to hate everything about him.

"I've got some money," Glen said. "Let me spend it on a pretty girl tonight."

"Find one of those and you're lucky," my mother said, turning away toward the front door.

"I already found one," Glen Baxter said. But the door slammed behind her, and he looked at me then with a look I think now was helplessness, though I could not see a way to change anything.

My mother sat in the back seat of Glen's Nash and looked out the window while we drove. My double gun was in the seat between us beside Glen's Belgian pump, which he kept loaded with five shells in case, he said, he saw something beside the road he wanted to shoot. I had hunted rabbits before, and had ground-sluiced pheasants and other birds, but I had never been on an actual hunt before, one where you drove out to some special place and did it formally. And I was excited. I had a feeling that something important was about to happen to me and that this would be a day I would always remember.

My mother did not say anything for a long time, and neither did I. We drove up through Great Falls and out the other side toward Fort Benton, which was on the benchland where wheat was grown.

"Geese mate for life," my mother said, just out of the blue, as we were driving. "I hope you know that. They're special birds."

"I know that," Glen said in the front seat. "I have every respect for them."

"So where were you for three months?" she said. "I'm only curious."

"I was in the Big Hole for a while," Glen said, "and after that I went over to Douglas, Wyoming."

"What were you planning to do there?" my mother asked.

"I wanted to find a job, but it didn't work out."

"I'm going to college," she said suddenly, and this was something I had never heard about before. I turned to look at her, but she was staring out her window and wouldn't see me.

"I knew French once," Glen said. "Rose's pink. Rouge's red." He glanced at me and smiled. "I think that's a wise idea, Aileen. When are you going to start?"

"I don't want Les to think he was raised by crazy people all his life," my mother said.

"Les ought to go himself," Glen said.

"After I go, he will."

"What do you say about that, Les?" Glen said, grinning.

"He says it's just fine," my mother said.

"It's just fine," I said.

Where Glen Baxter took us was out onto the high flat prairie that was disked for wheat and had high, high mountains out to the east, with lower heartbreak hills in between. It was, I remember, a day for blues in the sky, and down in the distance we could see the small town of Floweree and the state highway running past it toward Fort Benton and the high line. We drove out on top of the prairie on a muddy dirt road fenced on both sides, until we had gone about three miles, which is where Glen stopped.

"All right," he said, looking up in the rearview mirror at my mother. "You wouldn't think there was anything here, would you?"

"*We're* here," my mother said. "You brought us here."

"You'll be glad though," Glen said, and seemed confident to me. I had looked around myself but could not see anything. No water or trees, nothing that seemed like a good place to hunt anything. Just wasted land. "There's a big lake out there, Les," Glen said. "You can't see it now from here because it's low. But the geese are there. You'll see."

"It's like the moon out here, I recognize that," my mother said, "only it's worse." She was staring out at the flat, disked wheatland as if she could actually see something in particular and wanted to know more about it. "How'd you find this place?"

"I came once on the wheat push," Glen said.

"And I'm sure the owner told you just to come back and hunt any time you like and bring anybody you wanted. Come one, come all. Is that it?"

"People shouldn't own land anyway," Glen said. "Anybody should be able to use it."

"Les, Glen's going to poach here," my mother said. "I just want you to know that, because that's a crime and the law will get you for it. If you're a man now, you're going to have to face the consequences."

"That's not true," Glen Baxter said, and looked gloomily out over the steering wheel down the muddy road toward the mountains. Though for myself I believed it was true, and didn't care. I didn't care about anything at that moment except seeing geese fly over me and shooting them down.

"Well, I'm certainly not going out there," my mother said. "I like towns better, and I already have enough trouble."

"That's okay," Glen said. "When the geese lift up you'll get to see them. That's all I wanted. Les and me'll go shoot them, won't we, Les?"

"Yes," I said, and I put my hand on my shotgun, which had been my father's and was heavy as rocks.

"Then we should go on," Glen said, "or we'll waste our light."

We got out of the car with our guns. Glen took off his canvas shoes and put on his pair of black irrigators out of the trunk. Then we crossed the barbed-wire fence and walked out into the high, tilled field toward nothing. I looked back at my mother when we were still not so far away, but I could only see the small, dark top of her head, low in the back seat of the Nash, staring out and thinking what I could not then begin to say.

On the walk toward the lake, Glen began talking to me. I had never been alone with him and knew little about him except what my mother said — that he drank too much, or other times that he was the nicest man she had ever known in the world and that some day a woman would marry him, though she didn't think it would be her. Glen told me as we walked that he wished he had finished college, but that it was too late now, that his mind was too old. He said he had liked "the far east" very much, and that people there knew how to treat each other, and that he would go back some day but couldn't go now. He said also that he would like to live in Russia for a while and mentioned the names of people who had gone there, names I didn't know. He said it would be hard at first, because it was so different, but that pretty soon anyone would learn to like it and wouldn't want to live anywhere else, and that Russians treated Americans who came to live there like kings. There were Communists everywhere now, he said. You didn't know them, but they were there. Montana had a large number, and he was in touch with all of them. He said that Communists were always in danger and that he had to protect himself all the time. And when he said that he pulled back his VFW jacket and showed me the butt of a pistol he had stuck under his shirt against his bare skin. "There are people who want to kill me right now," he said, "and I would kill a man myself if I thought I had to." And we kept walking. Though in a while he said, "I don't think I know much about you, Les. But I'd like to. What do you like to do?"

"I like to box," I said. "My father did it. It's a good thing to know."

"I suppose you have to protect yourself too," Glen said.

"I know how to," I said.

"Do you like to watch TV?" Glen said, and smiled.

"Not much."

"I love to," Glen said. "I could watch it instead of eating if I had one."

I looked out straight ahead over the green tops of sage that grew at the edge of the disked field, hoping to see the lake Glen said was there. There was an airishness and a sweet smell that I thought might be the place we were going, but I couldn't see it. "How will we hunt these geese?" I said.

"It won't be hard," Glen said. "Most hunting isn't even hunting. It's only shooting. And that's what this will be. In Illinois you would dig holes in the ground to hide in and set out your decoys. Then the geese come to you, over and over again. But we don't have time for that here." He glanced at me. "You have to be sure the first time here."

"How do you know they're here now?" I asked. And I looked toward the Highwood Mountains twenty miles away, half in snow and half dark blue at the bottom. I could see the little town of Floweree then, looking shabby and dimly lighted in the distance. A red bar sign shone. A car moved slowly away from the scattered buildings.

"They always come November first," Glen said.

"Are we going to poach them?"

"Does it make any difference to you?" Glen asked.

"No, it doesn't."

"Well then we aren't," he said.

We walked then for a while without talking. I looked back once to see the Nash far and small in the flat distance. I couldn't see my mother, and I thought that she must've turned on the radio and gone to sleep, which she always did, letting it play all night in her bedroom. Behind the car the sun was nearing the rounded mountains southwest of us, and I knew that when the sun was gone it would be cold. I wished my mother had decided to come along with us, and I thought for a moment of how little I really knew her at all.

Glen walked with me another quarter mile, crossed another barbed-wire fence where sage was growing, then went a hundred yards through wheatgrass and spurge until the ground went up and formed a kind of long hillock bunker built by a farmer against the wind. And I realized the lake was just beyond us. I could hear the sound of a car horn blowing and a dog barking all the way down in the town, then the wind seemed to move and all I could hear then and after then were geese. So many geese, from the sound of them, though I still could not see even one. I stood and listened to the high-pitched shouting sound, a sound I had never heard so close, a sound with size to it — though it was not loud. A sound that meant great numbers and that made your chest rise and your shoulders tighten with expectancy. It was a sound to make you feel separate from it and everything else, as if you were of no importance in the grand scheme of things.

"Do you hear them singing?" Glen asked. He held his hand up to make me stand still. And we both listened. "How many do you think, Les, just hearing?"

"A hundred," I said. "More than a hundred."

"Five thousand," Glen said. "More than you can believe when you see them. Go see."

I put down my gun and on my hands and knees crawled up the earthwork through the wheatgrass and thistle until I could see down to the lake and see the geese. And they were there, like a white bandage laid on the water, wide and long and continuous, a white expanse of snow geese, seventy yards from me, on the bank, but stretching onto the lake, which was large itself—a half mile across, with thick tules on the far side and wild plums farther and the blue mountain behind them.

"Do you see the big raft?" Glen said from below me, in a whisper.

"I see it," I said, still looking. It was such a thing to see, a view I had never seen and have not since.

"Are any on the land?" he said.

"Some are in the wheatgrass," I said, "but most are swimming."

"Good," Glen said. "They'll have to fly. But we can't wait for that now."

And I crawled backwards down the heel of land to where Glen was, and my gun. We were losing our light, and the air was purplish and cooling. I looked toward the car but couldn't see it, and I was no longer sure where it was below the lighted sky.

"Where do they fly to?" I said in a whisper, since I did not want anything to be ruined because of what I did or said. It was important to Glen to shoot the geese, and it was important to me.

"To the wheat," he said. "Or else they leave for good. I wish your mother had come, Les. Now she'll be sorry."

I could hear the geese quarreling and shouting on the lake surface. And I wondered if they knew we were here now. "She might be," I said with my heart pounding, but I didn't think she would be much.

It was a simple plan he had. I would stay behind the bunker, and he would crawl on his belly with his gun through the wheatgrass as near to the geese as he could. Then he would simply stand up and shoot all the ones he could close up, both in the air and on the ground. And when all the others flew up, with luck some would turn toward me as they came into the wind, and then I could shoot them and turn them back to him, and he would shoot them again. He could kill ten, he said, if he was lucky, and I might kill four. It didn't seem hard.

"Don't show them your face," Glen said. "Wait till you think you can touch them, then stand up and shoot. To hesitate is lost in this."

"All right," I said. "I'll try it."

"Shoot one in the head, and then shoot another one," Glen said. "It won't be hard." He patted me on the arm and smiled. Then he took off his VFW jacket and put it on the ground, climbed up the side of the bunker, cradling his shotgun in his arms, and slid on his belly into the dry stalks of yellow grass out of my sight.

Then for the first time in that entire day I was alone. And I didn't mind it. I sat squat down in the grass, loaded my double gun, and took my other two shells out of my pocket to hold. I pushed the safety off and on to see that it was right. The wind rose a little then, scuffed the grass and made me shiver. It was not the warm chinook now, but a wind out of the north, the one geese flew away from if they could.

Then I thought about my mother in the car alone, and how much longer I would stay with her, and what it might mean to her for me to leave. And I wondered when Glen Baxter would die and if someone would kill him, or whether my mother would marry him and how I would feel about it. And though I didn't know why, it occurred to me then that Glen Baxter and I would not be friends when all was said and done, since I didn't care if he ever married my mother or didn't.

Then I thought about boxing and what my father had taught me about it. To tighten your fists hard. To strike out straight from the shoulder and never punch backing up. How to cut a punch by snapping your fist inwards, how to carry your chin low, and to step toward a man when he is falling so you can hit him again. And most important, to keep your eyes open when you are hitting in the face and causing damage, because you need to see what you're doing to encourage yourself, and because it is when you close your eyes that you stop hitting and get hurt badly. "Fly all over your man, Les," my father said. "When you see your chance, fly on him and hit him till he falls." That, I thought, would always be my attitude in things.

And then I heard the geese again, their voices in unison, louder and shouting, as if the wind had changed and put all new sounds in the cold air. And then a *boom*. And I knew Glen was in among them and had stood up to shoot. The noise of geese rose and grew worse, and my fingers burned where I held my gun too tight to the metal, and I put it down and opened my fist to make the burning stop so I could feel the trigger when the moment came. *Boom*, Glen shot again, and I heard him shuck a shell, and all the sounds out beyond the bunker seemed to be rising — the geese, the shots, the air itself going up. *Boom*, Glen shot another time, and I knew he was taking his careful time to make his shots good. And I held my gun and started to crawl up the bunker so as not to be surprised when the geese came over me and I could shoot.

From the top I saw Glen Baxter alone in the wheat field, shooting at a white goose with black tips of wings that was on the ground not far from him, but trying to run and pull into the air. He shot it once more, and it fell over dead with its wings flapping.

Glen looked back at me and his face was distorted and strange. The air around him was full of white rising geese and he seemed to want them all. "Behind you, Les," he yelled at me and pointed. "They're all behind you now." I looked behind me, and there were geese in the air as far as I could see, more than I knew how many, moving so slowly, their wings wide out and working calmly and filling the air with noise, though their voices were not as loud or as shrill as I had thought they would be. And they were so close! Forty feet, some of them. The air around me vibrated and I could feel the wind from their wings and it seemed to me I could kill as many as the times I could shoot — a hundred or a thousand — and I raised my gun, put the muzzle on the head of a white goose and fired. It shuddered in the air, its wide feet sank below its belly, its wings cradled out to hold back air, and it fell straight down and landed with an awful sound, a noise a human would make, a thick, soft, *hump* noise. I looked up again and shot another goose, could hear the pellets hit its chest, but it didn't fall or even break its pattern for flying. *Boom*, Glen shot again. And then again. "Hey," I heard him shout. "Hey, hey." And there were geese flying over me, flying in line after line. I broke my gun and reloaded, and thought to myself as I did: I need confidence here, I need to be sure with this. I pointed at another goose and shot it in the head, and it fell the way the first one had, wings out, its belly down, and with the same thick noise of hitting. Then I sat down in the grass on the bunker and let geese fly over me.

By now the whole raft was in the air, all of it moving in a slow swirl above me and the lake and everywhere, finding the wind and heading out south in long wavering lines that caught the last sun and turned to silver as they gained a distance. It was a thing to see, I will tell you now. Five thousand white geese all in the air around you, making a noise like you have never heard before. And I thought to myself then: This is something I will never see again. I will never forget this. And I was right.

Glen Baxter shot twice more. One shot missed, but with the other he hit a goose flying away from him and knocked it half-falling and flying into the empty lake not far from shore, where it began to swim as though it was fine and make its noise.

Glen stood in the stubbly grass, looking out at the goose, his gun lowered. "I didn't need to shoot that, did I, Les?"

"I don't know," I said, sitting on the little knoll of land, looking at the goose swimming in the water.

"I don't know why I shoot 'em. They're so beautiful." He looked at me.

"I don't know either," I said.

"Maybe there's nothing else to do with them." Glen stared at the goose again and shook his head. "Maybe this is exactly what they're put on earth for."

I did not know what to say because I did not know what he could mean by that, though what I felt was embarrassment at the great number of geese there were, and a dulled feeling like a hunger because the shooting had stopped and it was over for me now.

Glen began to pick up his geese, and I walked down to my two that had fallen close together and were dead. One had hit with such an impact that its stomach had split and some of its inward parts were knocked out. Though the other looked unhurt, its soft white belly turned up like a pillow, its head and jagged bill-teeth and its tiny black eyes looking as if it were alive.

"What's happened to the hunters out here?" I heard a voice speak. It was my mother, standing in her pink dress on the knoll above us, hugging her arms. She was smiling though she was cold. And I realized that I had lost all thought of her in the shooting. "Who did all this shooting? Is this your work, Les?"

"No," I said.

"Les is a hunter, though, Aileen," Glen said. "He takes his time." He was holding two white geese by their necks, one in each hand, and he was smiling. He and my mother seemed pleased.

"I see you didn't miss too many," my mother said and smiled. I could tell she admired Glen for his geese, and that she had done some thinking in the car alone. "It *was* wonderful, Glen," she said. "I've never seen anything like that. They were like snow."

"It's worth seeing once, isn't it?" Glen said. "I should've killed more, but I got excited."

My mother looked at me then. "Where's yours, Les?"

"Here," I said and pointed to my two geese on the ground beside me.

My mother nodded in a nice way, and I think she liked everything then and wanted the day to turn out right and for all of us to be happy. "Six, then. You've got six in all."

"One's still out there," I said and motioned where the one goose was swimming in circles on the water.

"Okay," my mother said and put her hand over her eyes to look. "Where is it?"

Glen Baxter looked at me then with a strange smile, a smile that said he wished I had never mentioned anything about the other goose. And I wished I hadn't either. I looked up in the sky and could see the lines of geese by the thousands shining silver in the light, and I wished we could just leave and go home.

"That one's my mistake there," Glen Baxter said and grinned. "I shouldn't have shot that one, Aileen. I got too excited."

My mother looked out on the lake for a minute, then looked at Glen and back again. "Poor goose." She shook her head. "How will you get it, Glen?"

"I can't get that one now," Glen said.

My mother looked at him. "What do you mean?" she said.

"I'm going to leave that one," Glen said.

"Well, no. You can't leave one," my mother said. "You shot it. You have to get it. Isn't that a rule?"

"No," Glen said.

And my mother looked from Glen to me. "Wade out and get it, Glen," she said, in a sweet way, and my mother looked young then for some reason, like a young girl, in her flimsy short-sleeved waitress dress, and her skinny, bare legs in the wheatgrass.

"No." Glen Baxter looked down at his gun and shook his head. And I didn't know why he wouldn't go, because it would've been easy. The lake was shallow. And you could tell that anyone could've walked out a long way before it got deep, and Glen had on his boots.

My mother looked at the white goose, which was not more than thirty yards from the shore, its head up, moving in slow circles, its wings settled and relaxed so you could see the black tips. "Wade out and get it, Glenny, won't you please?" she said. "They're special things."

"You don't understand the world, Aileen," Glen said. "This can happen. It doesn't matter."

"But that's so cruel, Glen," she said, and a sweet smile came on her lips.

"Raise up your own arms, Leeny," Glen said. "I can't see any angel's wings, can you Les?" He looked at me, but I looked away.

"Then you go on and get it, Les," my mother said. "You weren't raised by crazy people." I started to go, but Glen Baxter suddenly grabbed me by my shoulder and pulled me back hard, so hard his fingers made bruises in my skin that I saw later.

"Nobody's going," he said. "This is over with now."

And my mother gave Glen a cold look then. "You don't have a heart, Glen," she said. "There's nothing to love in you. You're just a son of a bitch, that's all."

And Glen Baxter nodded at my mother as if he understood something that he had not understood before, but something that he was willing to know. "Fine," he said, "that's fine." And he took his big pistol out from against his belly, the big blue revolver I had only seen part of before and that he said protected him, and he pointed it out at the goose on the water, his arm straight away from him, and shot and missed. And then he shot and missed again. The goose made its noise once. And then he hit it dead, because there was no splash. And then he shot it three times more until the gun was empty and the goose's head was down and it was floating toward the middle of the lake where it was empty and dark blue. "Now who has a heart?" Glen said. But my mother was not there when he turned around. She had already started back to the car and was almost lost from sight in the darkness. And Glen smiled at me then and his face had a wild look on it. "Okay, Les?" he said.

"Okay," I said.

"There're limits to everything, right?"

"I guess so," I said.

"Your mother's a beautiful woman, but she's not the only beautiful woman in Montana." I did not say anything. And Glen Baxter suddenly said, "Here," and he held the pistol out at me. "Don't you want this? Don't you want to shoot me? Nobody thinks they'll die. But I'm ready for it right now." And I did not know what to do then. Though it is true that what I wanted to do was to hit him, hit him as hard in the face as I could, and see him on the ground bleeding and crying and pleading for me to stop. Only at that moment he looked scared to me, and I had never seen a grown man scared before — though I have seen one since — and I felt sorry for him, as though he was already a dead man. And I did not end up hitting him at all.

A light can go out in the heart. All of this went on years ago, but I still can feel now how sad and remote the world was to me. Glen Baxter, I think now, was not a bad man, only a man scared of something he'd never seen before — something soft in himself — his life going a way he didn't like. A woman with a son. Who could blame him there? I don't know what makes people do what they do or call themselves what they call themselves, only that you have to live someone's life to be the expert.

My mother had tried to see the good side of things, tried to be hopeful in the situation she was handed, tried to look out for us both, and it hadn't worked. It was a strange time in her life then and after that, a time when she had to adjust to being an adult just when she was on the thin edge of things. Too much awareness too early in life was her problem, I think.

And what I felt was only that I had somehow been pushed out into the world, into the real life then, the one I hadn't lived yet. In a year I was gone to hardrock mining and no-paycheck jobs and not to college. And I have thought more than once about my mother saying that I had not been raised by crazy people, and I don't know what that could mean or what difference it could make, unless it means that love is a reliable commodity, and even that is not always true, as I have found out.

Late on the night that all this took place I was in bed when I heard my mother say, "Come outside, Les. Come and hear this." And I went out onto the front porch barefoot and in my underwear, where it was warm like spring, and there was a spring mist in the air. I could see the lights of the Fairfield Coach in the distance on its way up to Great Falls.

And I could hear geese, white birds in the sky, flying. They made their high-pitched sound like angry yells, and though I couldn't see them high up, it seemed to me they were everywhere. And my mother looked up and said, "Hear them?" I could smell her hair wet from the shower. "They leave with the moon," she said. "It's still half wild out here."

And I said, "I hear them," and I felt a chill come over my bare chest, and the hair stood up on my arms the way it does before a storm. And for a while we listened.

"When I first married your father, you know, we lived on a street called Bluebird Canyon, in California. And I thought that was the prettiest street and the prettiest name. I suppose no one brings you up like your first love. You don't mind if I say that, do you?" She looked at me hopefully.

"No," I said.

"We have to keep civilization alive somehow." And she pulled her little housecoat together because there was a cold vein in the air, a part of the cold that would be on us the next day. "I don't feel part of things tonight, I guess."

"It's all right," I said.

"Do you know where I'd like to go?" she said.

"No," I said. And I suppose I knew she was angry then, angry with life but did not want to show me that.

"To the Straits of Juan de Fuca. Wouldn't that be something? Would you like that?"

"I'd like it," I said. And my mother looked off for a minute, as if she could see the Straits of Juan de Fuca out against the line of mountains, see the lights of things alive and a whole new world.

"I know you liked him," she said after a moment. "You and I both suffer fools too well."

"I didn't like him too much," I said. "I didn't really care."

"He'll fall on his face. I'm sure of that," she said. And I didn't say anything because I didn't care about Glen Baxter anymore, and was happy not to talk about him. "Would you tell me something if I asked you? Would you tell me the truth?"

"Yes," I said.

And my mother did not look at me. "Just tell the truth," she said.

"All right," I said.

"Do you think I'm still very feminine? I'm thirty-two years old now. You don't know what that means. But do you think I am?"

And I stood at the edge of the porch, with the olive trees before me, looking straight up into the mist where I could not see geese but could still hear them flying, could almost feel the air move below their white wings. And I felt the way you feel when you are on a trestle all alone and the train is coming, and you know you have to decide. And I said, "Yes, I do." Because that was the truth. And I tried to think of something else then and did not hear what my mother said after that.

And how old was I then? Sixteen. Sixteen is young, but it can also be a grown man. I am forty-one years old now, and I think about that time without regret, though my mother and I never talked in that way again, and I have not heard her voice now in a long, long time.

Francine Prose

Other Lives

Climbing up with a handful of star decals to paste on the bathroom ceiling, Claire sees a suspect-looking shampoo bottle on the cluttered top shelf. When she opens it, the whole room smells like a subway corridor where bums have been pissing for generations. She thinks back a few days to when Miranda and Poppy were playing in here with the door shut. She puts down the stars and yells for the girls with such urgency they come running before she's finished emptying it into the sink.

From the doorway, Poppy and her best friend Miranda look at Claire, then at each other. "Mom," says Poppy. "You threw it *out*?"

Claire wants to ask why they're saving their urine in bottles. But sitting on the edge of the tub has lowered her eye level and she's struck speechless by the beauty of their kneecaps, their long suntanned legs. How strong and shaky and elegant they are! Like newborn giraffes! By now she can't bring herself to ask, so she tells them not to do it again and is left with the rest of the morning to wonder what they had in mind.

She thinks it has something to do with alchemy and with faith, with those moments when children are playing with such pure concentration that anything is possible and the rest of the world drops away and becomes no more real than one of their 3-D Viewmaster slides. She remembers when she was Poppy's age, playing with her own best friend Evelyn. Evelyn's father had been dead several years, but his medical office in a separate wing of their house was untouched, as if office hours might begin any minute. In his chilly consulting room, smelling of carpet dust and furniture polish and more faintly of gauze and sterilizing pans, Claire and Evelyn played their peculiar version of doctor. Claire would come in and from behind the desk Evelyn would give her some imaginary pills. Then Claire would fall down dead and Evelyn would kneel and listen to her heart and say, "I'm sorry, it's too late."

But what Claire remembers best is the framed engraving on Evelyn's father's desk. It was one of those trompe l'oeil pieces you see sometimes in cheap art stores. From one angle, it looked like two Gibson girls at a table sipping ice cream sodas through straws. From another, it looked like a skull. Years later, when Claire learned that Evelyn's father had actually died in jail where he'd been sent for performing illegal abortions, she'd thought what an odd picture to have on an abortionist's desk. But at the time, it had just seemed marvelous. She used to unfocus her eyes and tilt her head so that it flipped back and forth. Skull, ladies. Skull, ladies. Skull.

Dottie's new hairdo, a wide corolla of pale blond curls, makes her look even more like a sunflower — spindly, graceful, rather precariously balanced. At one, when Dottie comes to pick up Miranda, Claire decides not to tell her about the shampoo bottle.

Lately, Dottie's had her mind on higher things. For the past few months, she's been driving down to the New Consciousness Academy in Bennington where she takes courses with titles like "Listening to the Inner Silence" and "Weeds for Your Needs." Claire blames this on one of Dottie's friends, an electrician named Jeanette. Once at a party, Claire overheard Jeanette telling someone how she and her boyfriend practice birth control based on lunar astrology and massive doses of wintergreen tea.

"Coffee?" says Claire, tentatively. It's hard to keep track of what substances Dottie's given up. Sometimes, most often in winter when Joey and Raymond are working and the girls are at school, Dottie and Claire get together for lunch. Walking into Dottie's house and smelling woodsmoke and wine and fresh-baked bread, seeing the table set with blue bowls and hothouse anemones and a soup thick with sausage, potatoes, tomatoes put up from the fall, Claire used to feel that she must be living her whole life right. All summer, she's been praying that Dottie won't give up meat.

Now Dottie says, "Have you got any herbal tea?" and Claire says, "Are you kidding?" "All right, coffee," says Dottie. "Just this once."

As Claire pours the coffee, Dottie fishes around in her enormous parachute-silk purse. Recently, Dottie's been bringing Claire reading material. She'd started off with Krishnamurti, Rajneesh, the songs of Milarepa; Claire tried but she just couldn't, she'd returned them unread. A few weeks back, she'd brought something by Dashiell Hammett about a man named Flitcraft who's walking to lunch one day and a beam falls down from a construction site and just misses him, and he just keeps walking and never goes to his job or back to his wife and family again.

When Claire read that, she wanted to call Dottie up and make her promise not to do something similar. But she didn't. The last time she and Dottie discussed the Academy, Dottie described a technique she'd learned for closing her eyes and pressing on her eyelids just hard enough to see thousands of pinpricks of light. Each one of those dots represents a past life, and if you know how to look, you can see it. In this way, Dottie learned that she'd spent a former life as a footsoldier in Napoleon's army on the killing march to Moscow. That's why she so hates the cold. Somehow Claire hadn't known that Dottie hated the winter, but really, it follows: a half-starved, half-frozen soldier cooking inspired sausage soup three lives later.

"I meant to bring you a book," says Dottie. Then she says, "A crazy thing happened this morning. I was working in front of the house, digging up those irises by the side of the road so I could divide them. I didn't hear anything but I must have had a sense because I turned around and there was this old lady—coiffed, polyestered, dressed for church, it looked like. She told me she'd come over from Montpelier with some friends for a picnic and got separated. Now she was lost and *so* upset.

"I said, Well, okay, I'll drive you back to Montpelier. We got as far as Barre when suddenly her whole story started coming apart and I realized: She hadn't been in Montpelier for twenty years. She was from that Good Shepherd House, that old folks' home up the road from us. I drove her back to the Good Shepherd, what else could I do? The manager thanked me, he was very embarrassed she'd escaped. Then just as I was pulling out, the old lady pointed up at the sky and gave me the most hateful triumphant smile, and I looked up through the windshield and there was this flock of geese heading south." Dottie catches her breath, then says, "You know what? It's August. I'd forgotten."

What Claire can't quite forget is that years ago, the first time she and Joey met Dottie and Raymond, afterwards Joey said, "They don't call her dotty for nothing." It took them both a while to see that what looked at first like dottiness was really an overflow of the same generosity which makes Dottie cook elegant warming meals and drive senile old ladies fifty miles out of her way to Montpelier. On Tuesdays and Thursdays, when Dottie goes down to the Academy, she's a volunteer chauffeur service, picking up classmates—including Jeanette the electrician—from all over central Vermont. Even Joey's come around to liking her, though Claire's noticed that he's usually someplace else when Dottie's around.

Now he's in the garden, tying up some tomatoes which fell last night in the wind. Finding them this morning—perfect red tomatoes smashed on top of each other—had sent her straight to the bathroom with her handful of star decals. That's the difference between me and Joey, Claire thinks. Thank God there's someone to save what's left of the vines.

Joey doesn't see Claire watching him but Dottie does and starts to flutter, as if she's overstayed. She calls up to Miranda, and just when it begins to seem as if they might not have heard, the girls drag themselves downstairs.

"Why does Miranda have to go?" says Poppy.

"Because it's fifteen miles and Miranda's mom isn't driving fifteen miles back and forth all day," says Claire.

"But I don't want to go," says Miranda.

They stand there, deadlocked, until Poppy says, "I've got an idea. I'll go home with Miranda and tonight her mom and dad can come to dinner and bring us both back and then Miranda can sleep over."

"That's fine with me," says Claire.

"Are you sure?" says Dottie.

Claire's sure. As Dottie leans down to kiss her good-bye, Claire thinks once more of sunflowers, specifically of the ones she and Joey and Poppy plant every summer on a steep slope so you can stand underneath and look up and the sunflowers look forty feet tall.

Washing his hands at the sink, Joey says, "One day she's going to show up in saffron robes with a begging bowl and her hair shaved down to one skanky topknot and then what?"

Claire thinks: Well, then we'll cook up some gluey brown rice and put a big glob in Dottie's bowl. But this sounds like something they'd say at the New Consciousness Academy, some dreadful homily about adaptation and making do. All she can think of is, "I cried because I had no shoes until I met a man who had no feet," and that's not it.

One night, not long after Dottie started attending the Academy, they were all sitting outside and Dottie looked up and said, "Sometimes I feel as if my whole life is that last minute of the planetarium show when they start showing off—that is, showing off what their projector can do—and the moon and planets and stars and even those distant galaxies begin spinning like crazy while they tell you the coming attractions and what time the next show begins. I just want to find someplace where it's not rushing past me so fast. Or where, if it is, I don't care."

"I hope you find it," Joey said. "I really do." Later that night, he told Claire that he knew what Dottie meant. "Still," he said, "it was creepy. The whole conversation was like talking to someone who still thinks *El Topo* is the greatest movie ever made."

Joey had gone through his own spiritual phase: acid, Castenada, long Sunday afternoons in front of the tonkas in the Staten Island Tibetan museum. All this was before he met Claire. He feels that his having grown out of it fifteen years ago gives him the right to criticize. Though actually, he's not mocking Dottie so much as protecting her husband Raymond, his best friend. Remote as the possibility seems, no one wants Dottie to follow in Flitcraft's footsteps.

Now Claire says, "I don't think she'd get her hair permed if she was planning to shave it." Then she steels herself, and in the tone of someone expecting bad news asks if any tomatoes are left. Joey says, "We'll be up to our *ears* in tomatoes," and Claire thinks: He'd say that no matter what.

One thing she loves about Joey is his optimism. If he's ever discontent, she doesn't know it. Once he'd wanted to be on stage, then he'd worked for a while as a landscaper, now he's a junior-high science teacher —a job which he says requires the combined talents of an actor and a gardener. His real passion is for the names of things: trees, animals, stars. But he's not one of those people who use such knowledge to make you feel small. It's why he's a popular teacher and why Poppy so loves to take walks with him, naming the wildflowers in the fields. Claire knows how rare it is for children to want to learn anything from their parents.

When Claire met Joey, she'd just moved up to Vermont with a semi-alcoholic independently wealthy photographer named Dell. Dell hired Joey to clear a half-acre around their cabin so they could have a garden and lawn. Upstairs there's a photo Dell took of them at the time and later sent as a wedding present to prove there were no hard feelings. It shows Claire and Joey leaning against Joey's rented backhoe; an uprooted acacia tree is spilling out of the bucket. Joey and Claire look cocky and hard in the face, like teen-age killers, Charlie Starkweather and his girl. Claire can hardly remember Dell's face. He always had something in front of it—a can of beer, a camera. If he had only put it down and looked, he'd have seen what was going on. Anyone would have. In the photo, it's early spring, the woods are full of musical names: trillium, marsh marigold, jack in the pulpit.

On the day they learned Claire was pregnant and went straight from the doctor's to the marriage license bureau in Burlington, Joey pulled off the road on the way home and took Claire's face in his hands and told her which animals mated for life. Whooping cranes, snow geese, macaws, she's forgotten the rest. Now they no longer talk this way, or maybe it goes without saying. Claire's stopped imagining other lives; if she could, she'd live this one forever. Though she knows it's supposed to be dangerous to get too comfortable, she feels it would take a catastrophe to tear the weave of their daily routine. They've weathered arguments, and those treacherous, tense, dull periods when they sneak past each other as if they're in constant danger of sneezing in each other's faces. Claire knows to hold on and wait for the day when what interests her most is what Joey will have to say about it.

Some things get better. Claire used to hate thinking about the lovers they'd had before; now all that seems as indistinct as Dell's face. Though they've had eight years to get used to the fact of Poppy's existence, they're still susceptible to attacks of amazement that they've created a new human being. And often when they're doing something together — cooking, gardening, making love — Claire comes as close as she ever has to those moments of pure alchemy, that communion Poppy and Miranda must share if they're storing their pee in bottles.

Soon they'll get up and mix some marinade for the chickens they'll grill outside later for Dottie and Raymond. But now Joey pours himself some coffee and they sit at the table, not talking. It is precisely the silence they used to dream of when Poppy was little and just having her around was like always having the bath water running or something about to boil over on the stove.

First the back doors fly open and the girls jump out of the car and run up to Poppy's room. Then Dottie gets out, then Raymond. From the beginning, Raymond's reminded Claire of the tin woodsman in *The Wizard of Oz*, and often he'll stop in the middle of things as if waiting for someone to come along with the oil can. He goes around to the trunk and takes out a tripod and something wrapped in a blanket which looks at first like a rifle and turns out to be a telescope.

"Guess what!" When Raymond shouts like that, you can see how snaggletoothed he is. "There's a meteor shower tonight. The largest concentration of shooting stars all year."

The telescope is one of the toys Raymond's bought since his paintings started selling. Raymond's success surprises them all, including

Raymond. His last two shows were large paintings of ordinary garden vegetables with skinny legs and big feet in rather stereotypical dance situations. It still surprises Claire that the New York art world would open its heart — would have a heart to open — to work bordering on the cartoonish and sentimental. But there's something undeniably mysterious and moving about those black daikon radishes doing the tango, those little cauliflowers in pink tutus on points before an audience of sleek and rather parental-looking green peppers. And there's no arguing with Raymond's draftmanship or the luminosity of his color; it's as if Memling lived through the sixties and took too many drugs. What's less surprising is that there are so many rich people who for one reason or another want to eat breakfast beneath a painting of dancing vegetables.

Claire has a crush on Raymond; at least that's what she thinks it is. It's not especially intense or very troublesome; it's been going on a long time and she doesn't expect it to change. If anything did change, it would probably disappear. She doesn't want to live with Raymond and now, as always when he hugs her hello, their bones grate; it's not particularly sexual.

She just likes him, that's all. When it's Raymond coming to dinner, she cooks and dresses with a little more care than she otherwise might, and spends the day remembering things to tell him which she promptly forgets. Of course, she's excited when Dottie or anyone is coming over. The difference is: With Dottie, Claire enjoys her food. With Raymond, she often forgets to eat.

Barbecued chicken, tomatoes with basil and mozzarella, pasta with chanterelles Joey's found in the woods — it all goes right by her. Luckily, everyone else is eating, the girls trekking back and forth from the table to the TV. The television noise makes it hard to talk. It's like family dinner, they can just eat. Anyway, conversation's been strained since Dottie started at the Academy. Claire fears that Joey might make some semi-sarcastic remark which will hurt Raymond more than Dottie. Raymond's protective of her; they seem mated for life. It's occurred to them all that Dottie is the original dancing vegetable.

What does get said is that the meteor shower isn't supposed to pick up till around midnight. But they'll set up the telescope earlier so the girls can have a look before they're too tired to see.

Joey and Raymond and the girls go outside while Dottie and Claire put the dishes in the sink. Claire asks if Poppy was any trouble that afternoon and Dottie says, "Oh, no. They played in the bathroom so quiet, I had to keep yelling up to make sure they were breathing. Later they told me they'd been making vanishing cream from that liquidy soap at the bottom of the soap dish. I said, You're eight years old, what do you need with vanishing cream? They said, to vanish. I told them they'd better not use it till they had something to bring them back from wherever they vanished to, and they said, yeah, they'd already thought of that."

"Where did they *hear* about vanishing cream?" says Claire. She feels she ought to tell Dottie — feels disloyal for not telling her — to watch for suspicious-looking shampoo bottles on the upper shelves. But she doesn't. It's almost as if she's saving it for something.

"Speaking of vanishing," says Dottie. She hands Claire the book she'd forgotten that afternoon. It's Calvino's *The Baron in the Trees*. Claire's read it before, and it seems like the right moment to ask, so she says, "Does this mean that you're going to get up from the table one night and climb up in the trees and never come down again?"

Dottie just looks at her. "Me in the trees?" she says. "With *my* allergies?"

They're amazed by how dark it is when they go outside. "I told you," says Dottie. "It's August."

The grass is damp and cool against their ankles as they walk across the lawn to where Miranda and Poppy are taking turns at the telescope. "Daddy," Claire hears Poppy say. "What's that?"

Joey crouches down and looks over her shoulder. Claire wonders what they see. Scorpio? Andromeda? Orion? Joey's told her a thousand times but she can never remember what's in the sky when.

Before Joey can answer, Raymond pulls Poppy away from the telescope and kneels and puts one arm around her and the other around Miranda. "That one?" he says, pointing. "That one's the Bad Baby. And it's lying in the Big Bassinet."

"Where?" cry the girls, and then they say, "Yes, I see!"

"And that one there's the Celestial Dog Dish. And that" — he traces his finger in a wavy circle — "is the Silver Dollar Pancake."

"What's that one?" says Miranda.

"Remember *Superman II*?" Raymond's the one who takes the girls to movies no one else wants to see. "That's what's left of the villains after they get turned to glass and smashed to smithereens."

"Oh, no," say the girls, and hide their faces against Raymond's long legs.

Claire's tensed, as if Raymond's infringed on Joey's right to name things, or worse, is making fun of him. But Joey's laughing, he likes

Raymond's names as much as the real ones. Claire steps up to the telescope and aims it at the thin crescent moon, at that landscape of chalk mountains and craters like just-burst bubbles. But all she sees is the same flat white she can see with her naked eye. Something's wrong with the telescope, or with her. The feeling she gets reminds her of waking up knowing the day's already gone wrong but not yet why, of mornings when Poppy's been sick in the night, or last summer when Joey's father was dying.

By now the others have all lain down on the hillside to look for shooting stars. There aren't any, not yet. Claire wonders if Dottie is listening to the inner silence or thinking of past lives, if Raymond is inventing more constellations. She can't imagine what Joey's thinking. She herself can't get her mind off Jeanette the electrician and her boyfriend, drinking penny-royal tea and checking that sliver of moon to see if this is a safe night for love.

On the way in, Joey says, "Lying out there, I remembered this magazine article I haven't thought of in years, about Jean Genet at the '68 Democratic convention in Chicago. The whole time, he kept staring at the dashboard of the car they were driving him around in. And afterwards, when they asked him what he thought of it—the riots, the beatings and so forth—he just shrugged and said, 'What can you expect from a country that would make a car named Galaxy?'"

Over coffee, the conversation degenerates into stories they've told before, tales of how the children tyrannize and abuse them, have kept them prisoner in their own homes for years at a time. The reason they can talk like this is that they all know: The children are the light of their lives. A good part of why they stay here is that Vermont seems like an easy place to raise kids. Even their children have visionary names: Poppy, Miranda. O brave new world!

When Claire first moved here with Dell, she commuted to New York, where she was working as a free-lance costume designer. She likes to tell people that the high point of her career was making a holster and fringed vest and chaps for a chicken to wear on "Hee Haw." Later she got to see it on TV, the chicken panicky and humiliated in its cowboy suit, flapping in circles while Grandpa Jones fired blanks at its feet and yelled, "Dance!" Soon it will be Halloween and Claire will sew Poppy a costume. So far she's been a jar of peanut butter, an anteater with pockets full of velveteen ants, Rapunzel. Last fall Claire made her a caterpillar suit with a back which unzipped and reversed out into butterfly wings. Poppy's already told her that this year she wants to be a New Wave, so all Claire will have to do is rip up a T-shirt and buy tights and wraparound shades and blue spray-on washable hair dye.

Dottie is telling about the girls making vanishing cream when Joey pretends to hear something in the garden and excuses himself and goes out. Dottie says she wants to stay up for the meteor shower but is feeling tired so she'll lie down awhile on the living-room couch.

Claire and Raymond are left alone at the table. It takes them so long to start talking, Claire's glad her crush on Raymond will never be anything more; if they had to spend a day in each other's company, they'd run out of things to say. Still it's exciting. Raymond seems nervous, too.

Finally he asks how her day was, and Claire's surprised to hear herself say, "Pretty awful." She hadn't meant to complain, nor had she thought her day was so awful. Now she thinks maybe it was. "Nothing really," she says. "One little thing after another. Have you ever had days when you pick up a pen and the phone rings and when you get off, you can't find the pen?"

"Me?" says Raymond. "I've had decades like that."

Claire says, "I woke up thinking I'd be nice and cook Poppy some French toast. So I open the egg carton and poke my finger through one of those stuck-on leaky eggs. When I got through cleaning the egg off the refrigerator, the milk turned out to be sour. I figured, Well, I'll make her scrambled eggs with coriander, she likes that. I went out to the garden for coriander and all the tomatoes were lying on the ground. The awful part was that most of them looked fine from on top, you had to turn them over to see they were smashed. You know: first you think it's all right and then it isn't all right."

"I almost never think it's all right," says Raymond. "That's how I take care of that."

"Know how I took care of it?" says Claire. "I went crying to Joey. Then I went upstairs and got out these star decals I'd been saving, I thought it would make me feel better. I'd been planning to paste them on the ceiling over the tub so I could take a shower with all the lights out and the stars glowing up above and even in winter it would be like taking a shower outside." Suddenly Claire is embarrassed by this vision of herself naked in the warm steamy blackness under the faint stars. She wonders if Dottie is listening from the other room and is almost glad the next part is about finding the shampoo bottle.

"That's life," says Raymond. "Reach for the stars and wind up with a bottle of piss."

"That's what I thought," says Claire. "But listen." She tells him about calling the girls in and when she says, "Like newborn giraffes," she really does feel awful, as if she's serving her daughter up so Raymond will see her as a complicated person with a daily life rich in similes and astonishing spiritual reverses. Now she understands why she hadn't mentioned the incident to Dottie or Joey. She was saving it for Raymond so it wouldn't be just a story she'd told before. But Raymond's already saying, "I know. Sometimes one second can turn the whole thing around.

"One winter," he says, "Miranda was around two, we were living in Roxbury, freezing to death. We decided it was all or nothing. We sold everything, got rid of the apartment, bought tickets to some dinky Caribbean island where somebody told us you could live on fish and mangoes and coconuts off the trees. I thought, I'll paint shells, sell them to the tourists. But when we got there, it wasn't mango season, the fish weren't running, and the capital city was one giant cinderblock motel. There was a housing shortage, food shortage, an everything shortage.

"So we took a bus across the island, thinking we'd get off at the first tropical paradise, but no place seemed very friendly and by then Miranda was running another fever. We wound up in the second-biggest city, which looked pretty much like a bad neighborhood in L.A. We were supposed to be glad that our hotel room had a balcony facing main street. Dottie put Miranda to bed, then crawled in and pulled the covers over her head and said she wasn't coming out except to fly back to Boston.

"At that moment, we heard a brass band, some drums. By the time I wrestled the balcony shutters open, a parade was coming by. It was the tail end of carnival, I think. The whole island was there, painted and feathered and glittered to the teeth, marching formations of guys in ruffly Carmen Miranda shirts with marimbas, little girls done up like bumblebees with antennae bobbing on their heads. Fever or no fever, we lifted Miranda up to see. And maybe it was what she'd needed all along. Because by the time the last marcher went by, her fever was gone.

"Miranda fell asleep, then Dottie. I went for a walk. On the corner, a guy was selling telescopes. Japanese-made, not like that one out there, but good. They must have been stolen off some boat, they were selling for practically nothing. So I bought one and went down to the beach. The beach was deserted. I stayed there I don't know how long.

It was the first time I ever looked through a telescope. It was something."

For the second time that day, Claire's struck speechless. Only this time, what's astonishing is, she's in pain. She feels she's led her whole life wrong. What did she think she was doing? If only she could have been on that beach with Raymond looking through a telescope for the first time, or even at the hotel when he came back. Suddenly her own memories seem two-dimensional, like photographs, like worn-out duplicate baseball cards she'd trade all at once for that one of Raymond's. She tells herself that if she'd married Raymond, she might be like Dottie now, confused and restless and wanting only to believe that somewhere there is a weed for her need. She remembers the end of the Hammett story: After Flitcraft's brush with death, he goes to Seattle and marries a woman exactly like the wife he left on the other side of that beam. There's no guarantee that another life will be better or even different from your own, and Claire knows that. But it doesn't help at all.

There's a silence. Claire can't look at Raymond. At last he says, "If I could paint what I saw through that telescope that night, do you think I'd ever paint another dancing vegetable in my whole fucking life?"

For all Raymond's intensity, it's kind of a funny question, and Claire laughs, mostly from relief that the moment is over. Then she notices that Dottie has come in. Dottie looks a little travel-worn, as if she might actually have crossed the steppes from Moscow to Paris. She seems happy to be back. As it turns out, she's been closer than that. Because what she says is, "Suppose I'd believed that old lady and dropped her off in the middle of Montpelier? What would have happened then?"

Claire wants to say something fast before Raymond starts inventing adventures for a crazy old lady alone in Montpelier. Just then, Joey reappears. Apparently, he's come back in and gone upstairs without their hearing; he's got the girls ready for bed, scrubbed and shiny, dressed in long white cotton nightgowns like slender Edwardian angels. Claire looks at the children and the two sets of parents and thinks a stranger walking in would have trouble telling: Which one paints dancing vegetables? Which one's lived before as a Napoleonic soldier? Which ones have mated for life? She thinks they are like constellations, or like that engraving on Evelyn's father's desk, or like sunflowers seen from below. Depending on how you look, they could be anything.

Then Raymond says, "It's almost midnight," and they all troop outside. On the way out, Raymond hangs back and when Claire catches up with him, he leans down so his lips are grazing her ear and says, "I hope this doesn't turn out to be another Comet Kohoutek."

Outside, Claire loses sight of them, except for the girls, whose white nightgowns glow in the dark like phosphorescent stars. She lays down on the grass. She's thinking about Kohoutek and about that first winter she and Joey lived together. How excited he was at the prospect of seeing a comet, and later, how disappointed! She remembers that the Museum of Natural History set up a dial-in Comet News Hot-line which was supposed to announce new sightings and wound up just giving data about Kohoutek's history and origins. Still Joey kept calling long distance and letting the message run through several times. Mostly he did it when Claire was out of the house, but not always. Now, as Claire tries not to blink, to stretch her field of vision wide enough for even the most peripheral shooting star, she keeps seeing how Joey looked in those days when she'd come home and stamp the snow off her boots and see him — his back to her, his ear to the phone, listening. And now, as always, it's just when she's thinking of something else that she spots it — that ribbon of light streaking by her so fast she can never be sure if she's really seen it or not.

Tobias Wolff

Coming Attractions

Jean was alone in the theater. She had seen the customers out, locked the doors, and zipped up the night's receipts in the bank deposit bag. Now she was taking a last look around while she waited for her boss to come back and drive her home.

Mr. Munson had left after the first show to go ice skating at the new mall on Buena Vista. He'd been leaving early for almost a month now and at first Jean thought he was committing adultery against his wife, until she saw him on the ice one Saturday afternoon while she was out shoplifting with her girlfriend Kathy. They stopped by the curved window that ran around the rink and watched Mr. Munson crash into the wall several times. "Fat people shouldn't skate," Kathy said, and they walked on.

Most nights Mr. Munson came back to the theater around eleven. This was the latest he had ever been. It was almost twelve o'clock.

Someone had left an orange scarf on one of the seats in the back row. Under the same seat lay a partially eaten hambone and a bottle of hot sauce. The hambone still looked like what it was, an animal's leg, and when she saw it Jean felt weak. She picked up the scarf and left the food for Mr. Munson to deal with. If he said anything about it she would just play dumb. She put the scarf in the lost-and-found bag and walked toward the front of the theater, glancing from side to side to scan the lengths of the rows.

Halfway down the aisle Jean found a pair of sunglasses. They were Guccis. She dropped them in the bag and tried to forget about them, as if she were a regular honest person who did not steal lost items and everything else that wasn't bolted down, but Jean knew that she was going to keep the sunglasses and this knowledge made her resistance feel ridiculous. She walked a few rows further, then gave a helpless shrug as if someone were watching and took the sunglasses out of the bag. They didn't fit. Her face was too narrow for them, her nose too thin. They made everything dim and kept slipping down, but Jean left them on as she worked her way toward the front of the theater.

In the first row on the right, near the wall, Jean saw a coat draped over one of the seats. She moved along the row to pick it up. Then she stopped and took off the sunglasses, because she had decided to believe that the coat was not a coat, but a dead woman wearing a coat. A dead woman all by herself in a theater at midnight.

Jean closed her eyes and made a soft whimpering noise like a dreaming dog makes. It sounded phony to her, so she stopped doing it; she opened her eyes and walked back along the row and up the aisle toward the lobby.

Jean put the lost-and-found bag away, then stood by the glass entrance doors and watched the traffic. She leaned forward as each new line of cars approached, looking through her own reflected face for Mr. Munson's Toyota. The glass grew so foggy from her breath that Jean could barely see through it. She became aware of her breathing, how shallow and fast it was. The game with the coat had scared her more than she'd meant it to. Jean watched some more cars go by. Finally she turned away and crossed the lobby to Mr. Munson's office.

Jean locked the office door behind her, but the closed door made her feel trapped. She unlocked the door again and left it open. From Mr. Munson's desk she could see the Coke machine and a row of posters advertising next week's movie. The desktop was empty except for the telephone and a picture of Mrs. Munson standing beside a snowdrift back where the Munsons used to live — Minnesota or Wisconsin. Mrs. Munson had on a parka, and she was pointing at the top of the drift to show how tall it was.

The snow made Jean think of her father.

It was quiet in the office. Jean laid her head on her crossed arms and closed her eyes. Almost at once she opened them again. She sat up and pulled the telephone across the desk and dialed her father's number. It was three hours later there and he was a heavy sleeper, so she let the phone ring for a long time. At first she held the receiver tight against her ear. Then she laid it down on the desk and listened to it until she heard a voice. Jean picked up the receiver again. It was her stepmother, Linda, saying "Hello? . . . Hello? . . . Hello? . . ." Jean would have hung up on her but she heard the fear in Linda's voice like an echo of her own, and she couldn't do it. "Hello," she said.

"Hello? Who is this, please?"

"Jean," Jean murmured.

"Gee-Gee? Is this Gee-Gee?"

"It's me," Jean said.

"It's you," Linda said. "My God, you gave me a fright."

"I'm sorry."

"What time is it out there?"

"Twelve. Ten past twelve."

"It's three o'clock in the morning here, lambchop. We're later than you are."

"I know."

"I just wondered if maybe you thought we were earlier. Wow, just hang on till I get myself together." A moment later Linda said, "There. Pulse normal. All systems go. So where are you, anyway?"

"At work."

"That's right, your dad told me you had a job. Gee-Gee with a job! You're just turning into a regular little grownup, aren't you?"

"I guess," Jean said.

"Well, I think that's just super."

Jean nodded.

"I'm big on people doing for themselves," Linda said. "Fifteen isn't too young. I started work when I was twelve and I haven't stopped since."

"I know," Jean said.

Linda laughed. "Christ almighty, the jobs I've had. I could tell you stories."

Jean smiled politely into the receiver. She caught herself doing it and made a face.

"I guess you want to talk to old grumpy bear," Linda said.

"If that's okay."

"I hope it isn't bad news. You're not preggers, are you?"

"No."

"How about your brother?"

"Tucker isn't pregnant either," Jean said. "He hasn't started dating yet."

Linda laughed again. "I didn't mean *that*. I meant how *is* he?"

"Tucker's doing fine."

"And your mom?"

"She's fine too. We're all fine."

"That's great," Linda said, "because you know how your dad is about bad news. He's just not set up for it. He's more of a good news person."

Jean gave Linda the finger. She mashed it against the mouthpiece, then said, "Right." And Linda *was* right. Jean knew that, knew she wouldn't have said anything even if her father had come to the telephone except how great she was, and how great Tucker and her mom were, because telling him anything else would be against the rules. "Everyone's fine," Jean repeated. "I just had this urge to talk to him, that's all."

"Sure you did," Linda said. "Don't think he doesn't get the same urge sometimes."

"Tell him hi," Jean said. "Sorry I woke you up."

"That's what we're here for, dumpling. I'll see if I can get him to write you. He keeps meaning to, but letters are hard for him. He likes to be more hands-on with people. Still, I'll see what I can do, okay? You take care now."

Jean smashed the phone down and yelled, "Fool!" She leaned violently back in the chair and crossed her legs. "Stupid hag," she said. "Crone."

She went on like this until she couldn't think of anything else. Then she called her mother's apartment. Tucker answered the phone. "Tucker, what are you doing up?" Jean asked.

"Nothing," Tucker said. "You're supposed to be home. Mom said you'd be home now."

"And you're supposed to be in bed," Jean told him. She heard a woman's voice shrieking, then two gunshots and a blare of music. "I can't believe you're still up," Jean said. "Let me speak to Mom."

"What?"

"Let me speak to Mom."

"She's not here," Tucker said. "Jean, know what?"

Jean closed her eyes.

"There's a bicycle in the swimming pool," Tucker said. "In the deep end. Under the diving board. Mrs. Fox told me I could keep it if we get it out. It's red," he added.

"Tucker, where's Mom? I want to talk to her."

"She went out with Uncle Nick."

"Where?"

Tucker didn't answer.

"Where did they go, Tucker?"

Tucker still didn't answer. Jean heard the sound of police sirens and squealing tires, and knew that he was watching the television again. He'd forgotten all about her. She screamed his name into the receiver. "What?" he said.

"Where are the grownups?"

"I don't know. Jean, are you coming home now?"

"In a few minutes. Go to bed, Tucker."

"Okay," he said. Then he said, "'Bye," and hung up.

Jean got the telephone book out of the desk, but she could not remember Nick's last name. His number was probably lying around the apartment somewhere, in fact she knew it was, she had seen it, on her mom's bedside table or stuck to the refrigerator with a magnet. But if she asked Tucker to look for it he would get all confused and start crying.

Jean got up and stood in the doorway. A jogger wearing phosphorescent stripes ran past the lobby window. The Coke machine gave a long rattling shudder, then went off with a sigh. Jean felt hungry. She got herself a package of Milk Duds from the refreshment counter and carried them back to Mr. Munson's office, where she chewed mouthful after mouthful until her jaws were tired. Jean put the rest of the Milk Duds in her purse with the sunglasses. Then she took out the telephone book and looked for the name of her English teacher, Mr. Hopkins. Mr. Hopkins also taught Driver's Ed and Kathy said that he had practically climbed on top of her when they were doing parallel parking. Jean hated him for that. How could someone recite poetry the way Mr. Hopkins did and still want Kathy?

His number wasn't in the book. Jean kept flipping through the pages. She chose a name and dialed the number and a man answered right away. In a soft voice he said, "Yes." Not "Yes?" but "Yes," as if he'd been expecting this call.

"Mr. Love," Jean said, "have I got news for you."

"Who is this?" he asked. "Do you know what time it is?"

"The news just came in. We thought you'd want to hear it right away. But if you wish to refuse the call all you have to do is say so."

"I'm not sure I understand," Mr. Love said.

"Do you wish to refuse the call, Mr. Love?"

He did not answer right away. Then he said, "Don't tell me I won something."

"Won something? Mr. Love, that is the understatement of the century."

"Just a minute," he said. "I have to get my glasses."

"This *is* Mr. Love, I assume," Jean asked when he returned to the telephone.

"Yes, ma'am. One and the same."

"We can't be too careful," Jean told him. "We're not talking about a bunch of steak knives here."

"I've never won anything before," Mr. Love said. "Just spelling bees. When I was a kid I could spell the paint off the walls."

"I guess I've got you on the edge of your seat," Jean said.

Mr. Love laughed.

"You sound like a nice person," Jean said. "Where are you from?"

Mr. Love laughed again. "You're deliberately tying me up in knots."

Jean said, "We have a few standard questions we like to ask." She took the sunglasses from her purse and slipped them on. She leaned back and looked up at the ceiling. "We like to get acquainted with our winners."

"You've got me in a state," Mr. Love said. "All right, here goes. Born and raised in Detroit. Joined the Navy after Pearl Harbor. Got my discharge papers in San Diego, June forty-six, and moved up here a couple weeks later. Been here ever since. That's about it."

"Good. So far so good. Age, Mr. Love?"

"Sixty-one."

"Marital status?"

"No status at all. I'm a single man."

"Do you mean to say, Mr. Love, that you have lived more than half a century and never entered into holy matrimony?"

Mr. Love was silent for a moment. Then he said, "Come on now—what's all this about?"

"One more question, Mr. Love. Then we'll talk prizes."

Mr. Love said nothing, but Jean could hear him breathe.

She picked up the photograph of Mrs. Munson and laid it face down on the desk. "Here's the question, Mr. Love. I lie and steal and sleep around. What do you think about that?"

"Ah," Mr. Love said. "So I didn't win anything."

"Well, sir, no. I have to say no."

He cleared his throat and said, "I don't follow."

"It's a prank," Jean told him. "I'm a prankster."

"I understand that. I just don't see the point. What's the point?"

Jean let the question pass.

"Well, you're not the first to make a fool out of me," Mr. Love said, "and I suppose you won't be the last."

"I don't actually sleep around," Jean said.

He said, "You need to learn some concern for other people. Do you go to church?"

"No, sir. Sometimes back home we used to, but not here. Only once on Easter. The priest didn't even give a sermon. All he did was play a tape of a baby being born, with whale songs in the background." Jean waited for Mr. Love's reaction. He didn't seem to have one. "I don't actually sleep around," Jean repeated. "Just with one of my teachers. He's married," she added.

"Married!" Mr. Love said. "That's terrible. How old are you?"

"He thinks I'm brilliant," Jean said. "Brilliant and seductive. He kept staring at me in class. The next thing I knew he was writing poems on the back of my essays, and that's how it started. He's hopelessly in love with me but I could care less. I'm just playing him along."

"God in heaven," Mr. Love said.

"I'm awful to him. Absolutely heartless. I make fun of him in front of my friends. I do imitations of him. I even do imitations of him in bed, all the sounds he makes and everything. I guess you could say I'm just totally out of control. Don't ask me to tell you where it is, but I have this tattoo that says X-RATED. It's my motto. That and 'Live fast, die young.' Whenever I'm doing something really depraved I always say 'Live fast, die young.' I probably will, too."

"I'm at a loss," Mr. Love said. "I wish I knew what to do here."

He was quiet.

"Say something," Jean told him. "Bawl me out."

"I don't know you. I don't even know your name. I might be of some help if I knew your name."

"Fat chance," Jean said.

"Then I just don't know what to say."

Jean heard the snapping of the lock in the lobby door. "Adieu," she said, and hung up. She took the sunglasses off and put them in her purse, then stood and walked around the desk in time to see Mr. Munson swinging toward the office between a pair of crutches, one plaster-bound foot held cocked behind him. There was a bandage across his forehead. "Don't say a word," he told Jean. "I don't want to talk about it." Mr. Munson lurched past her into the office. "Just a little difficulty on the ice," he said bitterly. "Just a little taste of the old Munson karma." He took the bank deposit bag from the drawer where Jean kept it for him, unzipped it, leaned forward on his crutches, and shook the money onto the desktop. "Here," he said. Without looking up, Mr. Munson held out a five to Jean. "There's a cab waiting out front."

"A cab?"

"Do you expect me to drive in this condition? Look at me, for Christ's sake. I'm a mess."

"You don't look that bad," Jean told him.

"I look like the goddam *Spirit of Seventy-six* or something," Mr. Munson said. He lowered himself into the chair and propped his crutches against the desk. "I used to be good," he said, "I mean really good." He raised his eyes to Jean. "I'm nice to you, aren't I? I don't yell at you when you screw up. I don't say anything when you sneak your little friend in. You shouldn't look at me like that," he said. "You should try to look sorry."

Tucker was asleep on the floor in front of the television. Jean opened up the Hide-a-bed and managed to get him into his pajamas and between the covers without waking him up. Then she ransacked her mother's room for Nick's telephone number. She didn't find it, but she did find a new letter from her father. Jean sat on the bed and read the letter through, scowling at the sugary words he used, sometimes repeating them in a sarcastic tone. They still wrote each other love letters, her mother and father, but they had no right to; not now, not after what they'd done. It was disgusting.

Jean went to her own room. She read *Silas Marner* for a while, then got undressed and stood in front of the mirror. She studied herself. She turned and glanced coldly over her shoulder.

Jean faced the mirror again and practiced looking sad but brave. Then she got the sunglasses out of her purse and put them on, along with one of the blouses she'd stolen at Bullock's last weekend. She switched off all the lights except the swag lamp above her desk, so that she looked as if she were standing under a streetlight. The blouse hung halfway down her bare thighs. Jean turned the wide collar up, and lowered her eyelids, and let her mouth fall open a little. "I think of you all the time," she whispered, reciting her father's words, "every day and every night, dearest love, only love of my life." Jean moved her shoulders sinuously to make the sequins shimmer. "Dearest sackbutt," she said. "Dearest raisinbrain." She pursed her lips and made her eyelids flutter.

Tucker yelled something from the next room.

Jean went to the doorway. "Go to sleep, Tucker."

"I want Mom," Tucker said.

Jean took the sunglasses off. Tucker was sitting up in bed, looking wildly around as if he didn't know where he was. Jean walked across the room and sat down beside him. "Mom'll be home in a minute." Tucker's hair was sticking up all over, and Jean began to smooth it down. "You want a glass of water?"

"I want Mom."

"Listen, Tucker." Jean kept combing back his hair with her fingers. "Listen, tomorrow is going to be a really special day but it won't come unless you go to sleep."

He looked around the room again, then back at Jean. "Special how?"

"You'll see."

"You mean when I wake up?"

"Right, but first you have to go to sleep." Jean pushed against Tucker as she stroked his hair, and at last he relented and lay down again.

"Promise?" he said.

"Promise."

When Tucker was asleep Jean got up and went outside. She leaned against the door, her skin bristling with cold, and looked around at the other apartments. All of them were dark. Jean hugged herself and padded along the rough wooden walkway, down the steps to the courtyard.

The pool lights were still on so that nobody would fall in and sue. Still hugging herself, Jean tested the water with one foot. It was icy. Mrs. Fox must have turned off the heat. That was just like her, to turn the heat on in the summer and turn it off in the winter. Stupid crone. It wasn't even her money. Jean sniffed and rubbed her arms and stuck her foot in the water again, this time past the ankle. Again she looked at the dark windows all around. Then she peeled off the blouse, tossed it behind her, and jumped in.

Jean's heart clenched when she hit the water. She kicked herself back up, gasping for air, and grabbed the ladder. Tremors twitched across her shoulders. Her toes curled painfully, then went numb. Jean held on to the ladder and waited for the numbness to spread. She looked up. A plane was moving slowly across the sky. Jean timed her breathing to the blinking of its lights, and when she had calmed herself she took a series of deeper and deeper breaths until she had the one she wanted. Then she pushed off and dove toward the glowing red triangle at the bottom of the pool.

Her eyes ached. That was all she felt. Jean closed her fingers around the handlebars and tried to scissor-kick the bicycle up with her, but when she had it halfway to the surface it seemed to take on weight, and she had to let it go. It settled to the bottom without a sound, sending only a dull shock up through the water. Jean filled her lungs and went back under. She took hold of the handlebars again. She dragged the bike along the tiles to the side of the pool, where she went into a crouch and shoved away hard from the bottom. Kicking furiously, clawing the water with her free hand, Jean rose slowly toward the gleaming chrome of the ladder and just managed to grab the second rung as the bike began to pull her back down.

She let out the last of her air.

The bike was getting heavy. Jean brought her knees up and got her feet on the lowest rung. She rested a moment. Then she moved her free hand to the rail and began to straighten her legs, pushing herself up toward the light flashing on the surface just above her. She felt her mouth start to open. *No*, she thought, but her mouth opened anyway and Jean was choking when her head broke through to air. She coughed out the water in her throat and then gagged on the chlorine aftertaste until she almost puked. Her eyes burned.

Jean climbed the ladder to where she could work her hips over the edge of the pool and slide forward a bit. She let go of the rail and wiped her face. Her other arm was dead, but she knew the bike was still there because she could feel its weight in her shoulders and back. In a little while she would pull it out. No problem — just as soon as she got herself back together. But until then she couldn't do a thing but lie with her cheek on the cement, and blink her eyes, and savor the cold air that passed through her.

Zulfikar Ghose

A Translator's Fiction

North of Lima, on the coast of Peru — such was my experience during the five days that I had occasion to spend in that region — there is a sparkling clarity on winter afternoons that, as with the addition of water to certain liquors, begins to turn milky just before sunset: one imagines it is only the exhaustion of all the brilliance that had prevailed during the day and one looks at the empurpled western horizon in expectation of witnessing the sun's spectacular sinking, but the purple has already vanished, the fog has come in, and one realizes that phantom shadows have begun to waver over the land, and it is only a matter of minutes, while the sun has still not actually set, that darkness quite overwhelms the land. The following day, the risen sun does not dissipate the darkness, and just when one begins to despair of ever seeing again that glorious perspective of the Andes that, tourist guide in hand, one had seen from the southeastern corner of Plaza de la Constitución, looking east down Paseo Colón with its splendid rows of cypresses, suddenly, around eleven in the morning, it is as if the lights are brightly turned on to illuminate the stage for the first act, full of optimism and gaiety, of a drama destined to end four acts later in a tragedy on a darkened stage.

The theatrical image is the somewhat fanciful figure employed by my host, Señor Próspero Aguilar, from the terrace of whose house overlooking the Pacific I first saw the fog rising so dramatically. "Imagine," he said, "a theater. You know the play, can recite many of its lines from memory, but you are attending a new production, and suddenly you are assaulted by sensations you had not anticipated."

Señor Aguilar's metaphor perfectly mirrored what he talked about: the choice of his figure was not original, as he himself knew, though he made no apology for resorting to the familiar image; indeed, the glimmer in his eyes indicated that he was aware of enjoying the position of a critic who knew he himself was the ultimate, and finally the only, object of his own theory, but that was only his way of accommodating his listener: which is to say he made me feel quite at ease for there seemed to be no threat of originality in his speech. Once he had thus drawn me into his confidence, however, he astonished me with a twist in the conversation for which I had been unprepared — in the process perhaps giving me a clue (which I apprehended only in retrospect) that the regular tricks of my storyteller's trade were child's play to him. I had only remarked at the curious phenomenon of the weather; he, seeming to expatiate on that subject, giving me the impression that he was only uttering the usual baroque language which was no more than a civilized complement to the rather pleasant, albeit ordinary, Chilean wine that we drank, subtly transformed the subject and had me — me the novelist and he the critic! — entirely submerged in what he was amused later to hear me refer to as the Jamesian great glazed tank of fiction.

His narrative centered upon the life of an American named Tony Quaglino who had gone to Otavalo in 1969 as an emissary of one of those altruistic bodies, like the Peace Corps, seeking to escape the sense of desolation that tormented his generation, leaving the sooty air of urban New Jersey for what he resignedly expected would be a wilderness but what turned out to be a charming ancient civilization peopled by ruddy-complexioned Indians who grew corn and slaughtered pigs. Señor Aguilar paused after his introductory description of Quaglino — twenty-two years old, dark Italian type, guilty at his good fortune in not being drafted — and, leaning forward to place my glass on the table, I recounted briefly the conjectures that had come to my mind with its habit of inventing stories with only the slightest suggestion from life to prompt it. It was to be a story of a discovery of origins. Or about the disenchantment of naïve presumptions concerning a society in its innocence. Or perhaps about spiritual growth? "Ah, my friend," Señor Aguilar said, "you know too much about life, which serves you admirably with its terrible dramas for your stories, but what do you know of the soul's residence in darkness?"

I thought the last a rather extravagant phrase in the mouth of a critic famous in South America for his iconoclasm. "Not at all," he countered, remaining grim although my expression had been jocular, "and please let us not concern ourselves with a public mask." Surely, as my translator, he must understand that I knew nothing about life except for the annual list of precautions my doctor obliged me to take? But Señor Aguilar was no longer in a mood to share a joke and proposed we retire to the living room for it was beginning to be chilly on the terrace. Rising, I observed that the horizon had gone entirely a dark gray. "Quaglino's story will amaze you," he said, leading me into the house.

It took us a few minutes to settle ourselves in comfortable leather chairs with a small mahogany table between us. There was first the solemn business of obtaining ice from the kitchen and pouring out tall glasses of Scotch and soda, and, of course, it would have been impolite of me had I not, while my host silently prepared the drinks, expressed my admiration for the large Botero painting that hung on the wall, congratulating him from across the room for possessing so fine a picture. It occurred to me that something of Botero's humor was perceptible in the person of Señor Aguilar, who, like the artist's figures, was a globular creature. When I had first met him a few years earlier, he had suddenly said, after the small talk between author and translator had been exhausted, "Ironies attend our birth." He had proceeded to give an autobiographical example. "My humble parents, who could not write the language they spoke, named me Próspero, no doubt hoping that I would have better luck in the game of life, little knowing that I was destined to study the language of Shakespeare. But observe this further irony: given an exceptional talent with words, I was not given the magic wand of creation, only a ballpoint pen with which to make marks in the margins of others or to substitute their words with Spanish ones." He was the translator of my novel that I had had the temerity, or the foolishness, to entitle *Verónica and the Góngora Passion*, and had written in a language that had deliberate affinities with the style of G. K. Chesterton, with a pinch of suspense from Robert Louis Stevenson — a vain attempt to avoid the vulgarity of being considered *modern*, vain because British and American reviewers had ignored the book as one more experimental novel with inflated avant-garde pretensions. My poor Verónica died before she could be born. Señor Aguilar had said excitedly, "Ah, my ballpoint will yet be a wand!" and made the preposterous proposal that his translation be presented to the Spanish-speaking world as the original, allowing paperback houses in London and New York to bring out their editions as a translation. The critic, I observed to him, was ever an opportunist wanting to usurp the writer's eminence. "What do you want," he asked pointedly, "fame in this life and wealth for your heirs?" I did not understand his question, and he took my puzzled silence to indicate acquiescence in his fatal scheme — in due course, the English-language paperback edition was attacked for the translator's wooden, old-fashioned prose style, and my poor Verónica languishes as an old maid in one culture and drives men crazy with her gaudy whorishness in the other. I walked away from the Botero seeing that my host had placed the two glasses on the small mahogany table and had himself taken a seat next to it and waited to resume his story.

Of course, Quaglino's earlier experiences in the Ecuadorian interior were merely the predictable impressions of a young American whose only idea of a foreign world was a ten-day tour of Britain during his senior year in high school when without his conscious reflection the idea had been lodged in his mind that landscapes — moist, overcast, misty, the great elm trees a liquid shimmering in the middle distance — were most deeply colored when they were blurred, the general gray throbbing with an intense vivacity, all blue and green and yellow, but who had flown back to New York and blindly crossed the city and returned home without having the feeling that he had recently left it; so that his arrival in the Andes at first evoked the usual expressions of how charming this new world was, how terribly sharp its edges, how different was its pace — all the trite observations of a young man who was arrogantly convinced that he was experienced in life: had he not witnessed the maturing of his nation, beginning to doubt its role in the world, himself a spokesman for anguish, for repentance in a country where everyone had begun to talk feverishly, passionately; and had he not undergone personal initiations in the underworld of violent sex and drugs when only thirteen and fourteen, and been in the streets when the blacks rioted, smashing the plate-glass security of the fancy stores, setting fires in the nation's blood? His closest friend Jimmy had been drafted and in that tormented time that debauched the young, Jimmy, on the last night before he wore the uniform, rolled his father's blue Mustang from a cliff and sent it smashing among the rocks, and two months later, though it seemed he had only gone the weekend, taken the return flight home, Jimmy was delivered back to his country in a plastic bag. And the young women of his group, hysterical with losing their men to the whore ideology, among them Betsy whom he believed he loved, threw away the old Doris Day Susan Hayward expectations of their mothers' generation, and in the confusion of voices in the militant time, slogans everywhere, revisions of customs, everywhere the shrieking questions and accusations, demanded the male despise himself, and Betsy who, like a pagan bowing before the lingam, had been thrillingly idolatrous in their carnal exchanges, announced to him, standing erect in her black turtleneck and blue jeans, that she would never love a man again.

And, of course, Quaglino's first few months in the new world had been lost in the foreigner's eager exhibitions to be like the natives, strumming a guitar among peasants in a bar, and in expressions of an inflated approval of the indigenous culture. But then Fourth of July nostalgia took him to Quito and the embassy's barbecue and the consular section's amateur country western whining, mildly nourishing at first with flavors of home, triggered the mechanism of diabolical memory, of the stress of being, the brightness of the Andean sky inexplicably befogged in his vision, and he walked without thinking, but driven only to keep moving, gulping the thin air like one trying to allay an attack of nausea, until he arrived in the old city. All churches and preserved houses with geraniums in the window boxes. Iglesia de San Francisco, Iglesia de Santo Domingo, Capilla de las madres de San Diego. He opened the heavy wooden doors into the baroque interiors, columns and altars of gold, of gold the sacred heart on paintings. And there was that picture, the *Virgin of the Flowers*, the baby in the crook of her right arm, in the gilt frame with the painted frame of flowers around the oval window that revealed the dark interior where she sat, a flower in her left hand, and the child's hand at her breast about to reach for the flower, and Quaglino could not tell why the picture should draw all the air out of his lungs and fill them with black, boiling tar. It was dark in the church. A little murky light from the high begrimed windows seemed more like floating mist than a diffusion of the sun's rays and only served to make the shadows more intense. But the uncanny perception of the soul needs no external illumination, and Quaglino, who had seen a blurred grayish landscape become a vivid assault on his vision without remarking upon the curious phenomenon and perhaps had been in the grip of progressive disturbances that, confounding the visible ordinary reality, had been dismissed as aberrations, now felt a severe choking in his throat and at the same time a descent into darkness as if the mind had finally been able to release the spring that unlocked the door to ecstasy but, entering, found itself only in a void.

Quaglino never knew what happened, how he recovered his breath and walked away from the *Virgin of the Flowers*, from her oppressive innocence, from the fearful beauty of the child, how he left the city and found himself after a time, a moment, a year, that he had no way of measuring, beside a narrow river in a jungle. Who can believe the chronicler of illusions, and who, suddenly plunged into fissures that open in the human mind, can doubt the inventor of dreams fabricating the swirling misty forms that are the paradigms of a terrible reality? To remain conscious before a progression of mundane events is a sad burden that we must somehow not buckle under, but from nowhere, or from deep within the soul, comes the unexpected attack and this life is replaced by a memory, the blood that had coursed silently bursts into a million efflorescences, each one a life making a singular claim to the body from which it has been shed. It is a form of a profound distraction of the self, this casual glance that has you staring at the infinite.

A group of girls, six or seven, among them Tamarinha, all recent celebrants of a puberty rite, come to the river to wash off the ceremonious streaks of red urucu paint from their small conical breasts and slender thighs, found him where he lay in a swoon on the bank, smothering the little magenta flowers growing there in a wild profusion. Quaglino felt a shiver in his body hearing the ringing voices of the girls engaged in a boisterous splashing of one another and stood up with a start; in the same moment, the girls noticed him and went dead still, knee-deep in the water, confused and shocked as if there were another aspect of the rite, hitherto kept secret from them, that had still to be performed. But the tallest girl, Tamarinha, spoke, a long flow of guttural speech. Quaglino heard the sound of her voice come rippling in the air, wondered what meaning there must be in her words, but the hissing, squawking phrases flew past him without his being able to catch the significance of a single one. Encouraged by Tamarinha's boldness, and seeing that the man made no dangerous advance, the other girls began to hoot in a communal derision of the absurdity of his being, and in a moment had leaped out of the river and started to tear off his clothes. It was only when they saw the pale white skin of the naked man that bewilderment came over them, and they looked at one another with unspoken questions and suddenly ran off. Quaglino heard their shrieks as they fled into the darkness of the forest, and he went after them, abandoning his shredded clothes scattered among the trampled flowers. He stopped after a while, panting, noticing that the shrieking had ceased. The jungle was thick around him, long loops of creepers hung from the high trees. There was no path in the undergrowth of ferns where he stood. Not a bird broke the silence for some minutes. Then the twittering began, the voices of the girls warbling in little bursts, making cooing sounds, cackling sounds, now seemingly just behind the tree nearest him and now farther away. Blindly, he pursued the sounds. The voices broke more loudly as he came to the darkest part of the forest. "This way," they seemed to cry in a raucous bursting of sound, "come, follow quickly!" Warm now, the voices of the girls, reaching him in waves of harmony, sibilants stroking his body, and then screechy or riotous or playful, pulling him this way and that, as if they held him with a long cord tied to his waist.

When he found himself come at last to a clearing, he felt a sense of disappointment that it was only a small village with a cluster of a dozen huts that he had arrived at. A group of men and women, dispersing at the conclusion of some ceremony, noticed his appearance with mild curiosity and hardly any astonishment. Beads and macaw feathers adorned their bodies, the men smeared with ashes, the women covered from forehead to feet with geometrical red lines that created optical dislocations in their flesh. Gathered in a group like a receiving party, they stood looking at him as at a long-expected dignitary. Quaglino regarded the assembly with composure, experiencing no trepidation to find himself among savages. Indeed, he felt quite relaxed. Pools of light from the high sun breaking through the tall trees fell on the village. The huts were laid out in a circle with one larger edifice at the center. The fringe of the jungle that could be seen in between the huts was comprised of flowering bushes that, catching the scattered light in the general darkness, emitted an unnaturally bright vividness. A moaning kind of a sound, the undertone of the tribe's speech, rose among the men and the women, turned to a rapid chattering and stopped. Suddenly, the men gave a jubilant cry and rushed toward him. The women, remaining where they were, began to chant. He was taken away to the men's hut, the building at the center, where he got the impression that he was being treated with a jolly camaraderie, the men slapping his back and speaking to one another in a jovial manner while gesturing toward him with their eyes. A liquor was served and drunk with a great deal of laughter. The thick, creamy liquid seemed odorless and not too potent. The taste was not repulsive, as he had anticipated. Food was sent in. Fish and some roots ground and boiled into a mush. Not unpleasant; but as with the drink, he had tasted nothing. More liquor was passed around. The men began to sing, a nasal chanting.

Quaglino felt no apprehension at his situation, nor any curiosity as to what was about to transpire. To himself, he had become bodiless, a spirit only, his one possession the faculty of perception, which witnessed the shell of his life with the memory echoing in it of another life from which, too, the flesh had fallen: he was in a trance of being, a state not hallucinatory and not the infliction of a devilish curse, but that crossing of light forces in the mind, a projection of beams from several sources, creating where they overlap an unimagined illumination. The self, the soul then reside in darkness, paradoxically as if in the center of the sun.

He was kept in the men's hut for several weeks. The primitive world was remarkably familiar and without surprises. The men talked to him in their language, which he did not understand. He saw them go away fishing or hunting and heard the yells of the children when they returned with a catch. The women sat pounding roots outside their huts, or weaving baskets and hammocks. He was not even surprised by the extraordinary amount of ennui that the tribe had to bear, days of listlessness and unexpressed dolor.

When some prescribed duration of time had passed, when the shaman had counted so many swellings of the moon, so many afternoons when the clouds took on the shapes of beasts of prey and devoured the sky, a procession playing on homemade percussion instruments led Quaglino from the men's hut some distance to a wide pond full of water lilies and yellow hyacinths. There he was bathed, and emerging with refreshed eyes, with cooler breath, he saw beyond the chanting crowd of men the bushes and trees covered with flowers, trumpeting red blossoms and little purses of purple petals, and behind a group of yellow acacias a field of magenta flowers. Returning to the village, he was given a hut of his own where the women daily hung garlands of flowers across its open front to form a curtain. He smelled nothing, however, and tasted nothing, though food and drink were brought to him and the flowers were sprinkled at noon with water from the pond.

When another prescribed duration of time had passed, when the black clouds that brought torrential rains came no more and steam rose from the land under the noonday sun, the village commenced a celebration, eating the abundant fish from the swollen rivers, that ended on the fifth day with a procession that brought Tamarinha to his hut, her body painted with urucu, red triangles and circles all over her skin. He understood that he was being married to her, that she was his bride in the dark world, his virgin under the canopy of the jungle, that his coming to the tribe had been a portent, making him the messenger of potency, the agent of rebirth: in this bodiless life, in this casual sojourn within memory, he was the creator, his nonbeing the vessel from which must pour a vital reincarnation.

The son was born. In that unreal existence, as if the tribe around him were made up of figures in an anthropological study, his brain preoccupied itself with memories of another life — the rust spots on the door of the Mustang that he noticed just when Jimmy was letting the car roll to the edge of the cliff, the festive decorations in the store windows on Fifth Avenue each December when his parents took him to New York to see the bright lights, the Saturday nights smoking pot among compacted cars in a junk yard in Newark near a foul-smelling canal that carried industrial effluence to the river. A million details evoked again the reality and the fiction of a time now dead. Betsy had said, cruelly he then thought, "I have better things to do with my life than become a breeder." He had innocently asked, "Such as?" She had looked scornfully at him and answered in a harsh voice, "The planet's fucked, don't you realize that?" And pausing, staring at him with increasing scorn, she had added, "By *man!*" He was stunned that the vengeance taught her by her lately espoused rhetoric should unaccountably make him a particular victim. And his friend Dennis, who was dead set on enlisting if he did not get drafted, had said on being called up, "We should bomb them out of sight!" And added in his bellicose enthusiasm, "Russia and China, too!" Simon who was with them and who had realized that day that his resolution to escape to Canada would have to be carried out, had said weakly, "Come on, you can't mean that." Dennis had replied, "We've got the power, man, we've got the technology." Simon sighed and looked at Dennis in despair, saying in a soft voice, "Didn't you read about Lake Erie? Christ, technology isn't going to save us, *it* is the problem." Thus the echoes of chaos, of desperate passions, of accumulated guilts; thus the voices addicted to hope, to change; thus the fragmentation of that reality in his mind. But around him, Quaglino heard the alien voices chanting in celebration, saw processions of women at dawn and at dusk, their arms laden with flowers, come and deck the hut in which Tamarinha lay in the hammock with her child, and watched the tribe feast in jubilation. His memories of the other life, rehearsed in his own language, were more vivid than his immediate experience, which, as if happening to another, was not burdened by the torment of time and therefore passed without his senses being engaged. He remembered his months with Betsy before she changed her conviction, recalling in detail their love-making, but Tamarinha became a blank as soon as he turned his eyes away from her. The thought again came to him that he was simply not present in his body. And yet the son had been born and the birth the occasion for the tribe's enduring joy.

He was walking back one afternoon from the men's hut where he had been especially feasted and saw from a distance that the garlands of flowers hanging at the front of Tamarinha's hut formed a rectangular frame; going closer, he observed that clusters of smaller flowers on the inner edge of the frame created the effect of an oval window. Inside this window, Tamarinha was to be seen sitting in the hammock, the baby on her right thigh, with her right hand coming round the baby's back to support it, and her head leaning toward the baby's head where it rested against her right shoulder. Her eyes looked down on the flower that she held in her left hand as though she were offering it to the baby whose right hand, resting on her breast, seemed about to move to accept the flower. At Tamarinha's back, the two ends of the hammock described a perfect semicircle, but the light entering the hut gave the impression of continuing the curving line so that he saw a complete circle, the whole a diffused disc behind the mother and the child. A shudder ran through Quaglino's body that was a throbbing of a reawakening consciousness, and a blackness stormed into his brain as if his lungs had collapsed.

Señor Aguilar remained silent for several minutes. Then he shook his head and said, "The horror of such a life! The thought that had come to Quaglino's mind just before the blackness overwhelmed him was a shocking one, too abominable to utter. God forgive me if I must utter it, for without it Quaglino's story has no meaning. I derive some comfort from the fact that the vile, profane words are Quaglino's and not mine and it is with loathing, with terror, that I speak them: *Evil began with God.*"

I did not break the silence that again filled the room. On the wall, Botero's rotund figures smiled placidly in their ballooned world while my globular companion sat in a state of spiritual dejection brought on by the appalling narrative. Outside, it was completely dark. The fog was undoubtedly thick. But I remained silent not because I had been shocked by the ending of the story. Señor Aguilar had said I would be amazed by it, but he could not have suspected in what manner. The contract with the Buenos Aires publisher was still being negotiated; I had only the previous day, on my arrival, presented Señor Aguilar with a copy of the novella that, with my usual recklessness with titles, was called *The American and the Virgin*; and so far, Señor Aguilar, preoccupied with entertaining me, had not had the opportunity to go beyond touching the pages and performing the gracious gesture of gently removing the dust cover with its lurid illustration and passing his fingertips over the black cloth in which the slight volume was bound in order to express his delight in American book binding: in brief, he did not know the contents of the book, and yet he seemed already to know my story by heart.

Stanley Kunitz

Seedcorn and Windfall

We are always beginning again to live.

— MONTAIGNE

Anyone who forsakes the child he was is already too old for poetry.

*

What fascinates me about the logic of the imagination is how unpredictable it is in practice, how full of surprises. Blake's "crooked road," not the straight road of science and philosophy.

*

I like to think that it is the poet's love of particulars, the things of this world, that leads him to universals.

*

As modernists — aren't we all? — we are inclined to believe that the new age creates new forms. In reality, the sense of form is inherent in the race, substantially the same over the whole span of recorded history. Our artistic inventions, from age to age, are essentially modifications of old forms or new applications of them. In sum, form is a constant in art, as opposed to techniques and materials, which are variables.

*

A badly made thing falls apart. It takes only a few years for most of the energy to leak out of a defective work of art. To put it simply, conservation of energy is the function of form.

*

What makes form adventurous is its unpredictable appetite for particulars. The truly creative mind is always ready for the operations of chance. It wants to sweep into the constellation of the art-work as much as it can of the loose, floating matter that it encounters. How much accident can the work incorporate? How much of the unconscious life can the mind dredge up from its depths?

*

The poets of any culture inherit a common tradition, by which they are sustained and replenished. What makes them separate and distinctive is the use they make of their own past, which cannot be the same as anybody else's. The difference of memories is the difference of souls.

*

Once Theodore Roethke, in a heated defense of the melodic line that was his instrument of choice, accused Robert Lowell to his face of having "a tin ear." Cal tried to dismiss the incident as a piece of drunken foolery, but I know the charge rankled, for he recalled it to me years later after Ted had died. Poets sometimes forget their poems, but never the bad things said about them.

*

My dismay at the clutter on my desk is offset by my zest for the hunt among my papers. At an age when I should be putting my house in order, I keep accumulating bits of information, not for any particular reason and in spite of the absurdity, because I was born curious and don't know how to stop.

*

We have all been expelled from the Garden, but the ones who suffer most in exile are those who are still permitted to dream of perfection.

*

"Words, above everything else, are in poetry, sounds," said Wallace Stevens. Even when we read a poem silently, we tend to read it differently from prose, paying more attention to its rhythm and pitch and pace, its interplay of vowels and consonants, its line-by-line progression of subtle harmonies and discords corresponding with variable states of feeling or the flow of the mind itself. It is unfortunate that the word "texture," in critical terminology, is commonly employed as if it defined nothing more than a surface phenomenon rather than an intrinsic property of the medium.

*

But as I rav'd and grew more fierce and wilde
At every word,
Methought I heard one calling, *"Childe!"*
And I reply'd, *"My Lord."*

Those noble lines — resolving, absolving — take me back, through a chain of associations, to my undergraduate days at Harvard, where I came upon them and learned them by heart in a state of exaltation. Simultaneously they evoke the image of a young man with clear blue eyes and a lean, sensitive countenance. This was Robert Oppenheimer, my neighbor on Mt. Auburn Street. I thought of him then as being much more worldly and self-assured than I, with a physical grace and shining intelligence that made him stand out among his classmates, as did his taste for literature and the fine arts. How could one have predicted that this elegant youth, with so much civilization in him, was destined to occupy the center of the world's stage as "father of the atom bomb"? Freeman Dyson has written that Oppenheimer played the part of Prince Hamlet in the high drama of Los Alamos. Certainly, the story of his rise and fall has a tragic dimension. It is a story of genius and fame and power and conscience and intrigue and betrayal and ultimately of public humiliation and disgrace, till a malignancy of the throat finished him at sixty-two. "The physicists have known sin," he had confessed, "and this is a knowledge which they cannot lose." In a way, his lifelong attachment to the humanities served to separate him from his more single-minded colleagues in the wartime nuclear industry. He never lost his love for poetry, and no poem meant more to him than George Herbert's "The Collar," that passionate outcry of a man in spiritual doubt and torment. What chafed Herbert in his country parsonage was, emblematically, the clerical collar. Oppenheimer's collar was that of the modern scientist in bondage to the state and in the service of death—an unholy alliance.

*

Some artists, observed Juan Gris, "are like weavers who think they can produce a material with only one set of threads and forget that there has to be another set to hold them together." The odds are that at first, in the apprentice years, one has only a single set of threads to work with, just as one has, at that early stage, only a single Time, the present, to live in, and a single self to occupy one's thoughts. A poet without a history is not precluded from composing ingenious or melodious verses, but the achievement of a mature art is dependent on accumulations of information, associated with exercises of the spirit that imbue language with a quality of innerness, a richness of psychic texture.

*

In his book of essays, Robert Hass included an explication of one of my poems that differed radically from almost everything I thought I knew about its origin, circumstance, and meaning. Nevertheless, I felt no inclination to quarrel with his commentary. What he proposed was such a sensible and coherent interpretation of the text, consistent with the evidence available to him, that I was persuaded to accept his reading of the poem as being at least as valid as my own, even though most of his assumptions were demonstrably false.

*

No one gave better practical advice to young writers than Chekhov. He was particularly hard on examples of stylistic inflation, such effusions as "the setting sun, bathing in the waves of the darkening sea, poured its purple gold, etc." Brevity, relevance, and specification were his criteria of excellence. A passage in one of his letters reads: "In descriptions of nature you should seize upon the little particulars, grouping them in such a way that they make a clear picture, even for closed eyes. For instance, you can convey the full effect of a moonlit night if you write that on the mill-dam a little glowing star-point flashed from the neck of a broken bottle. . . ."

An entry in Chekhov's notebook, dated several years later, reveals how faithful he was to his own instructions: "A bedroom. The light of the moon shines so brightly through the window that even the buttons on his nightshirt are visible."

*

Never before, in this or any other country, have so many apprentice writers had the opportunity to study with their predecessors and ancestors. That is one explanation of why it is so difficult to detect and define a generational style in the work of our contemporaries. Instead we have an interfusion and amalgam of styles and influences, a direct transmission belt overleaping the age barrier, a two-way learning process culminating in the paradox of the young writing old, and the old writing young. Only journalists and cabalists continue to fight the war between "the ancients" and "the moderns."

*

Two infallible touchstones of the poetic art: transformation and transcendence.

*

Poetry is ultimately mythology, the telling of the stories of the soul. The old myths, the old gods, the old heroes have never died. They are only sleeping at the bottom of our minds, waiting for our call. We have need of them, never more desperately than now, for in their sum they epitomize the wisdom and experience of the race. At every true act of the imagination, whether in art or science, they stir fitfully. And the corollary is equally true: art and science cannot exist without myths and symbols.

*

A major crisis in the history of poetry occurred in the last century when the novel displaced the poem as the accepted medium for story-telling. One can argue that poetry gained something in exchange, gained a good deal, by moving inward, gradually forging a link with the new science of psychoanalysis, but it is clear that in the process of cultivating this art of introversion, poets managed to lose most of their audience. A poetry deprived of narrative is also in danger of cutting itself off from its mythological roots. This dilemma will not be solved by settling for an anecdotal art, which is a species of trivialization, or by attempting to return to straight-line, sequential narration, which offers minimal aesthetic satisfactions to the modern mind. Henry James experienced a comparable difficulty in the course of his arduous enterprise and had a revelation, which he reported in prose that seems to stutter with excitement: "I realise — none too soon — that the *scenic* method is my absolute, my imperative, my *only* salvation. *The march of an action* is the thing for me to, more and more, attach myself to. . . ."

*

Much of what passes for "meditative" poetry today suffers from the poverty of what it is meditating on.

*

Malraux said it takes sixty years to make a man, and then he is only fit to die.

*

Even on his deathbed, Samuel Johnson stayed true to his character and did not deviate from the Johnsonian style. When a friend offered to plump up his pillow, he summoned up the strength to reply, "No, it is doing all that a pillow can do."

*

When the Tzartkover Rabbi, celebrated in Hasidic lore, was asked his reason for failing to preach Torah for a long time, he gave as his answer: "There are seventy ways of reciting Torah. One of them is through silence."

*

Thoreau walked the long strand of Cape Cod "to see that seashore where man's works are wrecks; to put up at the true Atlantic House, where ocean is land-lord as well as sea-lord . . . where the crumbling land is the only invalid." To this day, at Race Point, the incoming breakers articulate their might with a long roar that changes pitch at the changing of the tides.

*

Be prepared for everything — even spontaneity.

*

In his enchanting autobiography, Konstantin Paustovsky tells the story of Bagrov, a young student revolutionary during the reign of Nicholas II, who shot Minister Stolypin dead at the Kiev opera and was sentenced to be hanged. He accepted his fate with equanimity: "What possible difference can it make to me if I eat 2,000 fewer meatballs in my life?"

*

Paustovsky's comment on the early days of the Bolshevik Revolution: "Events took place so quickly that you missed half of them by sleeping." That is the way I've always felt, even without the excuse of a revolution, and why I insist on staying awake each night until I fall apart.

*

Sometimes I feel ashamed that I've written so few poems on political themes, on the causes that agitate me. But then I remind myself that to be a poet at all in twentieth-century America is to commit a political act.

*

Of all modern institutions the State, which is the political arm of the economy, is the most terrifying, the most monstrous instrument of power. All societies profess that they are organized for the sake of human welfare and freedom, but in practice power becomes an end in itself, a self-perpetuating coalition of egoes, supported by bureaucracies that gradually suffocate the spirit of a people. "Society everywhere," wrote Emerson presciently, "is in conspiracy against the manhood of every one of its members. . . . The virtue in most request is conformity. Self-reliance is its aversion."

*

Throughout the course of history politicians have had reason to fear the wicked tongue of poets, but poets, at least in this country, do not fear politicians — they simply distrust anybody who makes a vocation out of the pursuit of power. They tend to agree with old John Adams that "Power always thinks it has a great soul and vast views beyond the comprehension of the weak and that it is doing God's service when it is violating all His laws."

*

In his 87th year, Miró told an interviewer that he felt closest to "the young — all the young generations." From childhood to age, he ruminated, "I have always lived a very intense life, almost like a monk, an austere life. It comes out in little leaves, floating about, dispersing themselves. But the trunk of the tree and the branches remain solid."

Yes, he admitted, his style had changed — changed several times, in fact, during his long life. But these changes did not imply a rejection of what he had done before. Looking back, he could see a continuity in the essence of his work, which is nourished at every stage "by all of my past, the great human past. And what looks like a zigzag is really a straight line."

*

Years ago I came to the realization that the most poignant of all lyric tensions stems from the awareness that we are dying every moment we live. To embrace such knowledge and yet to remain compassionate and whole — that is the consummation of the endeavor of art.

*

The first grand concept I had was that of death, my death, everyone's death. Through the circumstances of my childhood it was the fox at my breast, wrapped under my coat, a consuming terror. I could not sleep at night, thinking about dying. And then I realized that if I wanted to retain my sanity I had to learn how to live with this dreadful knowledge, transforming it into a principle of creation instead of destruction. The first step toward salvation was the recognition of the narrowness of my world of sympathies. My affections had to flow outward and circulate through the natural order of things. Only then did I understand that, in the great chain of being, death as well as life has its own beauty and magnificence.

Frank Bidart

Dark Night

(JOHN OF THE CROSS)

In a dark night, when the light
    burning was the burning of love (*fortuitous*
    night, fated, free, —)
    as I stole from my dark house, dark
    house that was silent, grave, sleeping, —

by the staircase that was secret, hidden,
    safe: disguised by darkness (*fortuitous*
    night, fated, free, —)
    by darkness and by cunning, dark
    house that was silent, grave, sleeping—;

in that sweet night, secret, seen by
    no one and seeing
    nothing, my only light or
    guide
    the burning in my burning heart,

night was the guide
    to the place where he for whom I
    waited, whom I had long ago chosen,
    waits: night
    brighter than noon, in which none can see—;

night was the guide
   sweeter than the sun raw at
   dawn, for there the burning bridegroom is
   bride
   and he who chose at last is chosen.

                    *

As he lay sleeping on my sleepless
   breast, kept from the beginning for him
   alone, lying on the gift I gave
   as the restless
   fragrant cedars moved the restless winds, —

winds from the circling parapet circling
   us as I lay there touching and lifting his hair, —
   with his sovereign hand, he
   wounded my neck—
   and my senses, when they touched that, touched nothing . . .

In a dark night (*there where I*
   lost myself, —) as I leaned to rest
   in his smooth white breast, everything
   ceased
   and left me, forgotten in the grave of forgotten lilies.

George Bradley

E Pur Si Muove

Of course it had been madness even to bring it up,
Sheer madness, like the sighting of sea serpents
Or the discovery of strange lights in the sky;
And plainly it had been worse than madness to insist,
To devote entire treatises and a lifetime to the subject,
To a thing of great implication but no immediate use,
A thing that could not be conceived without study,
Without years of training and the aid of instruments,
And especially the delicate instrument of an open mind;
It had been stubbornness, foolishness, you see that now,
And so when the time comes you are ready to acquiesce,
When you have had your say, told the truth one last time,
You are ready to give the matter over and say no more.
When the time comes, you will take back your words,
But not because you fear the consequences of refusal
(Who looks into the night sky and imagines a new order
Has already seen the instruments of torture many times),
Though this is the conclusion your inquisitors will draw
And it is true you are not what is called a brave man;
And not because you are made indifferent in your contempt
(You take their point, agree with it even, that there is
Nothing so dangerous as a new way of seeing the world);
Rather, you accept the conditions lightly, the recantation,
Lightly you accept their offer of a villa with a view,
Because you have grown old and contention makes you weary,
Because you like the idea of raising vines and tomatoes,
And because, whatever you might have said or suffered,
It is in motion still, cutting a great arc through nothingness,
Sweeping through space according to a design so grand
It remains, just as they would have it, a matter of faith,
Because, whether you say yea, whether you say nay,
Nevertheless it moves.

André Breton

Translated from the French by Bill Zavatsky and Zack Rogow

The Reptile Houseburglars

(TO JANINE)

On the clothes reel in the courtyard little Marie had just hung out the laundry to dry. It was a succession of still-recent dates: that of her mother's marriage (the beautiful wedding dress had been torn to pieces), a baptism, the curtains of her little brother's crib laughed in the wind like seagulls on the crags of the coast. The little girl blew out the detergent flowers like candles and convinced herself how slow life was. She started now and then to look at her slightly too-pink hands, and leaned back into the bucket of water for later on, when she'd have an anemone in her belt. Night began to fall. The details of nautical charts hardly mattered anymore; on the bridges, scarves of ocher smoke and goodbyes trailed on the ground. The laziness of distractions, the tempest of love, and numerous marigold insect storm clouds pass in succession across the "overalls" covered with sparks of milk. Marie knows that her mother is no longer in possession of all her faculties: for days at a time, her head covered with reflections more notched than in dreams, she bites laughter's necklace of tears. Does she remember having been beautiful? The people who'd lived in the region the longest were worried that the roofers would return to the town, they'd have preferred rain in their houses. But the sky! As the hives of illusion fill with strange poison, the young woman brings her arms up towards her head to say: leave me alone. She asks for a drink of volcano milk and they bring her mineral water. She folds her hands before picking a leaf, greener than the light of carafes, to write on. Underneath her shoulder we hear (the angels don't miss it when they arrive, guided by the trail of feathers she no longer wears): "Marie dear, one day you'll know what a sacrifice is on the verge of being consummated, I won't tell you any more about it. Go, my daughter, be happy. My child's eyes are curtains more tender than those in the hotel rooms where I lived in the company of aviators and green plants." The treasure buried in the fireplace ash decomposes into little phosphorescent insects which utter a monotonous song, but what could she say to the crickets? God didn't feel more loved than usual but the candelabra of the trees in bloom were there for a reason. Frivolous demons hid, changeable as spring waters which rush over the satin of stones and the black velvet of fish. What did Marie suddenly appear so attentive to? It's the month of August, and the cars have emigrated since the Grand Prix. Whom are we going to see appear in this lonely part of town, the poet running away from home modulating his lament over the pearl rails, the man in love running to catch up with his beauty on a thunderbolt, or the hunter crouched in grass that can cut you, and who is cold? The little girl throws in the towel, she's burning to know what she doesn't, the meaning of this long flight at ground level, the beautiful guilty stream which begins to flow. My God, and now she falls to her knees, and on the floor above the moans become less muffled, the face of the wall clock reflects everything that happens and a soul rises to heaven. Who knows; the four-leaf clover half-opens to the moon's rays; for the evidence you need only enter the empty house.

Shrivelled Love

When windows pierce dawn like desire and the jackal's eye, winches of silk hoist me onto catwalks in the suburbs. I call to a girl dreaming in the gilded cottage; she overtakes me on heaps of black moss and offers me her lips which are stones at the bottom of the swift stream. Veiled threats walk down building steps. The best thing to do is run away from the great feather cylinders when hunters limp across sodden fields. If we bathe in the watered silk of the streets, childhood returns to its homeland, a female greyhound. Man hunts his prey in the air and fruits dry on trays of pink paper, in the shadow of names magnified by forgetfulness. Joys and sorrows spread through the city. Gold and eucalyptus, with the same odor, attack our dreams. Among bridles and gloomy edelweiss lie underground shapes like stoppers on bottles of perfume.

Maps on the Dunes

(TO GIUSEPPE UNGARETTI)

The timetable of hollow flowers and prominent cheekbones invites us to leave volcanic saltshakers for birdbaths. On a red checkerboard napkin the days of the year are arranged. The air is no longer as pure, the road no longer as wide as the famous bugle. Perishable evenings, the place on a prie-dieu where knees go, are carried in a suitcase painted with fat wormy verses. Little corduroy bicycles revolve on the countertop. The fish's ear, more forked than honeysuckle, hears blue oils coming down. Among sparkling burnouses whose charge gets lost in the curtains, I recognize a man who's blood of my blood.

Stephen Dunn

Toward the Verrazano

Up from South Jersey and the low persistent
pines, pollution curls into the sky
like dark cast-off ribbons
and the part of us that's pure camera,
that loves funnel clouds and blood
on a white dress, is satisfied.
At mile 127, no trace of a tree now,
nothing but concrete and high-tension
wires, we hook toward the Outerbridge
past Arthur Kill Road where garbage trucks
work the largest landfill in the world.
The windscreens are littered, gorgeous
with rotogravure sections, torn love
letters, mauve once-used tissues. The gulls
dip down like addicts, rise like angels.
Soon we're in traffic, row houses, a college
we've never heard of stark as an asylum.
In the distance there it is, the crown
of this back way in, immense, silvery,
and in no time we're suspended
out over the Narrows by a logic linked
to faith, so accustomed to the miraculous
we hardly speak, and when we do
it's with those words found on picture postcards
from polite friends with nothing to say.

John Engels

Dead Dog

At the edge of everything that moves and speaks
is the stillness of the dead dog,
which for days has lain vividly crushed
into the coarse grain of the road.

No, this is not the first time
we have surprised ourselves coming on it,
for this is our usual way. The sea wind
buzzes in the dry beards of the palms.

The trees bend sharply inland. The air scours
the windows with fine dusts of sand,
though at times less voraciously,
and this is when we venture out, each time

freshly startled to come upon
such dispirit of form, lacking
the usual engagements of beauty.
We go on in something like wonder

or in something like love,
though it is true that at times
we are afraid at night, standing
on the seawall, our eyes grainy with salt.

We fear the seething space before us,
from which we know the sea to be crawling
blindly in, just as we fear the face
which on some nights we discover ourselves

to be aware of, glaring in
from the pelted darkness
outside the window, its claws fanned wide
at the ears to make the figure

of the fanged and resurrectionary skull.
Oh, then we draw back against
our headboards and hold to one
another. Meanwhile our room

empties itself of light.
Meanwhile there is a backrush of light
on that discountenance.

Allison Funk

New England Walls

They announce where one man's property begins
and ends. In New England you find them everywhere,
you said, ringing the acres of devil's paintbrush

and Queen Anne's lace, flush with the birches.
I told you it puzzled me that these walls did not budge,
flat rocks and triangles over round stones

that should have relented
during the hard winters here, the spaces
between them unsealed. We talked about our marriages,

which had hardened into mystifying shapes.
All boundaries are arguments
against passion, but one night

before taking the paths to our separate rooms
we stood amazed before a field
so flooded with moonlight it shone,

as if covered with snow. It was June,
the air was close, and I was drowsy,
but the confusion of seasons unearthed a tenderness.

Couldn't we have called it accidental
if we had dissolved among the little animals
and the grass? Why, in your black clothes,

did you come steadily back into focus,
a tree that would not blossom
even briefly?

The Marsh

The mist is about to give up its secret
again. Slowly, the marsh it mummified
as we slept asserts itself, cattails

and tall grass, in back of the house.
By six they have separated, body and soul.
At dawn only the geese are audible,

their foghorns sound from the half-buried pools.
Nothing will redeem their leaving,
not even the gold and cranberry

draping the stunted trees like covers
thrown over the furniture of the departed.
Our house is too close to the marsh —

in between is a splintery fence,
the bony shoulders we see over
to vapors rising each morning. Our love

may be a ghost, too.
Is there any place we have not looked
for its old body and embrace?

Tess Gallagher

Into the Known

(FOR BILL KNOTT)

A corpse has walked across my shadow.
How do I know? I was standing
so it fell darkly across the shadow of a tree
in water, and my shadow grabbed hold
in the branches and shouted, "I'm drowning!
Save me!" Okay, I said, and stepped
to the side a few paces, disengaging its
arms from the leaves rippling through
me. But two boys rowed over it, dipping
their oars through my breasts and
groin. "Save yourself!" my shadow cried.
But when I walked jauntily upstream, it
scraped along behind as usual, sure of
itself as a corpse is sure, so it speaks
to no one, yet holds our attention resentfully
like a cow in the roadway.

A gull rowed over me and I felt
feverish, as if my future meant to initiate
a moment I would soon have to avoid.
Time to rehabilitate your astonishment, I said
to myself and plunged on
into the known. A carriage
with two cream-colored horses pulls up, as I
knew it would, and my shadow gets out. She
comes up to me like she means to slap me,
but I turn my back quick! so she falls
over the necks of the horses and they tremble
and jangle their bits and lift their hooves
smartly in place on the pavement.

Yes, today a corpse put its inaugural hand
on my shoulder, on my shadow's silken
shoulder, like a sword through meringue.
Veil of white, veil of drowned breath—I was
sticky with it, plundered like a wren's nest.
Down I lay in the grass and down
like a dog to roll, but my shadow jumped
into me—retouching the real with
the real, as the mortician said.
Pianissimo, dread fumbled the length of me,
a safari of butterflies skimming the lunge
of a gravesite. I kept breathing

as long as I could, convulsively snatching
the breaths back into me, but my mind
kept seeing a sailboat with its sail
gone slack. And because I know something about
wind, how it fidgets and stampedes, then
forgets entirely so everything goes still,
I folded my hands on my breasts
and let things take their course, and let
the sun shine deeply upon me, and let
the carriage sulk near the walnut grove,
and the cream-colored horses neigh to other
horses and, in starlight, cloud-shadows
drowsy as a mind that can't shout, can't
beseech—let these drift over the beloved
corpse of my shadow. Suddenly then

I pull myself up! "Not me!" I say.
I make them dance—that mitten, my shadow—
that quisling, my corpse. I dance
like a woman led to a vault of spiders.
I tell the horses to
dance too. I still don't know
if we got out of it.

His Shining Helmet; Its Horsehair Crest

I was reading the novel
about a war fought on horseback, reading
with the pleasure of a child given horror as
splendor. The moment came when
the soldier rose in his saddle and
the rim of the saddle was shorn
away. There the story broke off.
Then the survey of fallen comrades and
the field trampled around those with
"wounds to the head and breast." Strange
how I thought of the horses during
these tinted portraits, the horses, mentioned
only as "he rode," "his mount
stumbled," or "he bent from
the saddle to retrieve the standard, then
galloped on."

I close the book and see then
the one they did not speak of—the one
wounded in the face, the one
with his hand caught in the mane of
his horse, which lies beside and
over him, its eyes still open and its breath
a soft plunging to which the novelist
would add a "light rain" or
"a distant thunder of cannons."

But in the closed book, this
is the long moment I look into—the future
in which the wounds, as they say in the manual,
will be "non-specific, though
fatal." How far
from the single admonition in the Hittite cavalry
instructions, simply to: "Kill
the horse."

The Hat

My father is going to divide
his land. He telephones to say
there are four pieces of paper in
the hat. He's going to draw for
me. "You don't live forever," he
says. When he's dead, he says,
then I'll have something. He has
put his hand into the hat, has picked
out my lot, my portion. And I know
before long, he'll see to it
I have what's coming to me. As
for the hat—it too goes
where it's taken.

With Stars

(FOR M. K.)

My mother speaks from the dark—why
haven't I closed my eyes? Why don't I
sleep? And when I say I can't, she
wraps the quilt around me and leads me
to the window. I am four years old and
a star has the power of wishes.
We stare out together, but she sees past
their fierce shimmering sameness, each
point of light the emblem
of some lost, remembered face. What
do they want? I ask. "Not to be
forgotten," she says, and draws me close.
Then her gaze sifts the scattered brilliance.
Her hand goes out—"There! that one!" so
her own mother, dead years back, looks down
on us. Sleep then like a hammer
among the orbiting dead.

Tonight it is the stars' reminding
keeps me up past midnight.
My mother's voice, as in that childhood room,
is with me so surely I might rush out
and find that window, those stars
no further than the next doorway, and her
there waiting—awake all night
because I was awake. "Go
to sleep," I'd say. "They want me
awake tonight." And she'd know who I meant—
those others still living and afar
because I think them there. And why not
give the dead this benefit of separations?
There were so many nameless before.
But oh, if one falls, if—
how can that child ever fall asleep
until sunrise?

Jorie Graham

Self-portrait As the Gesture Between Them

(Adam and Eve)

1

The gesture like a fruit torn from a limb, torn swiftly.

2

The whole bough bending then springing back as if from sudden sight.

3

The rip in the fabric where the action begins, the opening of the narrow passage.

4

The passage along the arc of denouement once the plot has begun,
    like a limb,
the buds in it cinched and numbered,
outside the true story really, outside of improvisation,
moving along day by day into the sweet appointment.

5

But what else could they have done, these two, sick of beginning,
revolving in place like a thing seen,
dumb, blind, rooted in the eye that's watching,
ridden and ridden by that slowest of glances the passage of time
staring and staring until the entrails show.

6

Every now and then a quick rain for no reason,

7

a wind moving round all sides, a wind shaking the points of view out
like the last bits of rain. . . .

8

So it was to have freedom she did it but like a secret thought.
A thought of him the light couldn't touch.
The light beating against it, the light flaying her thought of him,
trying to break it.
Like a fruit that grows but only in the invisible.
The whole world of the given beating against this garden
where he walks slowly in the hands of freedom
noiselessly beating his steps against the soil.

9

But a secret grows, a secret wants to be given away.
For a long time it swells and stains its bearer with beauty.
It is what we see swelling forth making the shape we know a thing by.
The thing inside, the critique of the given.

10

So that she turned the thought of him in her narrow mind,
turned him slowly in the shallows, like a thin bird she'd found,
turned him in this place which was her own, as if to plant him but
     never letting go,
keeping the thought of him keen, limbed and simple in a kind of winter,
keeping him in this shadowlessness in which he needn't breathe,
him turning to touch her as a thing turns towards its thief,
owned but not seizable, resembling, resembling . . .

11

Meanwhile the heights of things were true. Meanwhile the distance of
the fields was true. Meanwhile the fretting of the light against the backs
 of them
as they walked through the fields naming things, true,
the touch of the light along the backs of their bodies . . .

12

as the apple builds inside the limb, as the rain builds
in the atmosphere, as the lateness accumulates until it finally
is,
as the meaning of the story builds,

13

scribbling at the edges of her body until it must be told, be

14

taken from her, this freedom,

15

so that she had to turn and touch him to give it away

16

to have him pick it from her as the answer takes the question

17

that he should read in her the rigid inscription

18

in a scintillant fold the fabric of the daylight bending

19

where the form is complete where the thing must be torn off

20

momentarily angelic, the instant writhing into a shape,

21

the two wedded, the readiness and the instant,

22

the extra bit that shifts the scales the other way now in his hand,
the gift that changes the balance,

23

the balance that cannot be broken owned by the air until he touches,

24

the balance like an apple held up into the sunlight

25

then taken down, the air changing by its passage, the feeling of being
    capable,

26

of being not quite right for the place, not quite the thing that's needed,

27

the feeling of being a digression not the link in the argument,
a new direction, an offshoot, the limb going on elsewhere,

28

and liking that error, a feeling of being capable because an error,

29

of being wrong perhaps altogether wrong a piece from another set

30

stripped of position stripped of true function

31

and loving that error, loving that filial form, that break from perfection

32

where the complex mechanism fails, where the stranger appears in the
    clearing,

33

out of nowhere and uncalled for, out of nowhere to share the day.

Michael S. Harper

Josh Gibson's Bat

(COOPERSTOWN, N.Y.)

Doubleday Field

Empty at the corners,
the crowd bunched up
behind the backstop,
the screen, not high enough
for pop flies,
is crawling with kids,
not a ginger-colored coach
or resident,
on either foul line.

My kid, the first baseman,
with a pro mitt
and a hand-carved bat
made of ash
without his initials
measures for the fences —
he's got his 34"s
and is mad,
half the day spent
in front of coffin's corner,
replicas of the Negro Leagues,
and two hours in archives
looking at photos,
the thickest of Mays
and Jackie,
and they have his bat.

He remembers being called "Sambo,"
as his grandfather was
near Hamilton,
on the IBM Field in Oneonta;
he goes three for three
from the southpaw figures of speech
on the black and white scoreboard.

Like his ancestors
he's got a great sense of humor
but not the body of Mays,
too many tapes of Stevie Wonder,
the broad grin of Durocher
protecting him from the girls
who hide in the bleachers.

He figures to tool his bat
with the birthdates of these girls;
he says he cares about color,
the race music of his talk
in the tape-measured records
of the Group Areas Act
unwritten in tar and feathers,
a stand of buttermilk
and a fly stirring the batter
for pancakes in the wrong country.

My Students Who Stand in Snow

(IN MEMORY OF MLK, JR. 4/4/85)

Your tall, fresh faces stand up in snow,
melt some time later in another scene,
modest springs beneath the grass;
they graze, pummel, take off on wheels,
and drink, in cans and chairs all up for sale.

In every clearing a woman in a wagon takes a ride;
the robin (of hockey) is both puck and wing.

Sirens come off on Fridays when the Post is locked;
they go off in jeans, book jackets, clocks.

Once, on *his* day, we held hands before the chapel:
a few spoke, thirty or more in a looseleaf circle,
two urban boys shaking in their boots;
the boots stood up in their stockings of skin,
turned to parchment, made a chime.

From the open windows (on the green) the wings of others
took their places. When the stroke of April
began to sink in snowbank, mud, daffodil,
the black drake came to swim with the white.

Business came to terms; a sound trumpeted —
scenes of this music in clumsy turf, folds, follows.

Lecturing on the Theme of Motherhood

The news is of camps, outpost, little progress;
I expect a bulletin from you on the latest
police foray into the projects, get it,
equal pay before the law, the only amendment
where angels talk to one another
about Friday, no eagles in evidence,
a few terns, almost broken apart in bottlecaps,
but who manage to fly.

Your grandson, Patrice, is playing basketball
in his football jersey; he says he can't cut
T's lawn because the place is ragged with daffodils—
his first recognition that flowers are the plateau
above the grave. He lies down in the gravel
driveway when asked to do chores, too close
to the free-throw line to shoot left-handed,
his natural delusion to your changing my grip
on a spoon at the highchair. I don't remember
the candy, told so often you're bound to forget
disappearance, the odor of shad Aunt Ede would make
after her trip to DeKalb Avenue, holding up traffic,
mind you, with a cane, which she rapped on the headlights of the bus, its white aura frolicking
in the police van driven by her students she knuckled
in the South Bronx, just before it burned down.

Zbigniew Herbert

Translated from the Polish by John and Bogdana Carpenter

Report from the Besieged City

Too old to carry arms and fight like the others —

they graciously gave me the inferior role of chronicler
I record — I don't know for whom — the history of the siege

I am supposed to be exact but I don't know when the invasion began
two hundred years ago in December in September perhaps yesterday
    at dawn
everyone here suffers from a loss of the sense of time

all we have left is the place the attachment to the place
we still rule over the ruins of temples specters of gardens and houses
if we lose the ruins nothing will be left

I write as I can in the rhythm of interminable weeks
monday: empty storehouses a rat became the unit of currency
tuesday: the mayor murdered by unknown assailants
wednesday: negotiations for a cease-fire the enemy has imprisoned our
    messengers
we don't know where they are held that is the place of torture
thursday: after a stormy meeting a majority of voices rejected
the motion of the spice merchants for unconditional surrender
friday: the beginning of the plague saturday: our invincible defender
N.N. committed suicide sunday: no more water we drove back
an attack at the eastern gate called the Gate of the Alliance

all of this is monotonous I know it can't move anyone

I avoid any commentary I keep a tight hold on my emotions I write
    about the facts

only they it seems are appreciated in foreign markets
yet with a certain pride I would like to inform the world
that thanks to the war we have raised a new species of children
our children don't like fairy tales they play at killing
awake and asleep they dream of soup of bread and bones
just like dogs and cats

in the evening I like to wander near the outposts of the City
along the frontier of our uncertain freedom
I look at the swarms of soldiers below their lights
I listen to the noise of drums barbarian shrieks
truly it is inconceivable the City is still defending itself
the siege has lasted a long time the enemies must take turns
nothing unites them except the desire for our extermination
Goths the Tartars Swedes troops of the Emperor regiments of
        Transfiguration
who can count them
the colors of their banners change like the forest on the horizon
from delicate bird's yellow in spring through green through red to
        winter's black

and so in the evening released from facts I can think
about distant ancient matters for example our
friends beyond the sea I know they sincerely sympathize
they send us flour lard sacks of comfort and good advice
they don't even know their fathers betrayed us
our former allies at the time of the second Apocalypse
their sons are blameless they deserve our gratitude therefore we are
        grateful
they have not experienced a siege as long as eternity
those struck by misfortune are always alone
the defenders of the Dalai Lama the Kurds the Afghan mountaineers

now as I write these words the advocates of conciliation
have won the upper hand over the party of inflexibles
a normal hesitation of moods fate still hangs in the balance

cemeteries grow larger the number of defenders is smaller
yet the defense continues it will continue to the end
and if the City falls but a single man escapes

he will carry the City within himself on the roads of exile
he will be the City
we look in the face of hunger the face of fire face of death
worst of all — the face of betrayal

and only our dreams have not been humiliated

(1982)

To Ryszard Krynicki—a Letter

Not much will remain Ryszard really not much
of the poetry of this insane century certainly Rilke Eliot
a few other distinguished shamans who knew the secret
of conjuring a form with words that resists the action of time without
    which
no phrase is worth remembering and speech is like sand

those school notebooks of ours sincerely tormented
with traces of sweat tears blood will be
like the text of a song without music for the eternal proofreader
honorably righteous more than obvious

too easily we came to believe beauty does not save
that it leads the lighthearted from dream to dream to death
none of us knew how to awaken the dryad of a poplar
to read the writing of clouds
this is why the unicorn will not cross our tracks
we won't bring to life a ship in the bay a peacock a rose
only nakedness remained for us and we stand naked
on the right the better side of the triptych
the Last Judgment

we took public affairs on our thin shoulders
recording suffering the struggle with tyranny with lying
but—you have to admit—we had opponents despicably small
so was it worth it to lower holy speech
to the babble of the speaker's platform the black foam of the newspapers

in our poems Ryszard there is so little joy—daughter of the gods
too few luminous dusks mirrors wreaths of rapture
nothing but dark psalmodies stammering of animulae
urns of ashes in the burned garden

in spite of fate the verdicts of history human misdeeds
what strength is needed to whisper
in the garden of betrayal — a silent night

what strength of spirit is needed to strike
beating blindly with despair against despair
a spark of light word of reconciliation

so the dancing circle will last forever on the thick grass
so the birth of a child and every beginning is blessed
gifts of air earth and fire and water

this I don't know — my friend — and is why
I am sending you these owl's puzzles in the night
a warm embrace
                    greetings from my shadow

Beethoven

They say he became deaf—but it isn't true
the demons of his hearing worked tirelessly
and the dead lake never slept in the shells of his ears

otitis media then acuta
brought into the hearing mechanism
squeaky tones hisses

a hollow sound whistle of a thrush wooden bell of the forest
he took from it as well as he could—a high descant of violins
undergrown by the deep blackness of basses

the list of his illnesses passions failures
is as rich as the catalogue of completed works
tympano-labyrinthine sclerosis probably syphilis

finally what had to come came—immense stupor
mute hands thrashing dark boxes and strings
the puffed-out cheeks of angels acclaiming silence

typhus in childhood later angina pectoris arteriosclerosis
in the Cavatine quartet opus 130
you can hear shallow panting the compressed heart suffocation

messy quarrelsome with a pockmarked face
he drank beyond measure and cheaply—beer coachman's schnapps
weakened by tuberculosis the liver refused to play

> there is nothing to regret—the creditors died
> the mistresses cooks and countesses also died
> princes protectors—the candelabra sobbed

> as if he were still living he borrows money scrambles
> between heaven and earth to make contacts

> but the moon is the moon even without the sonata

The Power of Taste

(FOR PROFESSOR IZYDORA DAMBSKA)

It didn't require great character at all
our refusal disagreement and resistance
we had a shred of necessary courage
but fundamentally it was a matter of taste
                              Yes taste
in which there are fibers of soul the cartilage of conscience

Who knows if we had been better and more attractively tempted
sent rose-skinned women thin as a wafer
or fantastic creatures from the paintings of Hieronymus Bosch
but what kind of hell was there at this time
a wet pit the murderers' alley the barrack
called a palace of justice
a home-brewed Mephisto in a Lenin jacket
sent Aurora's grandchildren out into the field
boys with potato faces
very ugly girls with red hands

Verily their rhetoric was made of cheap sacking
(Marcus Tullius kept turning in his grave)
chains of tautologies a couple of concepts like flails
the dialectics of slaughterers no distinctions in reasoning
syntax deprived of beauty of the subjunctive

So aesthetics can be helpful in life
one should not neglect the study of beauty

Before we declare our consent we must carefully examine
the shape of the architecture the rhythm of the drums and pipes
official colors the despicable ritual of funerals

Our eyes and ears refused obedience
the princes of our senses proudly chose exile

It did not require great character at all
we had a shred of necessary courage
but fundamentally it was a matter of taste
                    Yes taste
that commands us to get out to make a wry face draw out a sneer
even if for this the precious capital of the body the head
                                        must fall

The Murderers of Kings

As Regis asserts they resemble one another
like twins Ravaillac and Princip Clément and Caserio
often they come from families of epileptics and suicides
they however are healthy that is ordinary
usually young very young and so they remain for eternity

their solitude for months years they sharpen their knives
and in the woods outside town conscientiously learn how to shoot
they work out the assassination are alone painstaking and very honest
they give the pennies they earn to their mothers take care of their
      brothers and sisters don't drink
have no friends or girls

                after the coup they give themselves up without
                resistance
bear tortures bravely don't ask for clemency
reject any accomplices suggested during the investigation
there wasn't a conspiracy truly they were alone

              their inhuman sincerity and simplicity
irritates the judges the defense the public greedy for sensation

          those who send souls
to the beyond are amazed at the calm of the condemned in their final hour

calm lack of anger regret or even hatred
almost radiance

           so their brains are ransacked
the heart weighed liver cut however no departure
from the norm is discovered

not one of them managed to change the course of history
but the dark message has gone from generation to generation
so these small hands are worthy of reflection
small hands in which the certainty of the blow is trembling

Mr. Cogito's Soul

In the past
we know from history
she would go out from the body
when the heart stopped

with the last breath
she went quietly away
to the blue meadows of heaven

      Mr. Cogito's soul
      acts differently

      during his life she leaves his body
      without a word of farewell

      for months for years she lives
      on different continents
      beyond the frontiers
      of Mr. Cogito

      it is hard to locate her address
      she sends no news of herself
      avoids contacts
      doesn't write letters

      no one knows when she will return
      perhaps she has left forever

Mr. Cogito struggles to overcome
the base feeling of jealousy

he thinks well of his soul
thinks of her with tenderness

undoubtedly she must live also
in the bodies of others

certainly there are too few souls
for all humanity

Mr. Cogito accepts his fate
he has no other way out

he even attempts to say
—my own soul mine

he thinks of his soul affectionately
he thinks of his soul with tenderness

      therefore when she appears
      unexpectedly
      he doesn't welcome her with the words
      —it's good you've come back

      he only looks at her from an angle
      as she sits before the mirror
      combing her hair
      tangled and gray

Mr. Cogito — the Return

1

Mr. Cogito
has made up his mind to return
to the stony bosom
of his homeland

the decision is dramatic
he will regret it bitterly

but no longer can he endure
empty everyday expressions
— comment allez-vous
— wie geht's
— how are you

at first glance simple the questions
demand a complicated answer

Mr. Cogito tears off
the bandages of polite indifference

he has stopped believing in progress
he is concerned about his own wound

displays of abundance
fill him with boredom

he became attached only
to a Dorian column
the Church of San Clemente
the portrait of a certain lady
a book he didn't have time to read
and a few other trifles

therefore he returns
he sees already
the frontier
a plowed field
murderous shooting towers
dense thickets of wire

soundless
armor-plated doors
slowly close behind him

and already
he is
alone
in the treasure-house
of all misfortunes

2

so why does he return
ask friends
from the better world

he could stay here
somehow make ends meet

entrust the wound
to chemical stain-remover

leave it behind in waiting-rooms
of immense airports

so why is he returning

— to the water of childhood
— to entangled roots
— to the clasp of memory
— to the hand the face
seared on the grill of time

at first glance simple the questions
demand a complicated answer

probably Mr. Cogito returns
to give a reply

to the whisperings of fear
to impossible happiness
to the blow given from behind
to the deadly question

Galway Kinnell

December Day in Honolulu

This day, twice as long as the same day in Sheffield, Vermont, where
    by five the stars come out,
gives the postman opportunity to boggle the bell thrice.
First, a letter from Providence lamenting the "siege against poets"—
    Wright, Rukeyser, Hayden.
Next, Richard Hugo's memoir of James Wright, which says "Yes. I
    knew him. I loved him."
Last, around the time of stars in Sheffield, a package holding four
    glass door knobs packed in a *New York Times* of a year ago, which
    Muriel Rukeyser had sea-mailed to me, to fulfill if not explain
    those words she used to whisper whenever we met: "Galway, I
    have your doorknobs."
The wails of a cat in heat—in ultra-heat, I should say, here everything's
    hot already—breaks in, like the voice of propagation itself:
This one or that one dies but never the singer: whether in Honolulu in its humid
mornings or in New York in its unbreathable dusk or in Sheffield now dark
but for chimney sparks dying into the crowded heaven, one singer falls but
another jumps into the empty place and sings . . .
The wails come more heavily. Maybe propagation itself must haul its
    voice all the way up from the beginning.
Or it could be it's just a very old cat, making its last appearance on the
    clanking magic circle of its trashcan lid, from its final life crying
    back—before turning totally faithful forever—an earlier, perhaps
    the first, life's first, irreplaceable lover.

Conception

Having crowed the seed
of the child of their hearts
into her in the dark middle
of the night, as cocks
sometimes cry out to a light
not yet visible to the rest,
and lying there with cock
shrugging its way out of her,
and rising back through phases
of identity, he hears
her say, "Yes, I am two now,
and with thee, three."

The Man Splitting Wood in the Daybreak

The man splitting wood in the daybreak
looks strong, as though if one weakened
one could turn to him and he would help.
Gus Newland was strong. When he split wood
he struck hard, flashing the bright steel
through air of daybreak so fast rock maple
leapt apart — as they think marriages will
in countries about to institute divorce —
and even willow, which though stacked
to dry a full year, on separating
actually weeps — totem wood, therefore,
to the married-until-death — sniffled asunder.
But Gus is dead. We could turn to our fathers,
but they protect us only through the harsh
grace of the numerals cut into their headstones.
Or to our mothers, whose love, so devastated,
can't, even in spring, break through the hard earth.
Our spouses weaken at the same rate we do.
We have to hold our children up to lean on them.
Everyone who could help goes or hasn't arrived.
What about the man splitting wood in the daybreak,
who looked strong? That was years ago.
I myself was that man splitting wood in the daybreak.

Driftwood from a Ship

It is the white of faces from which the sunburn has been suddenly
    scared away.
It has the rounded shoulders of those who fear they will pass the rest
    of their days alone.
The final moments of one it couldn't hold up — possibly the cook, who
    possibly could neither cook nor swim — have been gasped into it.
The black residue inside the black holes — three set close together, three
    far apart, three close — remember the hammer-blows' downward
    stages which shined nine nails permanently into their vanishing
    places.
A plane's long, misericording *shhhhhhhh's* long ago soothed away the
    halo fragments the sawmill's circular saw had tormented across
    its planes.
The pebbles it rubs itself into fuzz up all over it a first beard white
    right from the start.
Its grain cherishes the predicament of spruce, which has a trunk that
    rises and boughs that droop.
Its destiny is to disappear.
This could be accomplished when a beachcomber extracts its heat and
    resolves the rest into smoke and ashes; or in the normal way,
    through a combination of irritation and evanescence.

Stanley Kunitz

The Scene

(AFTER ALEXANDER BLOK)

Night. Street. Lamp. Drugstore.
A world of dim and sleazy light.
You may live twenty-five years more.
Nothing will change. No way out.

You die. You're born again and all
Will be repeated as before:
The cold ripple of a canal.
Night. Street. Lamp. Drugstore.

Three Small Parables for My Poet Friends

1

Certain saurian species, notably the skink, are capable of shedding their tails in self-defense when threatened. The detached appendage diverts attention to itself by taking on a life of its own and thrashing furiously about. As soon as the stalking wildcat pounces on the wriggler, snatching it up from the sand to bite and maul it, the free lizard scampers off. A new tail begins to grow in place of the one that has been sacrificed.

2

The larva of the tortoise beetle has the neat habit of collecting its droppings and exfoliated skin into a little packet that it carries over its back when it is out in the open. If it were not for this fecal shield, it would lie naked before its enemies.

3

Among the Bedouins, the beggar poets of the desert are held in contempt because of their greed, their thievery and venality. Everyone in the scattered encampments knows that poems of praise can be bought, even by the worst of scoundrels, for food or money. Furthermore, these wandering minstrels are notorious for stealing the ideas, lines, and even whole songs of others. Often the recitation is interrupted by the shouts of the squatters around the campfire: "Thou liest. Thou stolest it from So-and-so!" When the poet tries to defend himself, calling for witnesses to vouch for his probity or, in extremity, appealing to Allah, his hearers hoot him down, crying, "Kassad, kaddab! A poet is a liar."

James Laughlin

C'est à Mourir de Rire

que je te poursuis moi qui
suis un grepin crevé sans

grand'chose dans le jinjin
et toi un si joli lot avec

tant de tête mais on lit
comment Sigismundo a été

affolé par la belle Ixotta
et a même peut-être empois-

onné sa femme pour l'avoir
(je ne ferais rien de si

stupide que cela) et Goethe
agé de 73 ans cet été là

à Marienbad sentit le jean-
nu-tête et courut en bas de

son cabinet de travail lors-
qu'il entendit la chanson

de la gigolette dans l'allée
o si je dois périr c'est du

poison fraix et délicieux de
ton rire que je veux mourir.

W. S. Merwin

Koa

You were here

you were named for the most beautiful of trees
you are the color of the heart of the tree
you are gone like the tree from its wide place

everything that we loved was made of you
so that it would stay and be made of you
we call you by the name of the tree
and hear the lost leaves come running

if you still have a mind to be with us
be with us
be waiting on the road to the mountain
the mountain of searching the turning mountain
the still mountain

be at the gate when we come
and lead us home again

*

There you are in the clouds this morning of wind
nobody can see you

there is the light of your eyes there are your flying feet
there is your white silence
around us

in the stillness before the night ended
I went out and you were there
lying on the grass in the moonlight
you were the moonlight

never again to be seen or touched or lost

*

In the middle of the Pacific in the autumn
on a sea-cliff far down a dirt road
with you ten days dead ten nights
a noisy gang gathers in the dark and the drunk voices
and raw music drift through the black enduring leaves
you and I walked in the stream bed over the big smooth stones
we walked there in the day under the old mango trees
only last month I talked to you ahead of me

that day came down through the trees and filled
your long fur with light and you turned and looked back
now in the echoing night on the next ridge a dog is barking
the bark he barks from the top of the hill in the dark
when the first whale of the winter has been sighted
unseasonably early and before the moon comes up
rushing into the clouds like a sound you died in the night
out on the hill when this moon was still young

that is just past the full you were walking down there under
the trees again that afternoon it has been hot all summer
but you accompanied the day's departing guest
to the top of the hill and were blessed at the moment
of taking leave and were gone in your youth before the morning

*

Five years and a month you were my friend and joy
in a dark season you warmed me where the sun could not reach
in our happiness you were the color of our days
when you were not with me something of me was missing

late I have come to live where I love to be
with the woman I have looked for through all my lives
and to work at what I have wanted to say
since I was a child under the only tree

about the given earth and now what do I know
standing at night in the long wind without you

*

I think of you moving slowly into the darkness of the thicket
and becoming its darkness
no one calling you and the day breaking

and I think of you running like a light through the shadows
and racing toward me if I called
catching this hand in your mouth as you passed

*

The plovers are back
I always wondered whether you remembered them
when we saw them again in the autumn
flying over the open grass the first time
in pairs calling in the moonlight
knowing knowing

I try to see the world you would have seen
what you would have remembered
the night wings crying the trees in the moonless sky
your grass is dry out on the hill where you lay
you remembered the rain when it came
new from its great absence

*

Today I saw you
far out in the calm bay one wave running seaward
to the north where clouds were gathering

*

There was the light that came from you
into the morning
and filled the day's heart

W. S. Merwin / 133

and ran in the moonlight on the ridge
stroking the night

and there is the light that I remember
through the days and nights since you died
and it is not the same
now the fox flame burns a red path
through a country of smoke

and there is the light that has come back
twice since you left
the fur of the gray star the old sled bitch
waiting among the voices by the outer dwellings
in the snow

*

Now I have seen the white shadow
running to welcome me
under the night trees
I know the trees

just now I have seen the white
shadow racing to meet me under the same trees
that are there every day
where once I planted them
you were running to greet me as always

now you have that
white shadow under your eye
on the right
and on your foreleg and down along
your body
falling only on you
it seemed to me
a mark a trail of mist a reflection
oh even with that shadow what joy it was to see you
to feel the sound of your feet beating

Czeslaw Milosz

Translated from the Polish by the author and Robert Hass

Into the Tree

And he placed at the east of the garden of Eden Cherubim, and a flaming sword which turned every way, to keep the way of the tree of life.

— GENESIS, 3, 24

And he looked up and said, "I see men as trees, walking."

— MARK, 8, 24

The tree, says good Swedenborg, is a close relative of man.
Its boughs like arms join in an embrace.
The trees in truth are our parents,
We sprang from the oak, or perhaps, as the Greeks maintain, from the
    ash.

Our lips and tongue savor the fruit of the tree.
A woman's breast is called apple or pomegranate.
We love the womb as the tree loves the dark womb of the earth.
Thus, what is most desirable resides in a single tree,
And wisdom tries to touch its coarse-grained bark.

I learned, says the servant of the New Jerusalem,
That Adam in the garden, i. e., mankind's Golden Age,
Signifies the generations after the pre-adamites
Who are unjustly scorned though they were gentle,

Kind to each other, savage yet not bestial,
Happy in a land of fruits and springwaters.

Adam created in the image and in the likeness
Represents the parting of clouds covering the mind.

And Eve, why is she taken from Adam's rib?
— Because the rib is close to the heart, that's the name of self-love
And Adam comes to know Eve, loving himself in her.

Above those two, the tree. A huge shade tree.

Of which the counselor of the Royal Mining Commission says the
following in his book *De Amore Conjugiali*:

"The Tree of Life signifies a man who lives from God, or God living in
man; and as love and wisdom, or charity and faith, or good and truth,
make the life of God in man, these are signified by the Tree of Life, and
hence the eternal life of the man. . . . But the tree of science signifies the
man who believes that he lives from himself and not from God; thus
that love and wisdom, or charity and faith, or good and truth, are in
man from himself and not from God; and he believes this because he
thinks and wills, and speaks and acts, in all likeness and appearance as
from himself."

Self-love offered the apple and the Golden Age was over.
After it, the Silver Age, the Bronze Age. And the Iron.

Then a child opens its eyes and sees a tree for the first time.
And people seem to us like walking trees.

On Prayer

You ask me how to pray to someone who is not.
All I know is that prayer constructs a velvet bridge
And walking it we are aloft, as on a springboard,
Above landscapes the color of ripe gold
Transformed by a magic stopping of the sun.
That bridge leads to the shore of Reversal
Where everything is just the opposite and the word *is*
Unveils a meaning we hardly envisioned.
Notice: I say *we*; there, every one, separately,
Feels compassion for others entangled in the flesh
And knows that if there is no other shore
They will walk that aerial bridge all the same.

Consciousness

1. Consciousness enclosed in itself every separate birch
And the woods of New Hampshire, covered in May with green haze.
The faces of people are in it without number, the courses
Of planets, and things past and a portent of the future.
Then one should extract from it what one can, slowly,
Not trusting anybody. And it won't be much, for language is weak.

2. It is alien and useless to the hot lands of the living.
Leaves renew themselves, birds celebrate their nuptials
Without its help. And a couple on the bank of a river
Feel their bodies draw close right now, possessed by a nameless power.

3. I think that I am here, on this earth,
To present a report on it, but to whom I don't know.
As if I were sent so that whatever takes place
Has meaning because it changes into memory.

4. Fat and lean, old and young, male and female,
Carrying bags and valises, they defile in the corridors of an
        airport.
And suddenly I feel it is impossible.
It is the reverse side of a Gobelin
And behind there is the other which explains everything.

5. Now, not any time, here, in America
I try to isolate what matters to me most.
I neither absolve nor condemn myself.

The torments of a boy who wanted to be nice
And spent a number of years at the project.

The shame of whispering to the confessional grille
Behind which heavy breath and a hot ear.

The monstrance undressed from its patterned robe,
A little sun rimmed with sculptured rays.

Evening devotions of the household in May,
Litanies to the Maiden,
Mother of the Creator.

And I, conscience, contain the orchestra of regimental brasses
On which the moustachioed ones blew for the Elevation.

And musket volleys on Easter Saturday night
When the cold dawn had hardly reddened.

I am fond of sumptuous garments and disguises
Even if there is no truth in the painted Jesus.

Sometimes believing, sometimes not believing,
With others like myself I unite in worship.

Into the labyrinth of gilded baroque cornices
I penetrate, called by the saints of the Lord.

I make my pilgrimage to the miraculous places
Where a spring spurted suddenly from rock.

I enter the common childishness and brittleness
Of the sons and daughters of the human tribe.

And I preserve faithfully the prayer in the cathedral:
Jesus Christ, son of God, enlighten me, a sinner.

6. I—consciousness—originate in skin,
Smooth or covered with thickets of hair.
The stubbly cheek, the pubes, and the groin
Are mine exclusively, though not only mine.
And at the same instant, he or she—consciousness—
Examines its body in a mirror,
Recognizing a familiar which is not quite its own.

Do I, when I touch one flesh in the mirror,
Touch every flesh, learn consciousness of the other?

Or perhaps not at all, and she, unattainable,
Perceives in her own, strictly her own, manner?

7. You will never know what I feel, she said,
Because you are filling me and are not filled.

8. The warmth of dogs and the essence, inscrutable, of
    doggishness.
Yet I feel it. In the lolling of the humid tongue,
In the melancholy velvet of the eyes,
In the scent of fur, different from our own, yet related.
Our humanness becomes more marked then,
The common one, pulsating, drooling, hairy,
Though for the dogs it is we who are like gods
Disappearing in crystal palaces of reason,
Busy with activities beyond comprehension.

I want to believe that the forces above us,
Engaged in doings we cannot imitate,
Touch our cheeks and our hair sometimes
And feel in themselves this poor flesh and blood.

9. Every ritual, astonishing human arrangements.
The dresses in which they move, more durable than they are,
The gestures that freeze in air, to be filled by those born later,
Words that were pronounced by the dead, here and still in use.
And erotic: they guess under the fabric
Dark triangles of hair, are attentive to convexities in silk.
Faithful to the ritual because it differs so much from their natures,
And soars above them, above the warmth of mucous membrane,
On the incomprehensible borderline between mind and flesh.

10. Certainly, I did not reveal what I really thought.
Why should I reveal it? To multiply misunderstandings?
And reveal to whom? They are born, they mature
In a long pause and refuse to know what comes later.
Anyway I won't avert anything. All my life it was like that:
To know and not be able to avert. I must give them reason.
They have no use for lives lived sometime in the future
And the torments of their descendants are not their concern.

Poet at Seventy

Thus, brother theologian, here you are,
Connoisseur of heavens and abysses,
Year after year perfecting your art,
Choosing bookish wisdom for your mistress,
Only to discover you wander in the dark.

Ai, humiliated to the bone
By tricks that crafty reason plays,
You searched for peace in human homes
But they, like sailboats, glide away,
Their goal and port, alas, unknown.

You sit in taverns drinking wine,
Pleased by the hubbub and the din,
Voices grow loud and then decline
As if played out by a machine,
And you accept your quarantine.

On this sad earth no time to grieve,
Love potions every spring are brewing,
Your heart, in magic, finds relief,
Though Lenten dirges cut your cooing.
And thus you learn how to forgive.

Voracious, frivolous and dazed
As if your time were without end
You run around and loudly praise
Theatrum where the flesh pretends
To win the game of nights and days.

In plumes and scales to fly and crawl,
Put on mascara, fluffy dresses,
Attempt to play like beast and fowl,

Forgetting interstellar spaces:
Try, my philosopher, this world.

And all your wisdom came to nothing
Though many years you worked and strived
With only one reward and trophy:
Your happiness to be alive
And sorrow that your life is closing.

[TRANSLATED BY THE AUTHOR]

John Morgan

Letter from the Camp: the Pearl Fishers

Because we'd given in
to almost everything, our ranks
dissolve, sky-writing in a high mist.
Too skinny for games or laughter
we choke on the speckled air, tubercular,
as ghostly Mozart wafts
over the camp like mustard gas.

Oh, for a secret passage
out of the accumulated future of the race.
Recall Berlin, ten years ago
in subterranean light, two pearl fishers hung
among the pasty coral. Soft
in our bones we watched
through air

another world where lungs
are wasted — the fishes
still, suspended —
hearing as if in some third ear
waves breaking like stones
on a far shore, the tumble
of birth, the infinite suck of the sea.

Robert Pinsky

The Superb Lily

"He burned a great Worlde of Papers before he died,
And sayde, the Worlde was unworthy of them;
He was so superb" — the word

Meant *arrogant* once, the absolute of pride.
　　Presidents summered in my home town, once,
　　　And famous gamblers endowed

Fire houses: the Phil Daly Ladder and Hose
　　Survives Lincoln, Grant, Garfield and white,
　　　Sweet, Lillian Russell.

It's a dump now. But then, Winslow Homer chose
　　In his *Long Branch, New Jersey* to paint belles
　　　On the ocean bluffs, parasols

And bustles in the sun. All dead. "Superb Lily" —
　　A name W. C. Fields might call a lady.
　　　We called it *Swamp Lily* there:

Swollen perennial, that sucked bogs thirstily
　　In August, and in the droning air pulled
　　　Fiery petals back behind

Like arms with linked thumbs to show the throbbing-
　　Orange, purple-dotted tissue, moist
　　　Flamboyant endowment spread

To shoot out glandular dark purses bobbing
　　Almost vertical on the springy stamens,
　　　Phoenix of stagnant water.

Stanley Plumly

Above Barnesville

In the body the night sky in ascension —
the starry campion, the mallow rose, the wild potato vine.
You could pick them, though they'd die in your hand.
It's here, in the thirties, that the fathers panned for gold,
pick-and-shovel, five-to-a-dollar-a-day — you could survive
panning the glacial drift, the split rock, the old alluvial scar.
If you climb the brickpath back to the top of the hill,
for the long hard look, you can still see Quaker poverty,
the sheer tilt of the green-gray roll of the land,
the rock-soil thinning out, the coal breaking ground like ice.
Some of the farmers still use horses for fear of the height, the weight
    against them,
as all the working day you can walk to the abrupt edge
of property and watch machines opening the earth.
The valley, the locals call it,
a landscape so deadly the water pools to oil before it clears —
a kind of kerosene, a few dropped stars or sunlight.

Deep autumnal nights I imagine my parents lying side
by side on the good grass looking up at the coal and diamond dark,
as they will lie together for the rest of their lives.
The star lanes scatter, and disappear. I will be born
under the sign of the twins less than a mile from here,
with too much blood on the floor. My father, right now,
is turning toward my mother. In the doctrine of signatures
the body is divisible, the heart the leaf of a redbud
or the blue ash in a fire, the genitalia
the various and soft centers of the shell
or the long spathe and cleft, the pink pouch of the flower.
They will be waking soon.
Overhead the chill and endless pastoral of the sky, the constellations
    drifting.

For a moment the mirror is laid beside us—Cassiopeia, Ursa
Minor, the Plow—parts of the house, a door left open, a window,
so that we can see how far down into the earth the path is leading.

The word for wood is xylem, which is the living tissue,
and by a kind of poetry graduates inward
from summer to winter to sapwood to the heart.
I was with my father the day he found
the tree that had been gouged and rendered useless and cut down.
It was probably hickory or walnut, black, the dull bark split
and furrowed, like a field: it seemed a hundred feet,
most of it in branches, the feathering of leaves turning color at the top.
The size of it, so suddenly alone.
My father, in his anger, cut away until the wood was soft. . . .
In the rain the smell of tannin, fire and char, poignant on the air.
I remember how thin the upper branches were, intricate as nests,
how impossible to climb this high without falling, breaking through.
It seemed to have come down from the sky in stages—
the broken branches first, then the medulla and the root,
then, deep inside, the lumber flying at the brain.

At night, sometimes, you could hear the second shift,
and fantasize the train's elliptical passage through the town
or the mythical ocean pulling moonlight from your windows.
You could hear the celestial traffic taking off.
But in the morning, crack-white and plain, it would be nothing
but the earth made new again, a little less each time.
Once, one of those pure October days that seem to rise,
I came up over the scab-hill of a mine—all slag and oxidation,
the sick ground running orange in a stream, here and there
the skeletons of buildings. It looked like parts of a great abandoned
    house
ruined in a fire in the middle of a woods saved by snow.
It had seasons, memory—
nothing like the Dipper-sized machines digging into the hillsides by
    the houseful.
A month ago I could have picked wildflowers, corn-blues and
    goldenrod,
while in the summer I'd have never found the place in so much green.

In the constellation named for the bottles tossed to the side of the road,
for the poverty of leaves blowing one-way down the lane,
for the stones flecked like fish, for the water carried with both hands
    closed,
the stars are of the sixth and seventh magnitude.
You can hardly see them in the broken glass and the ash from the
    burn-off.
In the coal-colored dark it's all pinholes and candles,
and this is as close as we'll ever get,
as when we close our eyes something gossamer like nebula floats up.
I told my father not to die, but he didn't listen.
He got down on his knees as if to hold on to the earth,
as if to hide inside his body.
In the black and crystalline light of coal and rock,
through the flake and mica leaves, layer upon layer,
he would not climb the ladder so loved by believers.
For that I love him, and find him safe
in the least of things alive — dust on the road, wind at its back.

Those first cold nights you could taste the ice in the air.
North seemed to mean the stars, where the snow came from.
Even now you could see it start to fall. Sides of the trees white
with it, heelprints and tire-tracks white with it,
the little edges of the roofs, like the drawing in the kitchen, white with it.
If we could make it cold enough and snow enough, such silence!
Even now, with color in the leaves, you could almost see it falling.
My mother called it the ocean, the way it covered everything,
the way in the morning the light of it was blinding.
She'd watch it for hours, letting it fall.
I think of her following my father as if by a miracle of leverage,
the one pulling the other out to sea. I think of how I will follow her,
how she brought me here, half her body, half of the rest of her.
Those nights the constellation shapes glistened into water
I thought it was forever, I thought it was enough,
though I knew that if water rises stones will burn.

Susan Prospere

Star of Wonder

My mother lights the pilot light
　　　　　that guides us from one Christmas to another —

to the drumstick and the cat stealing milk from the creamer,
　　　the India rubber ball and the Tiny Tears doll
　　　　　　　　　　rocking in the cradle.

What mechanism in our heads makes us lie back,
　　　　　open our eyes, and cry real tears?

Put
　　away
　　　　the toys;
　　　　　　we are grown now.
The sheriff's star my brother wore
　　　　　　to keep law and order in childhood
hangs between styrofoam angels
　　　on a tree we fell at nighttime.

Pass the sherry, please, around the green tin trailer
　　　　　　　　we haul the tree in.
Here's to sugarplum visions while my father has his eyesight.

Here's to a smile and a penny whistle, here's to a promise,
　　　to stars blown through the sky with peashooters at bedtime.

Crossing our paths, here's to the deer
　　　　　　　captivated by our flashlights.

Good night.

We sleep in cigar box beds with four posts made of clothespins.
    Good night,
            good night to pick-up sticks and good night to my father
                placing smoke capsules in the Lionel steam engine.

He is taller than the train we leave on.

      All aboard   All aboard
                we go faster
                      faster
past the plastic houses and the bristle trees
              into the darkness under the wing chair.

Passion

For a dime in the 1930s my father bought a drawstring sack
                             of chinas and cloudies
and knelt on the ground where a house had burned
to play marbles in the evenings with his brother and first cousins,
forming a circle inside the space marked on the property
by a cistern, a chimney, and gallica roses.
In the dusk he fired shots that sent his opponents into purgatory.

He taught us what he could of courage and the science of the earth:
of litmus paper turned pink by the juice of a lemon
or blue when dipped in water and bicarbonate of soda,
of mercury that scatters and convenes in a shivery dollop,
and the power of a gyroscope balanced on a string, wheeling
                               down the airways.

What he didn't teach us is the mystery that holds a man
                             and woman together,
my brothers and I each with marriages dissolving.
The time my brother crawled under the house to fix the plumbing
in the wet darkness, he carried a pin-up lamp shaded with roses.
I think he was drawn by something provocative that we haven't
    discovered,
the electrical current from the lamp charging through his body
until he cried out to register the pain
of that terrifying moment when the voltage lit up his life.

James Reiss

Whitman at a Grain Depot

By a loading bay that smells of millet
I tell him about photos of the Okies
in pickups piled mattress-and-bedstead-high
before empty stretches reflected
in the hollows of their cheeks.

He reminds me that Matthew Brady traced
the worry lines of an earlier generation
bivouacked beside muskets, knowing no campfire
could warm fallen comrades,
no plow unplant the human harvest.

I tell him the First World War
was fought overseas by farm boys gassed
in fields seeded with mines, the orchards
ripe with snipers twenty years later.

Then was it wrong to call those barnyards lonely
because their owners were missing in action
and the horses stumbled up to their fetlocks in mud?
Is it wrong to compare corn tassels to the sun-
beaten hair of women on welfare?

A giant combine is parked by a silo here
where a spark could rain ash on our heads.
Surveying the stockpile of grain,
Whitman seizes a fistful
and calls it bone meal.

Ira Sadoff

The Way of All Flesh

All those sultry kisses,
addressed, like a waving hand
to the sinking ship, *Titanic*,
must not go to waste. Save
the kerchiefs and the ticket stubs,
those wishes, lost, for last good-byes.
All those foghorns, pulled-up
anchors, ghostly loves
and metabolic rushes
add up to a corpse whose body's
been given back to him, briefly,
like a miracle. So you rise
from the coffin of the single bed,
full of fresh ideas and plans
to beat the system, to meet your wife
halfway between the kitchen
and the steamy corridor. The body
travels. So those postcards
from Nape Neck and Cheek Bone,
from Pelvis and Wrist,
remind you of the summer romance
that lasted till October. And here,
in middle age, where passengers
have packed their recollections
for the final drowning, one wish
might stand for all of us: the porthole
opens on a turgid, salty, autumn sea:
your friend Lucille, whose thigh
you once spent all night nibbling,
comes back wanting, in her rowboat
full of greed, far more. *Amour*,
she says, *I'm lost*, and lingers
in your memory like the spray
before the breaking wave.

Sherod Santos

The Sea Change

The bay shines dull as lead today, and the blue-
Chevroned geese are through calling
To the east of here, their long line falling
Like a rope behind the scattered dunes,

Or rising all at once as the seawind drives them
Deeper into the south, into that lilac-mottled air,
Where the line grows thin, the horizon clears,
And their wings' inaudible commotion ends.

For years we lived in those same slow migrations
Of the heart, drawn by an impulse to love or despair
Toward some blurred relation between a here and there,
Or from an image of ourselves in a season's dissolution:

Twice we separated, and twice came back, and still
Not what we'd expected, separated for good,
And now you ask yourself, If two people could,
Would they endure all this for such exacting thrills?

It seems younger we must have felt otherwise.
Out walking along the beach we'd stare across
Those slow green breakers blown to wash
Then rushed out on the sand, as if the tide

Could turn more into itself than it turned away.
But this evening the shoreline only frightens me
With its heaps of kelp thrown back from the sea
As though from past affections; and the black sway

Of the patches out beyond the ocean's scree
Is like an image repeated in memory: of a day
To come when something inside will at last give way
And in a slow exhalation drift apart from me,

When the senses will rise up slowly from the dunes
And simply circle in the air, in their native blue.

Dennis Schmitz

Instructions for Fishing the Eel

December pools, latent, crosshatched
  in low wind
& the rest of the stream all exegesis.
Steelhead will nose
the water-seams around rocks
  where you can drop

yarn-flies or a roe-dip compound
  that bleeds red taste
around your hook,
  the fog head-high & bleeding

out of the nearby firs
hooked down by the same ice
  you sometimes pull through your reel
in stiff small O's that mean
  you've lost all weight

at the line's end: your connection,
  your tie to the it-world.
Your second lesson: when a fish
twists, leaps through

to our world to throw hook
  or die, contention stops—
where the line enters water
  is equipoise,
centering: fish & human at last
  in balance & glorying,

if either can, in the other.
Lastly, the steelhead's context
    is ocean; the hardest
lesson is to let go

what one can't be, first immersing
    the releasing hand,
dirtied by bait
but dry enough paradoxically to slime
    off in rainbows
the fish's protective coat: the hand's

reward is to feel
the no-shape of water, feel human warmth
drain away in the wetting.

Jaroslav Seifert

Translated from the Czech by Jeffrey Fiskin and Erik Vestville

When the Ashes

When the ashes bloom at home
their scent whispers through my window,
especially at dusk,
especially after rain.

The trees are a few minutes away,
down the street, around the corner.
This year, even before I limped down,
chattering jackdaws were already at work
on the red berries.

When I breathe in the rich fragrance
under the trees,
all around me life flexes
with pleasure as if stroked
gently by a woman's hand.

Burning Ship

I started out towards evening.
As a seeker is often anticipated,
one who waits is merely found.

I passed sleeping villages
where scraps of last summer's music
still ribboned ivied corners
until night caught up with me.

A flame flared in the dark.
Someone screamed: A ship's on fire!

A passionate tongue of flame
touched the naked water;
a young girl's shoulder trembled,
an ecstasy.

Beneath willows shuddering
over a well where darkness hides
from light, I saw her.

It was almost dawn.
She was tugging
a wet bucket
from the rim.
Timidly, I asked
if she had seen a flame?
She looked up startled,
turned her head away,
       and after a while nodded
       hesitantly.

Mortar Salvos

When the procession falls to its knees tomorrow,
you'll remain standing, festive and white
(little girls in white don't kneel),
silent as a handful of water.
Only mortars thunder, one after another,
on a distant hill.

We used to meet in the garden
by the local slaughterhouse,
in a stench of bucketed entrails
and pools of blood caked with green flies.

I picked handfuls of flowers for you.
No one could weave a prettier wreath.

Tomorrow when prayers begin,
a trifle long as usual,
I'll smile over your little tiara of flowers.

I watched your fingers tenderly
bend stem to stem, daisy to jasmine,
cockscomb to fragrant mint
when —
                my head spun.
You had such a strange look.
Lifting your skirt, you
scattered the lapful of petals
and I could see love
had only been napping in the heart above.

But it was so sudden,
your startled blood startled my heart.

The pounding was a festive salute
to passionate maiden beauty
which, until then, I had never known.

The Devil, naturally, stood by
in his hunter's costume
and, with a malicious twirl
of his mustachios,
noted my bewilderment
and your knees.

Tom Sleigh

Don't Go to the Barn

(FOR ROSE SLEIGH)

The brick of the asylum shimmered in the sun
As I watched the black hood of your depression
Lower down across your face immobile
But for the eyes staring off into the crystal

Blue bracing the scorched mountain.
Fire like a razor had swept the rock face clean. . . .
Cut off from your despair, I stared across the lawn
To your drug-blinkered gaze staring down

The shivering, flashing eyes of the aspen:
Blinking back that glare, I saw your heart eaten
By the gloom of the weather-warped barn
Off behind the orchard alleys convulsing

Into bloom, saw you walk into the shudder
Of blossoms rippling down in spasms
Of cool wind, the weeds you tread under
Springing back bristling, the tough, fibrous green

Closing in behind you, the chill brushings
Of the leaves feathering dew across your skin.
The barn like a grey flame burns above the bloom,
The hoof-cratered mud, glistening in the sun,

Squelching as you slog across the yard.
And now you enter into the raftered
Damp of lofty spaces cut by the veer
And slice of scaly wings, knot the knot hard,

Loop the rope around the beam, the zero
Of the noose dangling down: Your gaze swings
To mine, and I see your chances narrow:
Sprawled on the table, the volts axing

Through your skull, you jerk and shake,
Your body drugged to flab trembling and trembling,
Your teeth clenching jolt after jolt until crackling
In your brain a voice of fire speaks,

Divinely disapproving: "Don't go to the barn
And try to hang yourself. Don't go to the barn
And try to hang yourself. Don't go to the barn
And try to hang yourself. Rose, don't go to the barn."

Dave Smith

Cooking Eggs

Muse, you have left me at last. How did I come
to stand crowing, alone,
while the kitchen sizzles and smokes like fate?
Awkwardly aproned, uncertain,
I ply the clot of butter—what's enough?— but
let it burn until it reeks
in your overheated pan. Is this our history?
Preparations barely watched
unnerve me now: I'm confused about elements, times,
the small feet—remember?—
over linoleum: they've stolen my shoes ("Sorry,
Dad, Mom said OK!") Your door slammed
shut, woozy sentences left to hang unfinished, you
slipped from the sheets, easing
into the world. Today I woke with you gone,
and your gauzy gown's a dream,
so here I am trying to crack the shell cleanly,
to see again how it starts,
that eager, thin, pearly sliding-forth ooze you
managed with no hands almost,
awake or asleep. I watch it spurt and thicken
fast into creamy fingers
that wrinkle and brown, fissures of flesh, growths
of tissue that pop and blister
in self-begetting scars, and that smoky glaucoma
spreading over the heart.
How can I help getting gold on my hand like a smell
from your breastfalling hair,
which isn't with me anymore? I should have written
out what you did.
When I think of your biscuits the doorbell rings.
Each knob I touch turns something

wrongly off, or on. Small heaps of waste
everywhere accuse me. Morning
light you loved reveals the window's
smudged by something's smooch. I can't keep it up.
That's why today I abandoned all
for the shower that turned to ice, from which I
stepped forth, phone ringing,
to find no towel, so shivered myself dry, stood
amidst this mortgaged mess, and
saw the cardinals we've watched so many springs
they could be us. I notice
he's back first, red hot, croaking, clenching his limb.
Then she's there, black eye cocked
to check him as she vacuums the familiar dirt. She
lets him sing, half-listening,
too thin, eggless these days, yet she stands curious
as a girl sometimes when
he brings a worm down with a great gourmet flutter.
Sometimes she flies into the sun.
Then he bellows louder, as if the winter taught him
what love never could, crying
"Listen, you won't know me. I'm a brand new bird.
You hear? Come back.
I'm cooking all the time now. You'll be hungry, too."

Drag Race

(FOR NORMAN DUBIE)

Lying in bed I hear two come nose to nose
like fathers and sons, jockeying,
torque shaking the bodies
under the moonlight that shouts,
and the street goes instantly blacker
with rubber's balding death-howl
and the mind waking into panic
as if the house is exploding inside.
I smell the honeysuckle that accepts
again, as it must, the awful
drift of concussions, oil and smoke
snapping on houselights like fear
my father could never turn off.
Below, a boy's hand strikes the air
only, headlights lurch together,
locked to no horizon, wrestling
forth the veterans, also-rans of glory
who keep these crew-cut lawns,
their faces shrouded in curtains
the war brides hung years ago.
I could rise and walk among them,
my fatherly robe star-silvered,
unthreading with age and forgiveness,
saying sleep, it won't happen again,
not the dog's territorial wail,
not the voices belligerently boyish,
not the beer bottle spidering sidewalks,
not my father swinging the night
back, hunching upright in my face
to snarl in the moonlight
I'm going to die in a scummy ditch
where love doesn't mean a damn thing.
I could call out *You!* to the boy

already hiding in the sweet vines,
certain they'll pick him up, sure
in his head he isn't alone.
I could put my hand on him like a tall
tracking shadow and make him
shiver this warm night, his mouth
outrageous as the arguments of power.
For each of us I could say it's over, just
the black street all that's left.
I might say go home now. We might
stand so close and still the others
would believe we were learning
the secret of living together—
the paralysis of place
terrible and silent as nightmares
with porchlights flaring on, off,
inexplicable as tracers. But he
wouldn't listen, the light sheen
on him, holding like a fist.
Don't lie old man, he'd say, just
tell me what's going to happen.
Then I'd push him, tell him
get away punk, run, try to live,
each stunned throat of honeysuckle
understanding, nodding softly.

Cuba Night

The small of the back has its answers
for all our wrong turns, even the slightest,
those aches there's no name for, or source,
and the mole in the mirror, a black moon
of sudden importance can turn the hours
into love's rapt attention. As you shave
an innocent glance into the yard pulls
your gaze mulishly as if something's there
more than choice or will to live. Still,

the fly on its back, feet up in dead air
between the storm-doubled panes stiffens
some kind of reminder, redolent of a word
you don't speak, like history, but feel
as once you felt the shuffle and slap
of your father's feet on heartwood floors.
He would be bathed then, as you are now,
unshirted, coffee starting, his lathered,
clownish cheeks white, the dawn oozing red.

Quizzical, you hear the razor pull closer,
strokes deliberate so the skin bristles.
Is that it? The cafe, two men you were?
Standing outside, soft night, a radio,
the president declaring in the dirt one
line only war could cross. Your mother's
not yet meat somebody's death-trap Ford
will carve from breasts to groin-girdle.
Your father takes your teen-aged hand.

Up the block clusters of others leaned as
the dusk steadily bled all light from each
face, and a voice like Bob Dylan's said it

is history, and you said what? Same word
when a wife said I can't stand this anymore,
that had started with her crying yes, yes.
In the yard there's no smell of stale sheets,
no memory of a kiss like a feather, no
flare of Bikini atoll rerunning all night.

It's only the azaleas beginning to explode
that must have been planted in that year,
the smudged hand now earth's, first questions
he couldn't answer, his eyes brimming up.
Nobody you know's been to Cuba or can say
what history is. There's blood on your lip.
The mole's the same. You're starting over,
remembering the floor that seemed to shake
with speech, then with the unslipping of
her nakedness, soap-white. Then the shaving.

New England Mill

Locked down, hunched into itself,
flesh-colored scab ice
in places pink as silk or
bearing inexplicable stains
folds around the hulk
as cast-off garments
cling to the street people,

not quite enough coverage to reach
everywhere, the ragged trickle
from inside becoming a bruise,
blotchy as rust, like skin
exposed, calves, ankles of it
waiting for the sun's fever
and beautiful blue like
a flamelet. The granite

glitters most where sun comes,
less proposed than factual
as the goblets of the rich.
One thinks of these two
or three heirloom pieces
hauled over the Atlantic
by indentured girls who

sent them spinning in a vortex
of hands where, by luck or
penny-pinching histories,
they have come to display
themselves, unused, in a young
couple's pine hutch. But
iridescent coils of a late

afternoon sunset call back
the iron-cold rock, though we
want to see a man's last hair
breeze-drifted. Odd how it

seems the press of tissue
snoozing, brown tiny tendrils
green will spring through soon,

and no matter the hulk's heart
is past recovery, blackened,
echoingly empty as it holds
itself fetally like a man
at a city sidewalk grate.
Its mistakes were not ours
we want to exclaim, perhaps
no man's. How can we know

what the books tell us is
true? Yet we recall a gift
shop's bound photographs,
raffish poses in a company
posture, the river lighting
each face like a time
exposure that is endless,
the stark capes of trees —

all gone in this hard season.
Trying to refocus it all,
we see one hawking youth,
his jaw sharp as a stone wall.
His glance has bold confidence,
his hand is on her shoulder.
They know they are entering
our lives, making our future.

Tourists in winter, we back
with cameras onto the river
where they came, told how
its dark churning can't hurt.
We're safe enough to say
God forbid living like this.
We walk around whatever's
lying useless. The snap, snap
of shutters slamming is
like limbs breaking upwind.

Tomas Tranströmer

Translated from the Swedish by Samuel Charters

Gogol

His coat threadbare like a wolf pack.
His face like a marble chip.
Sitting in a circle of his letters in a grove that sighs
of scorn and mistake.
Yes, the heart blows like a piece of paper through the inhospitable
passageways.

Now the sunset slips over the countryside like a fox,
in a moment sets fire to the grass.
Space is filled with horns and hooves and below
the calèche glides shadowlike between my father's
illuminated estates.

Petersburg located at the same latitude as annihilation
(did you see the beautiful one in that leaning tower?)
and around blocks covered with ice still hovers like a jellyfish
the wretch in his overcoat.
And here, wrapped up in fasts, is the one who was surrounded by herds
    of laughter,
but a long time ago they departed for regions far beyond the tree line.

Mankind's staggering tables.
Look how the darkness is setting fire to the Milky Way.
So mount your fiery chariot and leave this land.

The Boat — The Village

A Portuguese fishing boat, blue, the wake roiling up a stretch of the
    Atlantic.
A long way out a blue point, but I'm there anyway, the six on board
    don't notice that we are seven.

I saw a boat like it being built, it lay like a large unstrung lute
in the poorravine, the village where you wash and wash with fury,
    patience, sadness.

Black with people on the beach. It was a meeting that was being
    dispersed, the loudspeakers carried away.
Soldiers led the speaker's Mercedes through the crowd. Words
    drummed against the metal-plated sides.

For Mats and Laila

The Date Line lies calm between Samoa and Tonga but the Midnight Line glides along over the ocean and the islands and the roofs of the huts. They're sleeping there on the other side. Here in Värmland it's midday, sunburning early summer day, I have thrown my baggage away. A swimming trip in the sky, how blue the air is. . . . Then suddenly I see the ridges on the other side of the lake; they're cut over. Like the shaved parts of the scalp on a patient who's going to have a brain operation. That has been there all the time. I didn't see it before. Blinkers and a crick in the neck. . . . The trip goes on. Now the landscape's full of streaks and lines, like in the old engravings where the people moved small between hills and mountains that were like ant hills and villages that were also thousands of streaks. And every human ant dragged his streak to the large engraving, there wasn't any real center but everything lived. Another thing: the figures are small, but each of them has his own face, the engraver has allowed them that, no, they're not ants. Most of them are simple people, but they can write their names. Proteus, however, is a modern person and expresses himself fluently in all styles, comes with "straight communication" or flourishes, depending on which gang he belongs to at the moment. But he can't write his name. He shrinks away from it like the werewolf from the silver bullet. They don't ask it of him either, not the hydra of the company, not the State. . . . The trip goes on. In that house lives a man who became desperate one night and shot with real bullets at the hammock hovering above the grass. And the Midnight Line gets nearer, it soon will have gone halfway around. (Don't tell me I'm trying to turn the clock back!) Tiredness will stream in through the hole the sun left.
. . . It never happened to me that the diamond of a certain moment made an irreparable crack over the picture of the world. No, it was the rubbing, the steady rubbing that wiped away the light strange smile. But something is becoming visible again with the rubbing, begins to be like a smile, you don't know what it can be worth. There's someone grabbing my arm every time I try to write.

Memory Sees Me

A morning in June when it is too early
to awaken but too late to sleep again.

Outside, the leaves' and bushes' seats are filled
with memories whose glances follow me.

They can't be seen, they blend themselves into
the background, like perfect chameleons.

They are so close that I can hear them breathing
though the sound of birds is deafening.

The Station

A train has rolled in. Here stands car after car,
but no door is opened, no one gets on or off.
Are there any doors at all? Inside it is swarming with
people who can't leave moving back and forth.
They stare out through the implacable windows.
And outside a man walks along the train with a sledgehammer.
He strikes the wheel, it clangs weakly. Except right here!
Here the tone swells incomprehensibly: a thunderclap,
the tolling of a cathedral bell, the round-the-world sailor's tolling
that lifts the whole train and the whole area's wet stones!
Everything sings. You will remember that. Travel on.

The Winter's Glance

Like a ladder I lean over and put
my face into the first floor of the cherry tree.
I am inside the bell of colors that rings with the sun.
I finish off the black-red cherries faster than four magpies.

Then suddenly I feel the chill from far off.
The moment blackens
and stays like the mark of the axe in the tree trunk.

From now on it's late. We go off half-running
out of sight, down, down into the antique sewer system.
The tunnels. We wander there for months
half out of duty and half in flight.

Brief devotions when some hatch opens above us
and a weak light falls.
We look upward, the starry sky through the grating of the sewer.

Molokai

We stand at the edge of the cliff and in the depths beneath us
gleam the roofs of the leper colony.
We could climb down, but we don't have time to make it back before
dark.
So we turn back through the forest, walk among trees with long blue
needles.
It is still. It is the stillness when the hawk comes.
It is a forest that forgives everything but forgets nothing.
Damien, out of love, chose life and oblivion. He found death and fame.
But we see these events from the wrong angle: a heap of stones instead
of the face of the sphinx.

The Gallery

I stopped over at a motel on E3.
In my room was a smell that I knew from before
in a museum's Asiatic collections:

masks Tibetan Japanese against a light wall.

It isn't masks now but faces

that penetrate the white wall of forgetfulness
to breathe, to ask for something.
I lie awake and see them struggle
and disappear and return.

Some borrow each other's shapes, change faces
deep within me
where forgetfulness and memory go on with their bargaining.

They penetrate the painting over of forgetfulness
the white wall
they disappear and return.

There is a sorrow here that doesn't call itself that.

Welcome to the real galleries!
Welcome to the real galleys!
The real gratings!

The karate boy who paralyzed a man
still dreams of fast profits.

This woman buys and buys things
to throw into the mouth of the empty space
that slinks behind her.

Mr. X doesn't dare leave his apartment.
A dark fence of ambiguous people
stands between him
and the horizon rolling steadily away.

She who once fled from Karelia
she who could laugh . . .
she appears now
but mute, turned to stone, a statue from Sumer.

As when I was ten years old and came home late.
In the stairway the lights were turned out.
But the elevator where I stood was lit, and the elevator
climbed like a diving bell through black depths
floor by floor while imagined faces
pressed against the grill.

But they are real faces now, not imagined ones.

I lie stretched out like a cross street.

Many climb out of the white mist.
We touched each other once, certainly!

A long light corridor that smells of carbolic acid.
The wheelchair. The teen-age girl
who is learning to talk after the car crash.

He who tried to call out under water
and the cold mass of the world squeezed in
through his nose and mouth.

Voices in the microphone said: Speed is power
speed is power!
Play the game, the show must go on!

In our careers we move stiffly step by step
as in a Noh play
with masks, shrieking song: Me, it's me!
The ones that lose out
are represented by a rolled-up blanket.

An artist said: Before, I was a planet
with its own thick atmosphere.
The rays from outside were broken up into rainbows,
continuous thunderstorms raged within, within.

Now I'm burned out and dry and open.
I don't have the energy of a child now.
I have a hot side and a cold side.

No rainbows.

I stopped over at the house where things could be heard.
Many want to come in there through the walls
but most don't find their way.

They are shouted down by the white noise of forgetfulness.

Anonymous song drowns in the walls.
Delicate knockings that don't want to be heard
drawn-out sighs
my old answers creeping homelessly.

Listen to society's mechanical self-reproaches
the large air conditioner's voice
like the artificial gale in the mine shafts
six hundred meters down.

Our eyes stay wide open under the bandage.

If I can at least get them to feel
that the shaking under us
means that we're on a bridge . . .

Often I have to stand completely motionless.
I'm the partner of the knife thrower in the circus!
Questions I threw from me in a fit of rage
come whining back

don't hit but nail down my shape
in coarse outline
stay there when I've left the place.

Often I have to remain silent. Willingly!
Because the "last word" is said again and again.
Because hello and goodbye . . .
Because a day like today . . .

Because the margins will finally rise
over their edges
and drown the text.

I stopped over at the sleepwalkers' hotel.
Many faces in here are desperate
others smoothed away
after their pilgrimage through forgetfulness.

They breathe disappear fight their way back
they see past me
they all want to go toward the icon of justice.

It happens, but seldom
that one of us really sees the other:

a person shows himself a moment
as in a photo but clearer
and in the background
something that is bigger than his shadow.

He stands full length in front of a mountain.
It's more a snail shell than a mountain.
It's more a house than a snail shell.
It isn't a house but has many rooms.
It's indistinct but overwhelming.
He grows from it and it from him.
It is his life, it is his labyrinth.

Chase Twichell

A Fire in the Mind

Sputnik, in Russian,
means "traveling companion."
1958: Father lifted his two children
asleep out of the car,
and shook them into sleep's equivalent,
a field of black grasses,
to watch the Soviet spark cross over.

In a photograph, also 1958,
he leans on his long-handled maul,
having split and stacked
what looks like
a snowbank of firewood.
Is that what burns?

Snow slaked his thirst.
He looks as though
he might love
with velocity,
with prowess and strangeness.

My body the orphan
calls out to that parent strangeness.

Not to the love that sleeps in heredity,
but to its counterpart,
the blood stung by companion fire.

Littered with fresh splinters
and the chainsaw's roughage,
the new stump beads with sap.
The green rings tighten in the tree.

After each bisection,
the wind scours
the wound to emptiness.
For love to persist,
the heart must keep its creases
sweet with corroborating dirt.

My father stared up
into the green-black galaxy,
the treasures sunken there.
Even now, years later,
I drift on that worldliness,
all love amassed so far.
I am not a flash of saintly fire.
I slake my thirst where I can,
and rest inside the tiredness
of this the long and only journey,
waking each time
to an advancing sadness and peace.
Each foreign heart
that passes near me
on its unknown trajectory
I call my relative,
my kindling spirit,
another rosy light transporting
its burden of pathos,
its cargo of soil.

Derek Walcott

Marina Tsvetayeva

Newspapers aged on the couch. The beach-house
loved its sunlit vacancy. The bed had a plaid
red and white coverlet. I watched the armoire's
mirror crossed and re-crossed by a fan's shadowy blade.

Parched as the beach, I went into the kitchen.
My thirst growled in the locked-off faucet.
I opened the fridge-door, but a white lichen
had frozen the trays like a Siberian forest.

I drank some iced-water in my self-allowed
happiness. The ceiling-fan whirred in peace.
I could see the tilted door of a broken cupboard
like a violin's cheekbone cradled against space.

Just as the blistered castaway craves water
instead of wine, your verse chilled every vein
from throat to foot, with the temperature
of the first spring from its original mountain.

Thought girdles earth in a second, so in this dacha
of immense absences, a door kept banging
against the past. The fly screen as abandoned
as a cashier's cage, when they arrest the cashier.

I put the bottle in and saw a station
with empty rails in snow, the ember of a train,
though August was scorching the white stone
around the lighthouse, where gulls return,

you slip from the door of your book in a black cloak
whose characters blur in rain, like the old mascara
of the Wailing Wall, or the plaster crack
in a doll's grin, her lashes lined with kohl.

Noon linen of Tsvetayeva, Marina your sea-sorrows
thorns on a driftwood branch! The godhead grows
bluer and emptier. Over drifts of prose
dilates the exclamation of your small figure.

And here's what's left: a sky-blue powder-box,
the frame of a window like a frontispiece
from which they peeled your photograph, dead clocks,
and hanging in a cupboard, a butterfly-lemon dress,

sand brushed from a bedsheet, the grave in a pillow,
an oceanic tear. The sea's mica sparkles in scales.
Time, that is half of eternity, like the sea in a window,
lifts like the muslin's stationary sails.

Storm Figure

Last night this century was a kerosene lamp
hallowing the bare boards of a kitchen-table.
With the poles down, its wick-smoke pined and flamed
and scorched the memory like a Hardy novel.

This wet dawn, walking barefoot from the beach-house,
you look down cold sand shuddering from dreck
to see a shawled, smoky figure where the brown shallows
roll fallen trunks like bodies after a shipwreck.

But this is the wrong ground. The Wessex coast
is in another century. The lamp's sheaf of flame,
erect in its window throughout the storm's harvest
was called fidelity, but has changed her name.

Still, the shallows' mutterings suit her
thunder-gone waiting, clouds blowing in smoky scraps,
breakers that chuff, slow, leaden swells of pewter,
the pier-piles rumbling, mosses gripped by crabs.

Street-lights cautiously re-dot the wrecked roads
with the morse of crickets, the century takes shape,
she is there in that drizzle whose gust recedes,
a figurehead fluttering without its ship.

Drop by slow drop the branch loses its pearls,
surf drags soiled petticoats through the beach's muck,
ice fetters her ankles fording the new rock-pools,
sheet-spray obscures her, but she is its water-mark.

The sea-light with its mullioned mackerel dances
over the smoked-out lamp by the double-bed,
and the wavering mirror from which a third face glances
then passes. The smiling muslin has resettled.

On drying scarps with tough tips of tidal grass
her shadow fades into half-clouding sand,
the surf draws up its hem, a seagull passes
arrowing in silence which is the soul's sound.

C. K. Williams

Travelers

He drives, she mostly sleeps; when she's awake, they quarrel, and now,
   in a violet dusk,

a rangy, raw-boned, efficient-looking mongrel loping towards them down
   the other shoulder

for no apparent reason swerves out on the roadbed just as a battered taxi
   is going by.

Horrible how it goes under, how it's jammed into the asphalt, compressed,
   abraded, crumpled,

then is ejected out behind, still, a miracle, alive, but spinning wildly on
   itself, tearing,

frenzied, at its broken spine, the mindless taxi never slowing, never noticing or caring,

them slowing, only for a moment though, as, "Go on," she says, "Go on,
   go on," face averted,

she can't look, while he, guilty as usual, fearful, fascinated and uncouth,
   can't not.

Girl Meets Boy

She would speak of "our relationship" as though it were a thing apart
    from either of us,
an entity with separate necessities, even its own criteria for appraisal,
    judgment, mode of act,
to which both of us were to be ready to sacrifice our own more momentary
    notions of identity.
It was as though there were a preexistent formula or recipe, something
    from a textbook,
which demanded not only the right ingredients — attentiveness, affection,
    generosity, et cetera —
but also a constant and rigorous examination and analysis of the shifting
    configurations
our emotions were assuming in their presumed movement towards some
    ultimate consummation
in whose intensity the rest of this, not in any way an end, would be re-
    deemed, would wither quietly away.

Books

Possibly because she's already so striking — tall, well-dressed, very clear,
    pure skin —
when the girl gets on the subway at Lafayette Street everyone notices
    her artificial hand
but we also manage, as we almost always do, not to be noticed noticing,
    except one sleeping woman
who hasn't budged since Brooklyn but who lifts her head now, opens
    up, forgets herself
and frankly stares at those intimidating twists of steel, the homely leather
    sock and laces,
so that the girl, as she comes through the door, has to do in turn now
    what is to be done,
which is to look down at it, too, a bit askance, with an air of tolerant,
    bemused annoyance,
the way someone would glance at their unruly, ferocious-looking but
    really quite friendly dog.

Philadelphia: 1978

I'm on my way to the doctor to get the result of chest X-rays because I
    coughed blood
a few weeks ago while we were still in California; I am more or less a
    wreck of anxiety
and just as I turn the corner from Spruce Street onto Sixteenth where
    my doctor's is,
a raggedy-looking guy coming towards me on the sidewalk yells to me
    from fifty feet away:
"I know that walk! I sure know *that* walk!" smiling broadly, with genuine
    good feeling.
Although I don't recognize him — he looks druggy, wasted — I smile back,
    then as we come closer,
he suddenly seems dubious, asking, "Don't I know you?" "Maybe not."
    "Weren't you in 'Nam?"
and — before I can answer — "Shit!" he spits out, "Shit!" furious with me:
    "You fucking *shit*!"

Self-knowledge

Because he was always the goodhearted one, the ingenuous one, the one
    who knew no cunning,
who, if "innocent" didn't quite apply, still merited some similar conno-
    tation of naiveté, simplicity,
the sense that an essential awareness of the coarseness of other people's
    motives was lacking
so that he was constantly blundering into situations in which he would
    take on good faith
what the other rapaciously, ruthlessly, duplicitously and nearly always
    successfully offered as truth . . .
all of that he understood about himself, but he was also aware that he
    couldn't alter at all
his basic affable faith in the benevolence of everyone's intentions and
    that because of this the world
would not as in a romance annihilate him but would toy unmercifully
    with him until he was mad.

Rungs

When we finally tracked him down, the old man (not really all that very
   old, we thought)
who'd made the comfortable, graceful, elegantly mortised chairs for all
   the farmers' kitchens
told us, never even opening the heavy iron gate into his yard, that he
   was through, retired,
done with it, and no, he didn't know anybody else who made them now,
   no one, he was the last.
He seemed to say it all with satisfaction, or he was anyway unmoved by
   what it may have meant,
leaving us to back away, apologize, get into our car to make an awkward
   U-turn in his unpaved lane,
suffering meanwhile modern pangs of conscience and regret for good
   things gone for good,
all the innocence the world was losing, all the chances we'd once had,
   and lost, for beauty.

Drought

A species of thistle no one had ever seen before appeared almost over-
    night in all the meadows,
coarse, gray-greenish clumps scattered anywhere the dying grass had
    opened up bare earth.
The farmers knew better or were too weary to try to fight the things, but
    their children,
walking out beside them through the sunset down the hillsides towards
    the still-cool woods
along the narrowed brooks, would kick the plants or try to pry them out
    with pointed sticks;
the tenacious roots would hardly ever want to give, though, and it was
    too hot still to do much
but crouch together where the thick, lethargic water filtered up and ran
    a few uncertain feet,
moistening the pebbles, forming tiny tide-pools where the thriving in-
    sects could repose and reproduce.

Guatemala: 1964

(FOR LOREN CRABTREE)

The Maya-Quechua Indians plodding to market on feet as flat and tough
    as toads were semi-starving
but we managed to notice nothing but their brilliant weaving and im-
    placable, picturesque aloofness.
The only people who would talk to us were the village alcoholic who sold
    his soul for *aguardiente*
and the Bahia nurse, Jenny, middle-aged, English-Nicaraguan, the sole
    medicine for eighty miles,
who Lord knows why befriended us, put us up, even took us in her jeep
    into the mountains,
where a child, if I remember, needed penicillin, and where the groups
    of dark, idling men
who since have risen and been crushed again noted us with something
    disconcertingly beyond suspicion.
Good Jenny: she had no time, she said, to tend the dying, but no where-
    withal to do much besides.

Love: Intimacy

They were so exceptionally well got-up for an ordinary Sunday afternoon stop-in at Deux Magots,
her in very chic deep black, him in a business suit, and they were so evi-
   dently just out of bed
but with very little to say to one another, much gazing off, elaborate
   lightings of her cigarettes,
her more proper than was to be believed, sipping with a flourished pinky
   at her Pimm's Cup,
that it occurred to me I was finally seeing one of those intriguing *Herald-
   Tribune* classifieds —
a woman's name, a number — for "escorts" or "companions," but then I
   had to change my mind:
she'd leaned towards him, deftly lifted a line of his thinning hair, and
   idly, with a mild pat,
had laid it back; not commiserating, really, just keeping record of the
   progress of the loss.

David Long

The Last Photograph of Lyle Pettibone

I took this early on a Sunday morning, the 26th of August, that blistering summer of 1917. I was using a Brownie Autographic, bought for eighteen dollars at the Stillwater Mercantile—you can see where I scratched the date and hour along the bottom of the negative. The people who'd been up all night were gone. Others would soon be rising and dressing for church, and stories would crackle through the streets, but I was alone then, or nearly so, crouched on the rails at the west edge of Stillwater, shivering. I could still smell the fire on my clothes, and the first light, when it finally arrived, came thickened with smoke. I made the picture, folded in the bellows of the camera, and walked back along the tracks toward home.

You asked me how I got started . . . it was then.

I was twenty-one that summer, caught between working as my father's factotum at the Dupree Hotel and being conscripted for the war. Some boys I knew had already left their jobs and shipped out; some others had fashioned hasty marriages . . . I'd see them walking through Depot Park with their pregnant wives after supper, heads bent to the grass. I wasn't so gung ho on the war myself. When the *Clarion* ran the first cull of Sperry County names, three hundred to the man, I was mortally relieved to skim to the end of it without seeing mine. But the relief wore thin before long. Flanders was falling, Russia was going to hell, American recruits were funneling into Pershing's army by the thousands. . . . As for matrimony, the only girl in Stillwater I'd cared for had gone East that May to study piano in earnest. Her name was Marcelle, and she wore a French braid that hung down her back like a bullwhip. Her picture shone at me mornings from the bevel of my shaving mirror. In her last letter, she told of going to the Opera House in Chicago to hear Irma Kincaid perform Chopin. *I know you'll think I'm just being dramatic, Willy, but Irma Kincaid has changed my life.*

I spent my free time staring at the town through the Brownie's viewfinder, developing what I saw in a room off the cold storage under the Dupree. I had a picture of the mayor with his foot planted ceremoniously on the running board of his new Saxon roadster . . . school-children poling their raft down McAfferty's Slough . . . drifters sleeping under a wagon behind the Pastime. "What do you want to take pictures of old bums for?" my sister Ellen would scold me mildly. "There's enough unpleasantness in life without going out and *scrounging* for it." "That's not what I'm doing," I'd tell her, "I'm just keeping my eyes open."

One afternoon I sweet-talked Ellen into sitting for me with her clothes off. We went up to an empty room on the top floor and I made dozens of pictures of her lolling on her quilt pretending she was one of the women on Calhoun Street. She was never a beauty, but her skin was white as bar soap, freckled pleasantly across the bosom, and she was capable of a wicked droopy-eyed smile. "How's this, Willy?" she'd ask, draping herself in a new travesty of wantonness. "You're one to reckon with, all right," I said, and we had a high time, the two of us, there under our father's roof. But when I mentioned the developing and printing, Ellen suddenly glazed with worry and told me she wouldn't allow it. "You have to promise me you won't print them," she said.

"You looked awfully good," I said. "Trust me."

"I'll trust you to never *ever* print those pictures," she said, and threw her robe around herself. "I'm not fooling."

And so I left her glaring out over the roofs of Stillwater, on the edge of tears. Later, I made the negatives and looked at them by myself against the lightbulb, then put them away in a drawer and never printed them up, more's the pity.

Of course, I took my father as well: a florid, girth-heavy widower of Scotch-French-Canadian stock, a man burdened by an ungenerous nature and nagging social aspirations, burdened, too, by a daughter who drank and a son he called a runt and a dreamer. . . .

But here's the first picture of Lyle Pettibone. He's down in front of the Montana Cafe, around the corner from where the IWW headquarters had been till that June, when the troopers had come after hours and shut it down. He's just endured another set-to with Wilbur Embree, who was on the town council, and E. C. Doyle, the banker, one of that high-minded crew that came to the hotel at noon every day to pack away one of Ellen's heavy lunches and smoke Cuban cigars with my father. By the time I got across the street, the shoving was done and Pettibone's copies of *Solidarity* were strewn down the boardwalk. Winded, hat aslant, he collected the papers in silence, waiting for the other men to get on with their rightful business. Men like Doyle and Embree thought harassment of unionists *was* their rightful business.

Pettibone was a tall man for those days, sober-looking as the Lutheran pastor, but it wasn't God on Pettibone's mind that summer, or not as yet. You can see his sawtooth of a nose, those chiseled-out cheeks . . . his voice was the same, sharp as a sickle, rife with a union spiel that either sickened and terrified you or sliced through all the built-up half-dead parts of you to a place that was still tender and ripe for such radical encouragement — depending on how you fell in the scheme of things. I'd heard where Helena had whistled through an ordinance to ban Wobbly organizers from public declamation, but Pettibone had spoken on our streets for weeks, and up in Depot Park as well. I'd watched him with his long arms thrown open to the sky, and I'd watched the people watching him, people of all kinds, in all kinds of costume, but mostly men I didn't recognize, shading their eyes, listening hard, and a few at the back I did know, taking notes.

They blamed the fire on him. Of course they did.

They'd been expecting something like it and then it happened and there was no question who was behind it and what it meant. All summer the *Clarion* had wailed and prophesied against the Wobbly Menace. Back in July, when trouble broke out down in Arizona, when they loaded Wobbly miners onto cattle cars and rode them out to the Mexican border and dumped them without so much as a tin cup full of water, Will McKinnon wrote that it wouldn't surprise him if citizens all through the West declared an open season on IWWs. He said we'd have a reign of terror. He wasn't personally in any position to advocate such a perversion of justice, but the deaf could've heard him pardon it. He worked that vein so hard, none of the *Clarion*'s right-thinking readers could've harbored any doubt that the IWWs were enemies of the flag, a plague on the country's war effort worse than slackers or pacifists or the few outright cowards dodging conscription. Of course, the Anaconda Company owned McKinnon, owned him outright, as they did damn near every other editor in Montana, then and for a long time after . . . but that distinction was lost on me at twenty-one. The town was afraid, you could feel that for certain. Myself, I was restless, and some afraid too, though not of Pettibone or what he said, not yet.

Well, I made that picture of Pettibone on the boardwalk and it wasn't until I started to thank him that he came to his senses and glowered at me.

"What're you doing?" he wanted to know.

It was so obvious I didn't know what to say. Nobody'd ever cared one way or the other if I took their picture, except that time with Ellen.

"Who's this for?" he said.

"It's not for anyone," I said. "I mean, it's for me."

He gave the street a sidelong check, but commerce had resumed around us.

"I liked hearing you talk the other day," I added suddenly . . . unaware until right then that I'd even listened. An illicit pleasure came crushing over me, so palpable Pettibone couldn't fail to witness it. He laid a hand on my shoulder and bent to squint me in the eye.

"You did," he said, solemn and testing, both. "What did you like about it?"

"I don't know," I said. "Sounded fair, what you were saying."

"We should live so long, you and I," Pettibone said.

Then he asked who I was. And I told him, leaving my father and his well-regarded name out of it.

"Willy the photographer . . ." Pettibone said. "You know there's going to be a strike . . . at the mill, here in Stillwater."

All I'd heard so far was the wary grumbling talk of the lunch crowd at the hotel, and McKinnon's. . . .

"I want you to come out to the mill and take some pictures," he said. "I think it would be very good if you would help us this way. You think you're up to that?"

I told him I was.

I told him he could count on me.

But a week later, when the strike came, I was back at the hotel re-shaking the back roof with my father. He could've paid to have it done — there were plenty who wanted a day or two's wage — but he was deviled to do for himself. He hauled his prosperity up the ladder, puffing and swearing at me. You'd think these would've been prime days for an innkeeper, Stillwater swelled out with newcomers as it was. A generation earlier there was woods here, and people still called it Stumptown sometimes, but no one worried anymore that Stillwater would prove another flash in the pan. Even so, these were not peaceable days for my father. Too many of the passers-through couldn't afford the Dupree. Some were family men who'd lost homesteads east of the mountains . . . honyockers they were called, immigrants lured West by the Great Northern to farm 320-acre parcels of dust. Many were single, though, with no change of clothes and—to my father's mind—unhealthy ambitions, or no ambitions at all. Anyone with a whisper of an accent, or a complexion darker than his own, he suspected of being an agitator. He rented rooms to strangers who could pay, but kept his eye on them, using spies like my sister and the hired girls who served them dinner. What he did with such intelligence as he came by, I didn't know.

We worked side by side on the roof all morning, and I itched to be out at the mill where I didn't belong, but I kept my tongue. I watched the traffic on Main and around the corner on First Street, and it passed for an ordinary day of high summer, though it was hard to pin down what was ordinary anymore. Just before lunch, my father pounded his thumb and cursed the Lord and flung the hammer across the alley, end over end . . . shattering the back window of the Mercantile. He stood on the ladder glaring down into the jagged hole, slack-jawed, as if now he'd surprised even himself.

We'd had strikes before, but nothing since 1909, and the tension was sharper now. What Pettibone was talking about was a general strike Big Bill Haywood and the Wobbly brass had called for the whole Northwest: pickers and harvest hands, miners, mill workers, and bindle stiffs who worked out of logging camps. They wanted five dollars for an eight-hour day and respectable living conditions in the camps. They wanted to run their union without being harassed and shot at and picked up for every kind of petty charge from vagrancy to suspicion of sedition. And they wanted the ones already in jail let go.

They were perfect fodder for the Wobblies. Nobody else was going to stand up for them, that was for damn sure. Timber beasts, people around here called them, illiterate footloose rabble. The mills and camps went through men like cans of beans. The Wobbly talk about One Big Union struck home. *An injury to one is an injury to all*, Pettibone and men like Pettibone said. *Live to be an old man or woman and hear the whistle blow for the bosses to go to work.* It sounded glorious, this talk, but the rest of it, the politics, the trashing of capitalism itself, that was only a far-fetched dream. They'd slept forty or fifty or sixty to a bunkhouse, doubled on straw-covered slabs, their clothes still rank and wet in the morning and no match for the ferocious cold. To a man they'd had lice and dysentery, and plenty had bronchitis they couldn't shake even when the summers finally came. And there weren't any over thirty with two hands full of fingers.

The Wobblies said you can forget about the sweet by-and-by, strike now, and they did.

For a few days, the *Clarion* ignored the strike, except for McKinnon's mighty editorializing, calling for federal troops to root out the IWWs. Then on the 20th of August he announced that the strike had proved a grand failure. But it hadn't . . . or it hadn't yet. For a time, it tied up three-quarters of the mills in the Northwest. But the strikers were isolated . . . nobody but the Lumbermen's Association and men like McKinnon knew for a fact how far it had gotten.

Now something let loose in McKinnon, and when it let loose in him it let loose all over the county. Other IWWs before Pettibone had stood up and said this wasn't their war, but this was Pettibone's favorite string to harp on. "Stay home," he preached to his people. "Fight your real enemy, fight the bosses." It was too much for McKinnon. *My friends*, he wrote, *treason is treason*. Nothing short of rounding up every last one of them would do, but authority was dragging its heels.

It was a dry summer, as I said. The streams ran low and the sloughs caked over and the grain heads shriveled before harvest. Out east of the mountains it was worse, of course, because the land was infinitely drier there to begin with, but even here in the valley the long afternoons of sun and the promise of a poor crop added to the strain. Early in August, a timber fire started up in Idaho near the Canadian line and burned eastward for eight days. It was far away, but you could smell it every morning and see the haze backed up against the mountains to the east. Someone called it sabotage, and a few probably believed it, though surely lightning had touched it off. The forest was government-owned up there, and the Wobs had no kick against that.

Anyway, sabotage was on people's minds. I never heard Pettibone favor it, for his thoughts were on the strike by then, and on the problem of keeping Wobblies out of the conscription. But others had. They called it soldiering on the job. Grain sacks would come unsewn. Shovel handles would break soon as they were passed around. Spikes would appear in logs bound for the headsaw. Whole shipments of cut timber would turn up four inches short. And nobody to blame. Hit the boss in the pocketbook and play dumb, that was the idea. But by that August sabotage had come to explain *anything* going haywire, from polluted wells to derailings of Great Northern. There were some who'd swear the drought itself was a Wobbly trick.

That Saturday, a week into the strike, the town was stuffed with people. Common sense said it was too hot to sit in the movie house, but some were braving it to watch Myrtle Stedman in a five-reeler called *Prison Without Walls*. There was a benefit for the Red Cross out at the Pavillion. At the hotel, we had a wedding party in progress — the Upshaws, important friends of my father, had married their oldest girl to a fellow from Spokane. The groom's mother was a disciple of Temperance, so the cut glass bowls on the buffet held a strawberry punch, but the men excused themselves now and again to work on flasks or bottles of ale my father'd stowed in crushed ice under a tarp on the back porch landing.

Earlier he'd called for pictures, and I'd lined the celebrants up and frozen them for posterity, still fresh. But now it was stifling inside. Even the cut flowers were droopy on their stems. The dining room was cleared of tables and Mort Pickerell's string band played and the guests danced. My sister Ellen looped freely about the room in the grasp of the groom's brother, her shoes off and her eyes half-shut. My father and Matthew Upshaw and the groom's father presided over it all, smiling heavily and dabbing at their foreheads with handkerchiefs.

I'd had enough of noise and pleasantry, and I thought I'd expire without some air. I headed out toward the kitchen and slipped up the back hall to my quarters on the third floor where I could sit in the window with my feet out on the peak of the porch roof. It was nine-thirty by my watch, just growing dark. The sky west of town was still aglow and overhead was a smear of deepening blues. Some of the mill workers had taken their last roll of wages over to Calhoun Street, I imagined, but most were down below, drinking. Men were spilling out the doorways of the Pastime, the Grandee, the Silver Dollar, and already there was yelling.

From up here, the town didn't look like so much, a few streets of commerce, a grid of frame houses stretching north to the Great Northern yard, south to the elevators, a little cluster of lights on the valley floor you could imagine snuffed out by the Lord's little finger. In a while, the evening wind came across the roofs. I stretched and breathed it in, expecting the smell of hay . . . not creosote and burning pitch. I jerked my head up and caught sight of the train yard. All up one siding, boxcars and flatbeds loaded with lumber were shooting out flames, full-blown at the western end, just getting going down by the station. For an instant, it seemed I was the only witness . . . then a few figures broke into running, and the headlamps of a few cars veered into Depot Square . . . then, all at once, the people on Main Street began to know.

David Long / 201

I hustled back inside and bolted into the hallway and down through the back wing . . . but a door opened in front of me and a man backed out, latching the door gingerly, as if he'd left someone sleeping. He straightened and saw me and stopped short.

It was Pettibone. What was he doing here? *My God!*

"William," he said. He looked enormously tired. His shoulders drooped and his hands hung from his sleeves like skinned rabbits.

"The train's on fire," I said.

The words didn't reach him at first.

"The train," I said. "The whole . . . all the lumber's burning."

There's no picture of Pettibone in the hallway, gazing down at me in bewilderment . . . except as I've called it to mind so many times. They say action was Pettibone's long suit, action and oratory. Still, with such a picture in hand, you'd see how the real man was given more to brooding and intellection. You'd see the incomprehension letting down into understanding and disappointment and weariness.

Then, standing opposite, we heard the fire bell. Pettibone returned a wayward suspender to his shoulder and peered over me at the empty hallway.

"I thought we were going to have pictures of the strike," he said.

"Well, I didn't make it," I started in, but Pettibone wouldn't have any use for cowardice, so I shut up. *I'll make it up to you*, I was thinking.

Pettibone shook his head. He turned and went back into the room and threw the bolt.

By the time I got to the fire, things were already out of hand. Not only were the cars burning, but a storage shed had caught, and the fire had leapt from it to a snarl of weeds and torn across them like a dam burst to a garage on Railroad Street. From the platform I could hear the popping glass and the whoosh of air, and from all sides commands and argument flaring and jumping from man to man. They'd managed to get some of the cars unhitched, but by the time they could get an engine jockeyed to the right track it was pointless to try and pull them all apart.

Some councilmen had arrived, and volunteer firemen, and men who worked the yard for the Great Northern, but for all this authority, nobody was in charge. A couple of hundred others pressed around, many come straight from the dance, the women in summer linen with flowers or hair ribbons worked loose, the men holding their jackets and staring. Through this crowd soon pushed some stalwarts of the Lumbermen's Association, including two of the mill owners, brothers named Kavanaugh, who'd made it in from a lodge on the lake with remarkable haste.

One boxcar was wheat, and two flatbeds were ties soaked in tar and creosote, but the other twenty-four were stacked full of contract lumber. The two Kavanaughs halted on the platform, observably angrier — and more stupefied — than the rest of us. They searched the line of fires, then turned and searched the line of flickering faces. In a moment they set off down the spur for a closer inspection, but the heat and the down-swooping coils of black smoke stopped them short, and they stood silhouetted in the cinders finally, gawking with the rest of us.

The firemen had now turned to that tongue of blaze threatening Railroad Street. The pumper and the chemical truck were pulled up at the edge of the heat. The south wall of Kramer's car barn was eaten away and smoke came chuffing through the roof shakes. If the firemen knew that railroad bums sometimes slept off bad weather or liquor in Kramer's loft, it didn't figure in their attentions. They sprayed down the sides of the next building up the line, some of the water turning instantly to steam. For a handful of minutes, the rest of that scraggly block — and who could tell what else — hung on the whim of the wind.

Then the crowd's first amazement burned off. The men in front got tired of standing around. Helplessness offended them. Shoving broke out by the depot doors. By the time I could worm myself near, one man had been wrestled to the pavement and another was being restrained by a beefy Sperry County deputy. They held the man down with a knee at his neck, like a calf for branding. In no time they'd been through his pockets and found his red card and showed it around for everyone, and the same with his friend's.

"No law against being in the union," the friend said, but he was a small man and surrounded.

"Don't give me law, mister," the deputy said.

Someone reached in and kicked at the down man's ribs, and the struggling started up again. A third man, who'd been standing by, was shoved forward.

"Here's another one," somebody yelled.

The depot door opened and the county sheriff stood illuminated by the fire, a man tall as Pettibone but solid as a steer. He eyed the boxcars, then popped open his watch and had a look at that, closed it with a patient click, then came striding down through the people to where the trouble was, one hand on his holster. Out the door behind him came the two preened heads of the Kavanaughs, but they slipped away into the commotion, and that was all I saw of them that night.

Maybe it was the sheriff who said it, or maybe the word was spat from some other mouth, but I heard it clear enough.

Pettibone.

I won't say I fit this all together right then, for I was a slow blossomer in most all things, matters of deceit included. But I worked my way out from the people and the rising clamor at the station and headed down through the alleys toward the Dupree.

I ran up through the shadows onto the back porch and my boot sent an empty bottle ringing across the landing, but no one was left to hear. The party had gone astray. Some of the guests had dashed off to the station, not being able to stand not going any longer, and some had come back and were loitering in the big room wondering what kind of mood to take up now. The bride and groom had departed. There was no sign of my father. Even the band had left their instruments on top of the piano and were gone.

I ran up the two flights of back stairs and down to the door where I'd had my sudden audience with Pettibone. No one answered my knocking. I put my ear to the door, but was breathing too hard to hear. Next thing, without a thought, I had my third-floor key out.

The curtains flapped into the room indifferently, those strips of cheap poplin my father assigned to his dollar-fifty rooms. The bed was stirred up, cigarettes were snuffed out in a water glass on the windowsill . . . that was it. I tried to fix Pettibone there in the room, that dark lankiness and agitation. And who it was *with* him . . . and what would possess him to trespass under my father's roof, so near the authorized gaiety downstairs? It occurred to me with a cold rush that I didn't know the first blessed thing about men like Pettibone . . . where they could find their respite in a town like ours, where they could turn when they had to.

When you thought of Stillwater, you thought of the railroad. You saw the depot in your mind's eye, looming at the end of Main, huge, white-painted, monument to the wheeling and dealing that secured us the GN's northern route, when everyone expected it to dip south to Sperry. It'd been my duty, since the age of fourteen, to loiter there, outside on a baggage cart by summer, inside on the curved walnut benches by winter, waiting for the train to disgorge guests for the Dupree.

But tonight, by the time I'd returned, the depot was ringed by men with guns.

Some were police and some were National Guard, and some were just men from town. They'd started rounding up Wobblies. The jail was too puny for such a job, so they were herded into the depot's generous waiting room. I climbed up on the back railing and stole a look through the stationmaster's window. Fifty or more of them were in there, packed together under the lights. They looked like they were waiting for a train, but where they were going they didn't need bags.

I tried to wiggle the window up enough to stick the Brownie through . . . but someone suckered me back of the knees and I fell from the railing and my head careened back against the concrete. The noise and the lights went dead for a moment, then came pounding back with the bang of my heart. I got up on all fours, but crumpled again with an awful pain and dizziness, and was a moment later hauled up by the back of the shirt and marched around into the light on spidery legs, then searched. The man was in uniform, no one I knew or who knew me. He stood me against the depot wall while he composed himself. I could feel the fires on my face. Burning like that, it seemed like they could burn forever. Nothing in focus, I strayed a few feet toward the tracks, but he had me again and prodded me past the windows and thrust me in.

The smoke was worse inside, trapped under shafts of heavy electric light. One guardsman had the door and there was one in each corner and one more perched in the ticket window with a shotgun cocked over his forearm, five in all, against a roomful of herded-up men.

"What you waiting for, bohunk?" the one at the door said.

I stumbled out into the middle. The nearest men looked me up and down and saw they didn't know me and turned back to themselves. I found space and collapsed to the bench and held my head. Slowly, the pounding lightened and my thoughts began to clear. I looked at the faces around me . . . and remembered the camera, felt it dropping from my hand again, falling away into the trampled shadows.

The door snapped open in a while and another man was driven inside. A languid wave rolled through the hanging smoke and broke against the far wall, then the air settled again. He was middle-aged, this one, with a dazed, swollen face and the tails of his shirt blood-soaked. He was as lost in here as I was . . . and I realized then that I knew him, or recognized him, from the photo I'd taken behind the Pastime, when he was sleeping under Von Ebersole's wagon. He was no Wobbly, this one.

For a time it was quiet. The heat grew and pressed in on us and the room took on a mean smell. Some of the men wouldn't sit down anymore.

"You," one was saying, up staring the nearest guardsman in the face. "How old you supposed to be?"

The guardsman was hardly older than me, a moon-faced boy in a clean uniform that didn't fit. He jockeyed the gun around in his arms and squinted off above our heads at the other guards, but the haze isolated him.

"Look at what they get to point guns at good union men," the man said, louder, narrowing in on the boy and his gun. Another two steps and he could wrap his hand around the muzzle. I couldn't tell how people would act anymore, what they'd give the most weight to any particular moment. I could see how the first shot would be touched off in panic and self-regard maybe, or would just expel itself like matter in a boil, then the others would have their reason and they'd lace us in a crossfire, and we'd be in no shape to say boo about it afterwards, though the guards would say plenty enough and McKinnon would write it up in a high style and people would believe it gladly and completely.

"Sit down, Blue," somebody called out.

This Blue rocked back on his heels and turned to us. He was drunk, or he'd been started that way when they'd caught up with him. His mouth was chapped with tobacco, his eyes flat and watery as he tried to light on the one who'd yelled at him.

"Shut him the hell up," someone farther back shouted.

Blue shook his head, stranded between us and the guard. "You pukes," he said. "You ain't worth boot grease."

There was nothing of Pettibone in him, nothing of entitlement or pride, I understood then, and got a sick feeling for us all.

Pettibone could've told us what they were doing: penning us up until morning when they could march us out in the daylight past the stench and ruin of the lumber train and load us onto cattle cars just readied for the purpose, the idea not even fresh, stolen from the Bisbee, Arizona, copper mines, or over at Everett, Washington . . . and haul us out of the valley and the county and the state on the suspicion of sabotage.

Pettibone could've stood up and told them — *us* — it wasn't his fire, and engendered a silence around him, in which every one of us at the station — Wobbly or no — would get clear-headed and remember that we weren't individually or in concert stupid enough to bolt up the line of train cars with gallon bottles of kerosene and punks, with the sun barely down and the town crawling with people and no realizable good to come from it, only trouble, which had materialized in force. It's true, Pettibone, by himself, or with the rest of us solidified around him, wouldn't have been able to *stop* the deportation, any more than he, or any of the others, right up to Big Bill Haywood himself, could stop the War Department from shipping IWWs off to Army camps, but with him there the men could've known the extent of what was going on and not gone at each other, empty-handed and down in their hearts. But, of course, Pettibone could not have risked being there himself.

The filigreed hands of the station clock said one-forty. The door to the tracks cracked open then and the sheriff pushed his way in, a gang of deputies in tow.

The room got quiet again, man by man.

The sheriff looked around for something to stand on, then just raised his voice. "Listen like this mattered," he said. "You're going to line up against that wall for me, that one with the bulletin board on it," he said. "Fast and orderly would be a good way."

After a decent interval, the nearest bunch rose as if their bones hurt and moved grudgingly toward the wall. A few more straggled over and I joined them and then most of the rest came, leaving Blue alone, slouched on the last bench, talked out. The boy guard moved in on him, happily, and pointed the gun at his face.

The sheriff drifted over to the two of them.

"Where's Pettibone?" he asked Blue.

Blue didn't say anything. He looked from the sheriff's face to the snout of the gun and down to his shoes.

The sheriff nodded. He picked his watch out again, opened it, and turned to compare it with the clock on the wall.

"All right," he said. He motioned to the boy to get Blue up and standing like the rest of us. Blue swung his arm out to bat the gun barrel away from his face, but the boy swiveled the butt around and cracked him in the temple and he went down across the bench and lay there, derelict.

The sheriff walked back over to us. "Where's Pettibone?" he said to the first man.

The man said he didn't know.

The sheriff watched him impassively. "If you knew, you'd tell me, wouldn't you," he said.

The man didn't say anything.

"I know what kind you are," the sheriff said, still eyeing him. "I know what you'd do."

He moved down the line, one deputy following along with a note pad, taking names. When he got to me he stopped and scowled.

It wasn't Pettibone, I thought, the sheriff hulking over me. *It could not have been Pettibone, even carried out by someone else's hand, could not have been.*

"Well, Mr. Dupree," the sheriff said. "Looks to me like it's time for you to get on home."

And like that, like sleight of hand, or worse, I was outside again, where it was cooler and the air was less concentrated and the crowd had been broken into factions and dispersed. The fires were still going but I didn't want to look at them anymore. I started back to the Dupree, despite myself. Where else was I going to go?

It occurred to me that I might walk up to that third-floor room and find the door open and the bed clean-made, and no vestige of Pettibone except in my imagination . . . my father's tremulous baritone reiterating in my mind's ear how untrustworthy I was, how weak to give myself over time and again to the made-up instead of the certifiably real and necessary. But if all that milled lumber was burning and the depot was full of men to be locked inside cattle cars, then anything else could, or could've happened, I was thinking. Salmon could come raining down out of the sky. I was halfway down Dakota Street near the Chinese laundry before I remembered the camera.

I knew I'd find it ruined, the lens shattered and the bellows ripped like a rag, but I had a sudden fierce desire to secure it and carry it home. I snuck back through the elms to the dark side of the depot and pawed through the heavy shadows beneath the railing, and down in the gap between some packing crates and the wall, then out on the grass, though that was too far for it to have flown. I was kneeling there, stupefied, my hands wet with dew, when a flurry of raised voices from up on the platform drove me back behind the boxes. In a moment, three men came past, one in uniform, the others decently dressed, men I knew I'd seen before but didn't know. They couldn't decide whether to run or walk fast. They crossed to a car waiting along the park and two got in. The other leaned down and kept talking, his free hand flitting like a huge bug against the streetlight.

Finally the headlamps came on and the two men drove off and the third stood looking after them, then did an about-face and peered back at the train yard and up at the putrid orange halo above it. Then he was gone too. I pulled myself up by the lid of the packing box and it came free in my hands, and there, swaddled in shavings, was the Brownie.

Try these other pictures: Pettibone and the woman — for it was now, in my mind, surely a woman, hard-faced comrade and lover under the guise of a traveling widow, whose room he had visited in the hotel — hurtling in a car away from Sperry County toward shelter and counsel at the Wobbly cabal in Spokane. Or Pettibone alone — just as likely — striding west on the GN tracks toward that skinny part of Idaho that should still have been Montana, satchels in either hand swinging like ballast, long legs hitting every second tie in perfect cadence. I could see him halting every little while to listen — for what, for dogs? They didn't have dogs, these officers or citizens who were after him, or have need of them apparently. Pettibone, his head cocked east, just the dimmest smudge of sky-reflected firelight glancing off his face, would hear only the yap and howl of a coyote, most of the timber wolves having retreated to British Columbia by our time, and the clamor of the town not carrying much beyond its boundaries, and the worst of *that* just spoken and confirmed between men in voices not meant to carry. . . .

Or picture any of the others I dreamed up, still hidden in the lee of the depot, the camera folded against my shirt, not twenty feet from where the sweating-out of Pettibone's actual whereabouts continued, the sheriff's shadow obliterating each man's night-beaten face in turn. What they'd have in common, these pictures, would be Pettibone in flight . . . for I couldn't shake the image of him in the upstairs hallway, face abruptly unleavened by the news I'd delivered and all the implication he wrung from it in a few consecutive instants. *Battles are won by the remnants of armies*, that was a Pettibone refrain, lifted maybe from an Old Testament litany of suffering and endurance. *Outnumber, outsmart, outlast them.* . . . I could only imagine him using his head start like a weapon.

And as for the Wobblies inside, it wouldn't matter if they knew or didn't know, if they broke ranks or not . . . whatever any of them said, it could be taken as more sabotage, more red-inspired trickery. These thoughts in mind, I tried out a new idea: that I might be forgiven for not telling what I knew, the truth about Pettibone and the fire . . . that my silence might even be strategic, the better part of valor. All of which was consoling . . . but missed the point entirely. For I'd managed all night not to ask myself the question that counted.

If it wasn't Pettibone's fire, whose was it?

McKinnon was right: it was the end of the Wobblies in Sperry County, beginning of the end even in Butte, union town above all others. "The expected has happened," he wrote in Monday's paper, the rest of the state and the Northwest looking on, meaning not the fire itself, which he decried separately, but the work of the twenty or so free-lance men who located Pettibone and took him into their collective custody, at roughly the same late hour of the night that the sheriff finally concluded that not one of those miserable Wobblies in the depot actually knew where Pettibone was.

Deportation by boxcar, that must've been the heart of the plan, as conceived, for the cars were too readily at hand, paid for by the sacrifice of a *portion* of the lumber train—but not the whole of it, certainly, and not those car barns down Railroad Street, and not the railroad bum charred to futility inside one of them. Nor the combustion of anger— most of all that—in no time surpassing their design. McKinnon played it straight. He passed the buck to Congress for not protecting industry, then turned his vitriol on Pettibone for a last time. "Hysterical," McKinnon said of Lyle Pettibone, "mentally unbalanced, preying on uneducated, unsophisticated laborers. . . ."

I left Stillwater.

The rest I know you're familiar enough with: the staff work I did those years for the *Post-Dispatch*, then my great fortune at meeting Roy Stryker who added me to the group he had at the Farm Security Administration, Dorothea Lange and Russ Lee and Walker Evans and those others making pictures of the tenants and croppers blown out of the Dustbowl . . . all of it, I can see now, fitting together, aiming me toward that day in 1941, outside General Tire in Akron, when some union men swarmed and beat down a strikebreaker, which was the shot they gave the Pulitzer for.

It's luck who gets the prize, that's an article of faith. But I took it as an honor, regardless . . . because even then, forty-four years old, older even than Pettibone had been, I would still sometimes hear my father's grinding deprecations of me and was tempted, despite the evidence, to believe in them . . . and because luck's not enough to explain what I was doing at General Tire that day, that change of shift. The tire workers, ganging in union regalia, with balled fists and nightsticks, and smiles burning into frantic bloom on their faces . . . and the scabs, this one here cut from the pack, bent double under one thickness of overcoat, nothing showing but a bony hand aimed at the sky like half a prayer . . . they knew what they were doing, all of them. And I knew my business by then as well, for it's a man's duty to find what he's good for, if he finds nothing else worth the cost of learning it. In all his days, in all his dogged sucking up to men of property and office my father never found this out.

That Sunday morning in Stillwater, after I'd talked myself home along the tracks, holding the folded Brownie inside my shirt, I slipped down into the cellar of the Dupree where it was cool and no one ever came—except my sister, in search of potatoes for the kitchen, or communion with her private store of red wine hidden among the Ball jars of Sperry County cherries. In a few minutes I had the film stripped, developed, and hanging by a clothespin to dry. I sat down in the dark and touched the clotted lump at the back of my head. I heard the morning commencing above me, the wince of guests reaching the bottom tread of the front staircase, one after another, pausing on the foyer carpet struck lavender by sunlight spewing through the transom, then crossing onto the bare floor of the dining room where the tables had been restored. I heard the hired girl's feet clipping back and forth to the kitchen, Ellen's dragging by the stove. I heard the waste water come coursing down the pipes and in a while I heard the church bells start in. Gradually, the dining room grew quiet. I got up and turned on the light and passed the negative before it. There they all were . . . the bride and her earnest groom, the mothers, Matthew Upshaw and my father and their friends, everyone shoulder to shoulder, dignified before the camera . . . and there at the end of the roll, Lyle Pettibone, uninvited, hanging from a trestle just west of town.

Louise Erdrich

The Air Seeder

1959

Gentlemen and Ladies of the Crop and Livestock Convention, I have come to unveil a miracle.

That's how I begin my spiel.

Each one of us survived the dustbowl, those clouds of blowing grit. Precious topsoil on the whim of the wind! Well gentlemen and ladies plowing caused that, tilling made it happen, and one way to stop that infernal process is not to till.

But . . .

Dramatic pause.

I have to till to plant, *you tell me. Well no more! Beneath this tarp I've got the answer to nature's prayers. Ladies and Gentlemen . . .*

I pull the string and drop the canvas.

THE AIR SEEDER!

And then I proceed to explain the mechanism. I point to the thin tubes that conduct the seeds from the box down to the surface. I explain how, assisted by a puff of the motorized bellows, each seed is blown gently into the earth. The Air Seeder does not disturb the earth, I tell them, thereby conserving moisture, reducing your topsoil loss

There are the usual questions, then, the usual agrarian scepticism. I caught the man's eye, a yearning guarded glance, while I was answering those questions, handing out leaflets, and demonstrating the process as best I could.

We were both at the Convention in Minneapolis. He was a slim man, balding early, with quick gray eyes and an easy manner about him, yet a waiting kind of air. He asked questions relating to process and durability. He liked the concept, he told me. Innovation was his game.

"I'm Demeray Pfef, in the land business down in Argus," he said. "I'd like to get into promotional work — put the town on the map, help agriculture.

"That's why I'm interested in your seeder," he went on.

I said it was the coming thing, showed him charts and farm news write-ups, but all the while I was thinking *why Argus?* It seemed like Argus popped up every time I turned around. Argus citizens were always shaking my hand. Or the newspapers—full of freak accidents, catastrophes, multiple births at Saint Adalbert's hospital in Argus. I wondered if someday I'd read my sister's name in these accounts, and I knew that it wouldn't matter if I did. I'd never call, visit, even write a letter. It had simply been too long. Yet I had a fascination, a curiosity that drew coincidence, and it was probably this that led me to ask the man, Pfef, to join me for a drink.

And, too, a salesman makes friends where he can.

We walked out of the convention room, crossed the lobby and entered the dim hotel bar.

"I'll stand you one," I said, putting down a five dollar bill when our drinks arrived. The waitress took the drinks' amount from the five and left the change on the table. I did not touch the change.

"Thank you very much." He took a slow drink, and said nothing else, which at first I found unsettling, but then, when I purposely waited also and didn't fill in the space he'd opened up, it was clear we had allowed our drinks to shift the ground between us.

"Are you from Minneapolis?" he asked. Somehow the subject seemed more personal now than when we spoke of his being from Argus.

"Here . . . different places," I told him.

"Which places?"

I paused, feeling the old discomfort over questions about my origin, yet wanting to reveal just enough to keep him asking that kind of question.

"Saint Jerome's," I said. "It's a home for orphans."

He clearly hadn't expected this. "I'm sorry," he said. "That's too bad."

I waved it off.

"For a while I lived in Florida, too. I'd heard my mother was down there. But I never found her."

He didn't have much to say about that either, but he kept that waiting look on his face and although I don't talk about myself much, try to keep my distance, I added what I never told anyone.

"I've got a sister," I said, "she lives in your town."

He looked expectant. Clearly, he knew everyone in Argus, and I realized I'd gone too far. He would tell Mary that he'd met me if I told him her name, which he clearly anticipated. I'd considered giving him a business card, but now I'd have to be more cautious.

"But I don't know who she is," I back-pedaled, "could be just a rumor. That kind of thing always happens in an orphan's home. Other kids pretend they've seen your files, or the matrons make up stories . . ."

"You believe it though," he said, looking straight into my eyes with conviction. At that moment, the ground dwindled considerably between us as it always does when one person admits to observing another that closely, and meets your eyes. It was now my turn to say something that would penetrate still farther. I took my chance.

"Let's have dinner in my hotel room," I said.

His stare changed to surprise. We'd downed three quick drinks by then, and the five he'd insisting on putting down also lay broken between us. Three drinks was where I started feeling loose, and as I watched him stand up I knew the same was true of him.

"What luck," he said, rummaging below his seat. "I dropped my pamphlets."

His hips were fine and thin, I noticed, but he wasn't strong or muscular. There was more to admire about my appearance. I lifted weights, swam laps, or ran an occasional five miles even when I was on the road. I took care of myself mentally too. I'd had enough disappointments in other people, and perhaps because of them I never let anything go far enough to cause me discomfort.

"Coming?" I asked.

He had recovered his pamphlets. He stood up and smiled a quick nervous smile, different from the waiting smile, and together we walked down the carpeted corridor, up two flights of stairs, and entered my room. It was a single room, dominated by a bed with a bright orange bedspread. Pfef managed to avoid looking at the bed by making a beeline for the window and admiring my view. Which was of the parking lot.

There really were menus in the bedside table drawer, and I was honestly hungry. I found that once we were alone in the room I didn't even care much what happened, one way or the other. It wasn't that Pfef was unattractive, it was his sudden nervousness that bored me, the awkward pretense when it was he who put his hand out once, stopping mine, when I'd tried to lay down another bill for drinks.

I sat on the bed and opened the menu. I knew what I was hungry for but it wasn't available.

"Game hens," I compromised, "even though they'll send them dry and tough."

He relaxed, sat down in the little chair beside the bed, and picked up a menu.

"The Prime Rib. That's my choice."

"We're settled then." I phoned the desk. While we waited for the trolley I poured him a shot from the bottle in my suitcase.

"Is this your only water glass?" he wondered, politely, before raising it to his lips.

"I'm not particular," I said, taking a pull from the bottle, "not like you."

He had been the one with the bold observant statements downstairs, but once I tagged him he flushed and fell silent, swirled the whiskey in his glass and then got the waiting look on his face again.

So I didn't say anything, just took the glass from his hand.

"The dinner," he said in a faint voice.

But he bent forward anyway. I held his shoulders and drew him to me. Then we lay back on the startling spread.

By the time the bellhop knocked on the door we were back where we'd started, dressed, the only difference being now we shared the water glass. The truth is I liked drinking from a glass.

The boy just shoved the cart in, put his hand out for the tip, and left us. Maybe he thought we were plotting gangsters, or knew the truth. Pfef ate quickly, avidly, with obvious relief. It had not been as bad as he thought, I guessed, or now that it was over he could put it behind him, pretend it never happened, go quietly back to Argus and tell his wife how well the convention had gone and ply her with some Minneapolis souvenir to oil the creaky little hinge of his guilt. I knew his type, the pretense.

"I've never done this before," he said.

I just turned away and carved the tiny birds, remembering the guarded yearning, his waiting eye. He was married for sure, at least I assumed it. He wore a wedding type ring and had a cared-for look—pressed, shined and starched.

"So how's the little woman?" I could not help myself. I said this with a sneer.

He looked up, uncomprehending, wiped his chin. I tapped his hand.

"Oh," he said, "I was engaged once, long ago."

"I bet you were."

Then he turned the tables, or tried to.

"What about you?" he asked.

"What about me?"

"You know."

"You mean women?" He nodded. I told him I'd known plenty and very closely, although the truth is I had always found their touch unbearable, a source of nameless panic.

"I'd never marry one though," I told him. "They give me vertigo." I said this rather sly, offhand. I'd learned that word from a Hitchcock movie that certainly had not played in Argus yet.

But he knew what the word meant.

"Why don't you let me try and find your sister?" he asked. This came out of the blue, unexpected, and when he looked at me with his clear sad eyes, I suddenly had the feeling that had always frightened me with women too. The black feeling with no reference, the ground I'd stood on giving way, the falling noplace. Maybe it was true about him, the awkwardness, no experience, the frightening possibility that he wanted to get to know me.

"I'm done," I said, shoving away my plate and, just to do something, just to stop the feeling, wheeling the cart madly out the door too. I came back in the room and leapt onto the bed. I had to stop myself from falling. So I jumped. I felt silly and light, bouncing in the air. I felt like a child who would ruin the bedsprings.

"You'd better stop," Pfef said, shocked, dropping meat from his fork. "The management."

"Screw the management," I laughed at his maidenly face. "I've got a trick I'm going to show you." I didn't actually have anything in mind but as I bounced, hitting the ceiling almost, I was suddenly inspired. I'd watched hard-muscled boys so closely on the diving boards downtown. They sprang up, whirled over, threw themselves precisely through the air in a somersault and split the water harshly with their toes. I would do the same. I took a great bounce. Then I tucked, spun, whirled, and I still believe that if it hadn't been for Pfef's sudden cry I would have cleared the bed and landed perfectly on my feet. But the cry of alarm threw me off. I kept my body tucked too long and hit the floor at the foot of the bed, in an area so small it seemed impossible I could have landed perfectly within it, but I did, and broke my neck too.

I knew it the instant I hit. I stayed conscious.

"Pfef," I said, the moment he bent down, "don't touch me."

He had the sense not to, the sense to call the hospital, the sense to sit beside me without talking and keep the orderlies from moving me until the doctor ordered up a plank. The stupid thing I kept thinking all this time, too, was not about my neck or how I could be paralyzed for life. For some reason I had no fear of it. No fear of anything. I looked at Pfef and the way he stared back, purely stricken, eyes naked, I knew if I wanted I could have him for life. But I didn't even think about that. It was my sister I thought about.

"Her name's Mary," I said out loud. "Mary Lavelle."

And then the injection took hold, the black warmth. I realized the place I'd landed on was only a flimsy ledge, and there was nothing else to stop me if I fell.

William Trevor

Bodily Secrets

At fifty-nine, she was on her own, the widow of the O'Neill who had inherited the town's coal business, who had started, as an enterprise of his own, the toy factory. Her children had flown the nest, her parents and her parents-in-law were no longer alive. Her husband had been in his lifetime a smallish though heavily built man, with wide shoulders and an unrelenting, cropped head, like a battering wedge. His cautious eyes had been set well apart beneath woolly eyebrows; small veins had reddened his nose. He had died at the age of sixty-three, falling down in the big, airy hall of Arcangelo House and afterwards not regaining any real awareness of who he was or what had happened. He had built Arcangelo House after he and his wife had stayed in an Italian hotel of that name when they visited Rome on the occasion of Holy Year.

A beauty once, she was a handsome woman still, tall and imposing in her middle age, with a well-covered look that reflected her liking for sweet things. Her grey hair was shaded towards its original brown, and discreetly burnished; she bought clothes extravagantly. She made up her face with precision, taking her time over it; and attended similarly to her fingernails and, in season, her toenails. She had borne four children in all, two of her three daughters being married now, one in Dublin, the other in Trim; the third was a nurse in Philadelphia. Her son, married also, ran the coal business but was more interested in developing a thousand acres of turf bog he had bought and which he saw as the beginning of an enterprise which he believed would in time outstrip his father's and his grandfather's already established empire. He had inherited their entrepreneur's spirit, and since he'd first been aware of the role laid down for him he had seen himself as their rival. He was married to Thelma, daughter of a Portarlington publican, a girl whom Mrs. O'Neill did not care for, considering her common. Particularly she did not care for the thought that one day Thelma would take her own place in Arcangelo House.

From the garden and the upstairs windows the house offered, over fields, a view of the town that was interrupted only by the toy factory.

When the wind blew from the south it carried sounds rendered faint over the distance: the cries of children, a car being started somewhere, the saws in the timber works, the grind of a heavy lorry on Daly's Hill. And no matter where the wind came from there was always the bell at the convent, and the bell of Our Lady in Glory, and the Protestant bell on Sundays. At night the street lights and the lights of houses were spread out prettily—the town seen at its best, as Mrs. O'Neill often reflected. But increasingly in the vacuum that Arcangelo House had become she reflected also that she felt like a pebble in a drum, and said as much to her bridge companions. They urged her to sell it and build a bungalow, but privately she felt that a bungalow was not her style.

When her husband had died Mrs. O'Neill had been fifty-six, and although they had regularly disagreed in their thirty-seven years of marriage, they had more often been affectionate companions. They had shared two interests in particular: golf and their children. Together they had attended the occasional race-meeting; and while her husband had not played bridge, she in turn had not inclined to join him in the bar of the Commercial Hotel, where he liked to spend an evening or two a week. Every summer they went to Lahinch or Bundoran for the golf, and for several years after Holy Year they had returned to Rome, to the hotel which had given their house its character and its name. Often, on a night which wasn't a bridge night, Mrs. O'Neill wondered about the future and whether she should indeed sell Arcangelo House. When the television came to an end she sat alone in the big open drawing-room, feeling just a little lonely and vaguely wishing that there was another interest in her life besides bridge and golf and her grown-up family. Time had dulled the loss that widowhood had brought, but in no way had it filled the vacuum that was somehow more apparent as time progressed. Once she'd been the centre of things in Arcangelo House, looking after everyone, in charge of other people's lives. "Ah, come on now," she'd said a thousand times to the husband who'd died on her. "You're as big a baby as any of them." In her days as a beauty she had more or less designed the house herself, standing over Mac-Guire the architect and endeavouring to picture for him a cool, well-organised hotel in Rome. It still pleased her that she had succeeded so well, not that Arcangelo House was to everyone's taste, she was well aware of that: it was too different, too modern, in a way too grand. But old Canon Kenny, the most educated man for miles about, said he would wager money that the house was the most intriguing to be found outside Dublin. It had been featured in *Social and Personal* and Mac-

Guire, who was inordinately proud of it, had once asked if a German architect, on a motoring holiday, might come and see it. How could she just leave it all? The garden, once little better than waste-land, had gorgeously matured. The portico, with its clean white arches, was rich with different clematis from June to August. The patio was warm enough to have breakfast on in March. Yet the accomplishing of what she'd wanted in the house and in the garden belonged to the time when she'd been in charge, and were a reminder that nothing now was changing or taking shape due to her efforts.

Occasionally, pursuing such lines of thought, she wondered if she would marry again. She couldn't help herself; she had no desire to re-marry, yet widows did so, it was something that quite often occurred. At the golf club there was Sweetman, a few years younger than herself, a bachelor all his life, pleasantly sociable but bleary when he had drink taken, and according to Dolores Fitzfynne a tightwad. There was O'Keefe, who was her own age, but it was hard to think of O'Keefe without thinking also of the Mrs. O'Keefe there had been, a drear of a woman who had played neither golf nor bridge, who hadn't even had children: O'Keefe had been infected by her dreariness or else had in-fected her in the first place. There was no one else, except perhaps Agnew, with his long, thin face and his hands, which were long also, gesturing in the air, and his faintly high-pitched voice. He was younger than the others, younger than she was herself by seven or eight years, yet she often thought of him in this connection. She thought about him in a different way on the morning her son, Cathal, decreed that the toy factory would have to go. For seventeen years Agnew had been its manager.

In a blue and yellow Paisley dressing-gown which she'd had all her married life she sat on the edge of her bed, listening to her son saying that the people at the toy factory could easily be absorbed elsewhere, that for a long time now he had systematically been running the business down. The toy factory had been profitable only in the im-mediate postwar years, unable ultimately to sustain the competition which had so ominously built up: long before his death her husband had been saying it would sooner or later have to close. It was a tiny concern, the loss would not be great.

"All they're making now are the fox terriers," Cathal said on the telephone, referring to wooden fox terriers on wheels.

"The building?" she said. "Best to have it down, wouldn't it?"

"I could bail garden peat there. I'm going into that, you know."

She did not say anything. She did not trust this dark-faced son she'd given birth to. Ceasing to be a toy factory, the building would be expanded when it became the location for one of his enterprises. There might be noise, even a smell of chemicals: you simply couldn't guess what would come along in order that more money might be made. And why should it matter since only a lone woman lived near by?

"We'll have to see," she said.

"Ah, of course, of course. No hurry at all."

She did not ask about Agnew. She could not see him being absorbed into the turf business or the coal business, and in any case Cathal didn't like him. Cathal would have him out on the street while you'd wink.

Cathal had his father's wedge of a head, his forehead and wide-apart, narrow eyes. He was the first of their children to be born, the one who had received more attention because the others were girls. Heir to so much, he had been claimed by a thrusting entrepreneur's world from infancy. The girls, except for Siobhan in Philadelphia, had been more mundanely claimed by men.

She wouldn't have minded any of the others being in Arcangelo House, but Thelma had a greedy way of looking at her, as if she couldn't wait to get into the place. Mrs. O'Neill dearly wished that her son hadn't married this girl, but he had and that was that. She sighed as she replaced the receiver, seeing Thelma's slightly puffy face, her nose too small for the rest of it. She sat for a moment longer, endeavouring to release her imagination of that face and in the end succeeding. Then she dressed herself and went down to the toy factory. Agnew was in the inner office, standing by the window, his back to her as she entered.

"Mr. Agnew."

"Ah, Mrs. O'Neill. Come in, come in, Mrs. O'Neill." He moved so swiftly in turning to greet her that she was reminded of the assured way he danced the quickstep. He came every December to the Golf Club Dance even though he was not a club member and had once confided to her that he had never played the game. "Croquet," he'd confided also. "I used to be quite snappy at croquet." He had his own expressions, a way of putting things that sometimes sounded odd. Typical that he should mention an old-fashioned game like croquet.

"I hope you're not busy, Mr. Agnew. I'm not disturbing you, am I?"

"Heavens above, why would you be? Won't you take a chair, Mrs. O'Neill? A cup of tea now?"

There was always this formality. He offered it and seemed shyly to demand it. Her husband had always used his surname, and so did Cathal; at the Golf Club Dance she'd heard other men call him by his initials, B. J. She couldn't in a million years imagine him addressing her as Norah.

"No, I won't have tea, thank you."

"A taste of sherry at all? I have a nice sweet little sherry—"

"No, thanks. Really, Mr. Agnew."

He smiled, gently closing a glass-fronted cabinet he had opened in expectation of her accepting his hospitality. He was wearing a brown suit chalked with a pinstripe, and a brown silk tie. He said:

"Well, it seems we have come to the end of the road."

"I know. I'm awfully sorry."

"Mr. O'Neill saw it coming years ago."

Yes, I'm afraid he did."

He smiled again; his voice was unperturbed. "The first day I came up to Arcangelo House I was terrified out of my wits. D'you remember, Mrs. O'Neill? Your husband had an advertisement for the job in the *Irish Times*."

"It seems an age ago."

"Doesn't it, though? An age."

His long face had acquired a meditative expression. He drew a packet of cigarettes from a pocket of his jacket and opened it slowly, folding back the silver paper. He advanced a single cigarette by knocking the packet on the surface of his desk. He leaped towards her, offering it. His wrists were slim and tanned: she had never noticed his wrists before.

"Thank you, Mr. Agnew."

He leaned across the desk again, holding the flame of a cigarette lighter to the tip of her cigarette. It gleamed with the dull patina of gold, as slender as a coin.

"No, I don't entirely know what I'll do." He lit his own cigarette and then held it, dangling, in his long fingers.

"Cathal should have something for you. It was my husband's intention, you know, that everyone at the toy factory should be offered something."

She wanted to make that clear; she wanted to record this unequivocal statement in the inner office so that later on, if necessary, she could quote herself to Cathal. She inhaled some smoke and released it luxuriously through her nostrils. She was fond of the occasional cigarette, although she never smoked when she was on her own.

"I'm not so sure I'd entirely fit in, Mrs. O'Neill. I don't know anything about selling turf."

She mentioned coal, which after all was the fuel that had made the O'Neills wealthy. There was still a thriving coal business, the biggest in the county.

He shook his head. His hair, once reddish, was almost entirely grey now. "I don't think," he said, "I'd be at home in coal."

"Well, I only thought I'd mention it."

"It's more than kind, Mrs. O'Neill."

"My husband wouldn't have wanted anyone not looked after."

"Oh, indeed I know it."

She stared at the lipstick mark on her cigarette and then raised the cigarette to her mouth again. It was awkward because she didn't want to walk out of the factory smoking a cigarette, yet it was too soon to crush it out on the ashtray in front of her.

"If there's any way the family can help, you'll say, Mr. Agnew?"

"I suppose I'll go to Dublin."

The remark was not accompanied by one of his glancing smiles; he gave no sign whatsoever that he'd touched upon a fascinating topic. No one knew why he spent weekends occasionally in Dublin, and a certain curiosity had gathered round the mystery of these visits. There was some secret which he kept, which he had not even confided to her husband in his lifetime. He came back melancholy was all her husband had ever reported, and once or twice with bloodshot eyes as if he had spent the time drinking.

"Though I'd rather not end up in Dublin," he added now. "To tell you the full truth, Mrs. O'Neill, it's not a city I entirely care for."

She bent the remains of her cigarette in half, extinguishing it on the ashtray. She stood up, thinking it odd that he'd said Dublin wasn't somewhere he cared for since he visited it so regularly.

"The toy factory was a favourite of my husband's. It saddened him to see it decline."

"It had its heyday."

"Yes, it had its day."

She went, walking with him from the office, through a shed full of unassembled terriers on wheels. The white cut-out bodies with a brown spot around the tail, the brown head, the little platform that carried the wheels, the wheels themselves: all these dislocated parts lay about in stacks, seeming unwanted. No one was working in the shed.

He walked with her through other deserted areas, out on to the gravel forecourt that stretched in a semicircle around the front of the small factory. A man loaded wired cartons on to a lorry. They were still meeting orders in England, Agnew told her. The paint shop was as active as ever, three girls on full time.

He held his hand out, his long, narrow features illuminated by another smile. His palm was cool, his grip gentle. He asked her not to worry about him. He assured her he'd be all right.

There were gusts of laughter in the club-house. Dessie Fitzfynne had told a Kerry joke, concerning eight Kerry gardai and a cow. Dolores Fitzfynne, who'd just gone round in 82 and wanted to talk about that instead, requested that he shouldn't tell another. Sweetman was talking about horses, arranging something about going to the Curragh. Sweetman loved getting parties together to go racing or to Lansdowne Road, or for a weekend down in Kelly's at Rosslare. Paunchy and rubicund, Flanagan kept saying it was his turn and what did anyone want?

"I heard the factory's winding up," the solicitor, Butler-Regan, remarked in his rowdy voice and she nodded, suddenly feeling dismal. She had forgotten about the toy factory while she'd been on the golf-course, going round in 91, taking a three to get out of the rough at the eighth. She'd been playing with Dessie Fitzfynne, opposing Dolores and Flanagan. They'd been beaten, of course.

It was silly to feel dismal just because the facts of commerce dictated the closure of an unprofitable concern. As both Cathal and Agnew had intimated, the end had been a matter of anticipation for years. Only sentiment had prevented such a decision in the lifetime of her husband.

"Ah well, there you are," Butler-Regan said noisily. "'Tis better let it go, Norah."

Flanagan handed her another gin and French even though she hadn't asked for one. Overhearing the reference to the toy factory, he said:

"I hear Agnew's wondering what to do with himself."

"The bold Agnew!" Butler-Regan laughed. He, too, was paunchy and rubicund. He added, laughing again, shouting through this laughter, "Oh, Master Agnew'll fall on his feet, I'd say."

They all liked Agnew even though he was so different. He was an easy companion for half an hour or so if you happened to run into him in the bar of the Commercial Hotel; he was always willing to drop into conversation with you on the street. He had digs with the Misses Malone in a house called St. Kevin's, where he was regularly to be seen tending the front garden, behind silver-painted railings set in a low concrete wall. He also walked the Misses Malone's dog, Judy, about the town and on Sundays he attended the Protestant Church unless he happened to be in Dublin.

"We'd all miss Agnew," Flanagan said. "That wild Protestant man." He laughed, making much the same explosive sound that the solicitor did. Did any of them realise, she wondered, that Agnew's quickstep put them all to shame every December?

"Oh, wild is right," Butler-Regan agreed. "Wasn't he in the city again a week ago?"

The two men laughed in unison, the burst of noise causing Rita Flanagan to glance sharply across the bar to ascertain if her husband was already drunk. In dog's-tooth skirt and soft fawn golfing-jacket, Mrs. O'Neill wondered what any of them would think if they knew that quite involuntarily as she stood there, she had begun to speculate on the possibility of not remaining for ever the widow she presently was. She sipped her gin and French, not taking part in a conversation about Sweetman's outing to the Curragh. In the same involuntary manner she found herself following a thread of thought that led her back to her wedding day. The O'Neills had insisted on paying for the reception, since her own family were not well-to-do. Old Canon Kenny — neither old nor a canon then — had conducted the service, assisted by a curate called Prendergast, who had later left the priesthood. They had gone to Bray for their honeymoon and on their first night in the International Hotel she had been jittery. She hadn't known how it should be, whether she should simply take her clothes off or wait for him to say something, whether or not there was going to be preliminary kissing. She'd gone as red as anything after they'd come up from the restaurant. "I think that waiter knew," she'd whispered on the stairs, not noticing that there was a maid just behind them. He'd been jittery too, and in the end it was she who inaugurated the kissing and in fact had taken his tie off. What on earth would it be like being in a bedroom in Bray with Agnew? There was fat on her shoulders now, which hadn't been there before, and naturally her thighs and her hips were no longer the same. Her body had been forgotten in that particular way for many years before her husband's death, almost since the birth of Siobhan. They had come to occupy separate bedrooms in Arcangelo House, having reached the decision that Cathal and the three girls were enough. At first, when it was safe to do so, she had visited the other bedroom, but the habit had dwindled and then ceased. Would it be a form of unfaithfulness to resume it in different circumstances now? It wasn't easy to guess how such things stood at fifty-nine.

O'Keefe, the widower of the woman who'd been a drear, approached her with the usual sorrowful look in his eyes, as if he still mourned the wife who had played neither bridge nor golf. The eyes themselves, lurking in their despondent wateriness behind spectacles, had pinkish rims and were the only feature you noticed in O'Keefe's flat face, except possibly his teeth, which moved uncomfortably in his jaw when he ate. He was eating now, chewing crisps from a transparent Tayto bag. His hair was like smooth lead; his bony limbs jutted from his clothes. There was no doubt whatsoever that O'Keefe, the manager of a butter business, was looking for a housekeeper in the form of a second wife. There was always a nudge or two in the clubhouse when he approached Mrs. O'Neill for a chat.

"Ah, didn't I have a terrible round? Did you see me in front of you, Norah? Wasn't I shocking?"

She denied that. She hadn't noticed his misfortunes, she said, which indeed she hadn't. She might have added that the butter manager couldn't be shocking if he tried for the rest of his life.

"I've been meaning to ask you," he said. "Would you be interested in a bunch of sweet-peas from the garden, Norah?"

She drank more gin and French. She had plenty of sweet-peas at Arcangelo House, she replied, though it was very good of him to offer her more.

"Or the asparagus fern? D'you grow that stuff?"

"I grow asparagus all right. Only I eat it before the fern comes."

"Ah well, why wouldn't you, Norah?"

Sweetman, at the bar, was sweating like an animal. No woman in her senses would want to marry Sweetman. His trouble with perspiration ironically denied his name, and the cageyness Dolores Fitzfynne claimed for him would hardly have been easy to live with. He had a tendency towards forgetfulness when his round came up in the clubhouse and, according to Dolores, the parties he organised for race-meetings or Lansdowne Road were done so to his own pecuniary advantage. "Too mingy with himself to look sideways at a woman," Dolores had said, and probably she was right. He was a surveyor with the county council; and if he gave you a lift in his car he had a way of mentioning the high price of petrol.

She watched Sweetman while O'Keefe continued in his tedious manner, offering her marigold plants. It had surprised her when Agnew had said he'd never in his life played golf. She'd thought afterwards that he would probably have been good. He had the look of someone who had been athletic in his time. His dancing suggested ballsense, she didn't know why.

"To tell you the honest truth, I don't much care for marigolds."

"The wife loved them. Give Mrs. O'Keefe a box of marigolds and she'd be pricking them out till Kingdom come."

He wagged his head; she nodded hers. She allowed a silence to develop in the hope that he'd go away. He said eventually:

"D'you ever watch that thing they have, *Dynasty* is it called?"

"I watch it the odd time."

"Will you tell me this, Norah: where do they get the stories?"

"I suppose they invent them."

"Isn't America the shocking place though?"

"I have a daughter there."

"Ah sure, of course you have."

At the bar Butler-Regan looked as though he might sing. Very occasionally he did, striking the bar rumbustiously with his fist, trying to make people join in. The club secretary, Dr. Walsh, had had to speak to him, explaining that it wasn't usual to sing in a golf club, even adding that he didn't think it quite the thing for a solicitor to sing anywhere. But Butler-Regan had done so again, and had again to be warned. It was said that his wife, who like the late Mrs. O'Keefe played neither bridge nor golf, had a terrible time with him.

"Does your girl ever remark on the *Dynasty* thing to you?" O'Keefe was enquiring. "I mean, if it might be accurate?"

"Siobhan has never mentioned *Dynasty*."

"Well, isn't that extraordinary?"

Ten minutes later the drinking in the clubhouse broke up and Mrs. O'Neill drove back to Arcangelo House. She made scrambled egg and watched a film about drug-running on the television. The police of several nations pursued a foursome of gangsters and finally ran the ringleader to earth in Los Angeles. She dozed off, and when she woke up a priest with a Cork accent was talking about the feast of Corpus Christi and she listened to him until he'd finished and then turned the television off.

In her bedroom she did something she had not done for ten years at least: before she slipped into her nightdress she paused in front of the long looking-glass of her wardrobe and surveyed her naked body. It was most certainly no longer her best feature, she said to herself, remembering it when she was a child, standing up in the bath to be dried. She remembered being naked at last in the bedroom of the International Hotel in Bray, and the awkward voluptuousness that had followed. The bearing of four children, her fondness for sweet things, the insidious nips of gin in the clubhouse: in combination they had taken a toll, making clothes as necessary as all that meticulous care with make-up and hair. The first time she'd been pregnant, with Cathal, she had looked at herself in this same looking-glass, assuring herself that the enormous swelling would simply go away, as indeed it had. But nothing would go away now. Flesh hung loosely, marked with pink imprints of straps or elastic. If she slimmed herself to the bone there would be scrawny, empty skin, loops and pockets, hollows as ugly as the bulges. She drew her nightdress over her head and a pattern of pink roses in tight little bunches hid what she preferred not to see, transforming her again into a handsome woman.

Agnew had sensitive skin, yet could not resist the quality of finely woven tweed. He chose the sober colours, the greys and browns and inconspicuous greens. He bought his Donegal tweed in Kevin and Howlin's in Dublin and had the suits made up by a tailor in Rathmines. Because of his sensitive skin he had the trousers lined.

Agnew had never worn these suits to his office in the toy factory, for they did not seem to him to be sufficiently matter-of-fact for business. He wore them at weekends, when he went to church and on Sunday afternoons when he drove out to Rathfarran and walked around the cliffs, ending up in Lynch's Bar down by the strand, where by arrangement he took his Sunday supper. He wore them also on the weekends when he went to Dublin.

He would miss the cliffs and the strand, he reflected at breakfast one morning, a few weeks after his visit from Mrs. O'Neill. He would miss the toy factory too, of course, and people he had come to know in a passing kind of way, without intimacy or closeness but yet agreeably.

In the snug, overcrowded dining-room of the terraced house called St. Kevin's he broke a piece of toast in half and poured himself more tea. He had been fortunate in St. Kevin's, fortunate because he was the only lodger and because the Misses Malone had never sought to share a meal with him, fortunate that the house was clean and the cooking averagely good. He'd been fortunate that his interest had never flagged in the job at the toy factory. He would take away with him a sample of every single wooden toy that had been manufactured during his time there: the duck with the quivering bill, the kangaroos, the giraffes, the little red steam engines, the donkeys and carts, the bricks, the elephants, the fox terriers on wheels, and all the others. He was proud of these toys and of his part in their production. They were superior in every possible way — more ingeniously designed, constructed with greater craftsmanship, more fondly finished — than the torrent of shoddiness that had flooded them out of existence.

"I'll miss you too," he said aloud in the overcrowded dining-room, staring down at the spaniel, Judy, who was wagging her tail in the hope of receiving a rind of bacon. She would eat rinds only if they were so brittle that they broke between her teeth. This morning, Agnew knew, what he had left would not satisfy her: the bacon had not been overdone. He lit a cigarette, folded the *Irish Times*, which earlier he had been reading, and left the dining-room, pursued by the dog. "I'm off now, Miss Malone," he called out in the hall, and one of the sisters called back to him from the kitchen. Judy, as she always did, followed him through the town to the toy factory, turning back when he reached the forecourt.

A woman called Mrs. Whelan who came to the factory three mornings a week to attend to whatever typing there was and to keep the books up to date, was to finish at the end of the week. She was there this morning, a prim, trim presence in navy-blue, conscientiously tapping out the last of the invoices. The final delivery was due to be dispatched that afternoon, for Cathal O'Neill had already laid down the peremptory instruction that further orders must not be accepted.

"Good morning, Mrs. Whelan."

"Good morning, sir."

Interrupted for the briefest of moments, she went on typing: she would be extremely useful to someone else, Agnew reflected, if she managed to find a position that suited her. "I think I'm going to start clearing the inner office," he said, passing into it reluctantly, for it was not a task he anticipated with any pleasure. What on earth was he going to do with himself? Fifty-one was far too young simply to retire, even if he could afford to. It was all very well saying he couldn't see himself in the fuel business, either coal or turf, but what alternative was there going to be? In the failing toy factory he had had a position, he had been of some small importance, and he had often wondered if he himself — and the predicament he must find himself in when the factory closed — hadn't been an element in his late employer's sentiment. Had Mr. O'Neill lived, the toy factory might have struggled on until a convenient moment was reached, when its manager might gracefully retire. Still, a father's sentiment rarely passed to a son, nor could it be expected to.

He took his jacket off and hung it up. As he did so the telephone rang and the widow of his late and sentimental employer invited him to what she described as a very small party on Sunday evening. It would be in his honour, he said to himself after he had politely accepted. It was the kind of thing people did; there might even be a presentation in the conventional way, of cutlery or Waterford glass or a clock.

"Now, this is bloody ridiculous!" Cathal glared at his mother, squinting in his extreme rage.

She remembered that squint in his pram. She remembered how his face would turn scarlet before exploding like a volcano, how he would beat his fists against her when she tried to lift him up. His father had had a bad temper also, though over the years she had learnt to ignore it.

"It isn't ridiculous at all, Cathal."

"You are fifty-nine years of age."

"I'm only too well aware of that."

"Agnew's our employee, for God's sake!" He said something else and then broke off, his shout becoming an incompressible stutter. He began again, calming down and collecting himself. "My God, when I think of Agnew!"

"I invited Basil Agnew —"

"Basil? *Basil?*"

"You knew his name was Basil. B. J. Agnew. It's on all the letters."

"In no way did I know the man's name was Basil. I didn't know what his bloody name was."

"Don't be violent, Cathal."

"Aw, for God's sake now!" He turned away from her. He crossed the Italianate drawing-room and stood with his back to her, morosely looking out of the window.

"I invited Basil Agnew to a little evening I had and he stayed on afterwards to help me clear up a bit. The Flanagans were there, and the Fitzfynnes and a few others. It was all quite above board, Cathal. Father Doherty was there, quite happy with the arrangement."

"You were seen out at Rathfarran with Agnew. You were in Lynch's with him."

"That was later on, the following Sunday it was. And of course we were in Lynch's. We had two glasses of whiskey each in Lynch's, and then we had our supper there."

"Will you for God's sake examine what you're doing? You hardly know Agnew."

"I've known him for seventeen years."

Cathal mentioned his father, who God rest him would be disgusted if he knew, and probably he did know. He could not understand, Cathal repeated for the third time in this tempestuous conversation, how any sane woman could behave like this.

"Well, I have behaved like this, Cathal. I have been asked a question by Basil Agnew and I have answered in the affirmative. I wanted to tell you before I spoke a word to Father Doherty."

"Agnew's a Protestant."

"We'll be married by Father Doherty. Basil isn't the least particular about matters like that."

"I bet you he isn't. The bloody man—"

"I must ask you, Cathal, not to keep referring to Basil Agnew as a bloody man. I do not refer to Thelma as a bloody woman. When you informed me in this very room that you intended to marry her I held my peace."

"The man's after your money and that's all there's to it."

"You're being most unpleasant, Cathal."

He almost spat. As a child, he had had a most unpleasant habit of spitting. His eyes savaged her as he continued violently to upbraid her and insult the man she had agreed to marry. He left eventually, barging his way out of the drawing-room, shouting back at her from the hall before he barged his way out of the house.

That evening her two married daughters, Eileen in Dublin and Rose in Trim, telephoned her. They were more diplomatic than Cathal, as they had always been. They beseeched her not to be hasty;

both offered to come and talk it all over with her. She had written to them, she said; she was sorry Cathal had taken it upon himself to get in touch with them, since she had particularly asked him not to. "It's all in my letter," she assured her daughters in turn. "Everything about how I feel and how I've thought it carefully over." The two men they'd married themselves were, after all, no great shakes: if you were honest you had to say that, one of them little better than a commercial traveller, the other reputed to be the worst veterinary surgeon in Trim. Yet she hadn't made much of a fuss when Eileen first brought her mousy little Liam to Arcangelo House, nor over Rose's Eddie, a younger version of Dessie Fitzfynne, with the same stories about Kerrymen and the same dull bonhomie. "It'll work out grand," she said to her daughters in turn. "Was I ever a fool in anything I did?"

The following morning Thelma came round and in her crude way said how flabbergasted she was. She sat there with her vacant expression and repeated three times that you could have knocked her down with a feather when Cathal had walked in the door and informed her that his mother was intending to marry Agnew. "I couldn't close my mouth," Thelma said. "I was stirring custard in the kitchen and declare to God didn't the damn stuff burn on me. 'She's after getting engaged to Agnew,' he said, and if you'd given me a thousand pounds I couldn't go on with the stirring."

Thelma's rigmarole continued, how Cathal had stormed about the kitchen, how he'd shouted at the children and knocked a pot of black-currant jam onto the floor with his elbow, how she'd had to sit down to recover herself. Then she lowered her voice as if there were other people in her mother-in-law's drawing-room. "Isn't there a lot of talk, though, about what Agnew gets up to when he goes off to Dublin for the two days? Is it women he goes after?" While she spoke, Thelma nodded vehemently, answering her own question. She'd heard it for certain, she continued in the same subdued voice, that Agnew had women of a certain description up in Dublin.

"That's tittle-tattle, Thelma."

"Ah sure, I'd say it was, all right. Still and all, Mrs. O'Neill."

"What Mr. Agnew does with his own time is hardly the business of anyone except himself."

"Ah sure, of course 'tisn't. It's only Cathal and myself was wondering."

The moon that was Thelma's face, its saucer eyes and jammy red mouth, the nose that resembled putty, was suddenly closer than Mrs.

O'Neill found agreeable. It was a way that Thelma had when she was endeavouring to be sincere.

"I had an uncle married late. Sure, the poor man ended demented."

You are the stupidest creature God ever put breath into, Mrs. O'Neill reflected, drawing herself back from her daughter-in-law's advancing features. She did not comment on Thelma's uncle any more than she had commented on the burning of the custard or the loss of the pot of blackcurrant jam.

"You know what I mean, Mrs. O'Neill?" The subdued tones became a whisper. "A horse-trainer's widow in Portarlington that went after the poor old devil's few pence."

"Well, I'm most certainly not after Mr. Agnew's few pence."

"Oh no, I'm not saying that at all. I'd never say a thing like that, Mrs. O'Neill, what you'd be after or what he'd be after. Sure, where'd I find the right to make statements the like of that?"

Thelma eventually went away. She would have been sent by Cathal, who would also have written to Siobhan. But Siobhan had always possessed a mind of her own and in due course a letter arrived from Philadelphia. *I'm delighted altogether at the news. I kind of hoped you'd do something like this.*

It had never, in the past, occurred to Agnew to get married. Nor would he have suggested it to his late employer's wife if he hadn't become aware that she wished him to. Marriage, she had clearly decided, would be the rescuing of both of them: she from her solitariness in Arcangelo House, he from the awkwardness of being unemployed. She had said she would like him to oversee the demolition of the toy factory and the creation of an apple orchard in its place. This enterprise was her own and had nothing to do with Cathal.

The women she played bridge with still addressed him friendlily when he met them on the street or in a shop. Her golfing companions — especially Flanagan and Fitzfynne — had even been enthusiastic. Butler-Regan had slapped him on the shoulders in the bar of the Commercial Hotel and said he was glad it hadn't been O'Keefe she'd gone for. Only O'Keefe had looked grumpy, not replying to Agnew's greeting when they met in Lawlor's one morning, both of them buying cigarettes. Dolores Fitzfynne telephoned him at the toy factory and said she was delighted. It was a good idea to plant an apple orchard on the site of the factory, Cox's and Beauty of Bath, russets and Bramleys and Worcesters. In the fullness of time the orchard would become her own particular interest, as the toys had been her husband's and the turf-bogs were her son's. It was a pity that the family were almost all opposed to the match, but naturally such a reaction was to be expected.

She was aware of eyes upon them when they danced together in the clubhouse, bedecked with Christmas decorations. What did these people really think? Did all of them share, while appearing not to, the family's disapproval? Did fat Butler-Regan and fat Flanagan think she was ridiculous, at fifty-nine years of age, to be allowing a man to marry her for her money? Did Dolores Fitzfynne think so? Mrs. Whelan, who had been his secretary for so long at the toy factory, always attended the Golf Club Annual Dance with her husband; the Misses Malone, his landladies for the same period of time in the terraced house called St Kevin's, came to help with the catering. Did these three women consider her beneath contempt because she'd trapped a slightly younger attractive man as a companion for her advancing years?

"I've always liked the way you dance the quickstep," she whispered.

"Always?"

"Yes, always."

The confession felt disgraceful. Cathal and Thelma, dancing only yards away, might talk all night about it if they knew. With O'Keefe, she wouldn't have had to be unfaithful in that way.

"You're not entirely devoid of rhythm yourself."

"I've always loved dancing actually."

O'Keefe would have asked for more, and for less. Some hint of man's pride would have caused him scrupulously to avoid touching a penny of her money, nor would he have wanted to go planting apple-trees under her direction. But O'Keefe would have entered her bedroom and staked his claim there, and she could not have borne that.

"We'll be married this time next week," he said. "Do you realise that?"

"Unless you decide to take to the hills."

"No, I'll not do that, Norah."

The Artie Furlong Band, new to the clubhouse this year and already reckoned to be a success, played an old tune she loved: "Smoke Gets in Your Eyes." His step changed easily, he scarcely touched her as he guided her through the other dancers. Sweetman was appalling to dance with because of his perspiration troubles, Dessie Fitzfynne's knees were always driving themselves into you, Butler-Regan held you far too tight. She'd go on playing bridge and golf after they were married, no reason not to. He'd said he intended to continue exercising the Misses Malone's spaniel.

"You're sure about this?" he whispered, bending his long face closer to hers, smiling a little. "You're absolutely sure, Norah?"

She remembered thinking how she couldn't imagine him ever calling her Norah, and how strange his own Christian name had felt when first she'd used it. She would never know him, she was aware of that; nor could he ever fully know her. There would never be the passion of love between them: all that must be done without.

"I'm sure all right."

The music ceased. They went to get a drink and were joined immediately by the Fitzfynnes and Rita Flanagan. Thelma came up and said one of the children had spots all over his stomach. Cathal kept his distance.

"We're drinking to the happy couple," Dessie Fitzfynne shouted, raising his glass. Thelma scuttled away, as if frightened to be seen anywhere near such a toast.

"Cheers to the both of you," Rita Flanagan shrilled, and in another part of the decorated clubhouse Butler-Regan the solicitor began to sing.

She smiled at the glasses that were raised towards them. "That's very kind of you," he said quietly. "We're touched."

She would have liked to add something, to have sorted out falsity from the truth. He was indeed marrying her for her money. But he, in return, was giving her a role that money could not purchase. Within a week the family would no longer possess her. Cathal's far-apart eyes would no longer dismiss her as a remnant of the dead.

"We're going to have an orchard, you know, where the toy factory is now."

They looked a bit surprised, at first not quite grasping her meaning and then wondering why she should mention an orchard just then.

"Our wedding present to one another," he explained. "Norah's trees and I shall tend them."

The band struck up again, drowning the raucous singing of Butler-Regan. Cathal at last approached his mother and asked her to dance, as every year he did on this Christmas occasion. But he did not at last say that he hoped it would work out all right, Agnew and herself in Arcangelo House. She had paid some price, Cathal believed, apart from the financial one. But Cathal, really, was not right and for him, too, she would have liked to sort out falsity from the truth.

"Well, that is that," he said, turning off the television on a Sunday night, after he had returned from Dublin. He lurched a little as he moved towards her, holding out his packet of cigarettes. He had said, before their marriage, that he often became intoxicated in the course of these weekends. He met his friends and they went from place to place, all of them men who enjoyed the company of men. Sometimes, left alone, or unlucky in the new companions he had met, he wandered the quaysides of the city, thinking about the sailors of the ships. On the strand at Rathfarran his face had been averted when he told her this, and when he finished she had not spoken. Dessie Fitzfynne and Sweetman liked men's company also, she had thought, and so had her husband in his lifetime. But that, of course, was not the same.

"I don't think I'll go back there." He swayed, like Flanagan did in drink. "God knows, I don't want to."

He always said that. He always offered her a cigarette after turning off the Sunday television. A moment later he made the renunciatory statement.

"It doesn't matter." She tried to smile, imagining him in the public houses he had told her about, his dignified presence mocked by a man who was once particularly his friend, a waiter who no longer liked him.

"I dread for your sake that someone will find out one of these days. I hadn't thought of that when we married."

"I knew what I was doing. You told me the truth, and you're honourable for that."

When he told her she had not confessed a truth as well: that clothes and make-up disguised a loss she found it hard to bear. She was haunted by herself, by the beauty that had been there in a hotel in Bray. Lingering in the clubhouse on these Sunday nights, she drank more gin and French than usual, knowing he would be tipsy, too, when he returned. Once they'd fallen asleep in their chairs, and she'd woken up at twenty past three and crept away to bed. He'd seemed like a child, one arm hanging down, fingers resting on the carpet. On the strand at Rathfarran he'd told her he never wanted to go to sleep on these Sunday nights because he hated waking up so. In his bedroom at St

Kevin's, the door locked against indiscreet entrance by one or other of the Misses Malone, he had sat with the whiskey bottle he'd bought for the purpose in Dublin. She listened while he'd told her that; concerning herself, there'd been no need to say what she might have because, being the man he was, he guessed.

They passed together through the hall of Arcangelo House and mounted the stairs to their separate bedrooms. They paused before they parted, offering in their tipsiness a vague, unstated reassurance. Tomorrow none of this would be mentioned; their common ground would not be traversed on a mundane Monday morning. For a moment on the landing outside their bedrooms they spoke of the orchard that would replace the toy factory, and trees they would watch growing up.

T. Coraghessan Boyle

The Hat

They sent a hit squad after the bear. Three guys in white parkas with National Forestry Service patches on the shoulders. It was late Friday afternoon, about a week before Christmas, the snow was coming down so fast it seemed as if the sky and earth were glued together, and Jill had just opened up the lodge for drinks and dinner when they stamped in through the door. The tall one—he ordered shots of Jim Beam and beers for all of them—could have been a bear himself, hunched under the weight of his shoulders in the big quilted parka, his face lost in a bristle of black beard, something feral and challenging in the flash of his blue eyes. "Hello, pretty lady," he said, looking Jill full in the face as he swung a leg over the barstool and pressed his forearms to the gleaming copper rail, "I hear you got a bear problem."

I was sitting in the shadows at the end of the bar, nursing a beer and watching the snow. Jill hadn't turned up the lights yet and I was glad—the place had a soothing underwater look to it, snow like a sheet stretched tight over the window, the fire in the corner gentle as a backrub. I was alive and moving—lighting a cigarette, lifting the glass to my lips—but I felt so peaceful I could have been dozing.

"That's right," Jill said, still flushing from the "pretty lady" remark. Two weeks earlier, in bed, she'd told me she hadn't felt pretty in years. What are you talking about? I'd said. She dropped her lower lip and looked away. I gained twenty pounds, she said. I reached out to touch her, smiling, as if to say twenty pounds—what's twenty pounds? Little Ball of Suet, I said, referring to one of the Maupassant stories in the book she'd given me. It's not funny, she said, but then she'd rolled over and touched me back.

"Name's Boo," the big man said, pausing to throw back his bourbon and take a sip of beer. "This is Scott," nodding at the guy on his left, also in beard and watchcap, "and Josh." Josh, who couldn't have been more than nineteen, appeared on his right like a jack-in-the-box. Boo unzipped the parka to expose a thermal shirt the color of dried blood.

"Is this all together?" Jill asked.

Boo nodded, and I noticed the scar cut along the ridge of his cheekbone, thinking of churchkey openers, paring knives, the long hooked ivory claws of bears. Then he turned to me. "What you drinking, friend?"

I'd begun to hear sounds from the kitchen—the faint kiss of cup and saucer, the rattle of cutlery—and my stomach suddenly dropped like an elevator out of control. I hadn't eaten all day. It was the middle of the month, I'd read all the paperbacks in the house, listened to all the records, and I was waiting for my check to come. There was no mail service up here of course—the road was closed half the time in winter anyway—but Marshall, the lodge owner and unofficial kingpin of the community, had gone down the mountain to lay in provisions against the holiday onslaught of tourists, ski-mobilers and the like, and he'd promised to pick it up for me. If it was there. If it was, and he made it back through the storm, I was going to have three or four shots of Wild Turkey, then check out the family dinner and sip coffee and Kahlua till Jill off work. "Beer," I said.

"Would you get this man a beer, pretty lady?" said Boo in his backwoods basso, and when she'd opened me one and come back for his money, he started in on the bear. Had she seen him? How much damage had he done? What about his tracks—anything unusual? His scat? He was reddish in color, right? Almost cinnamon? And with one folded ear?

She'd seen him. But not when he'd battered his way into the back storeroom, punctured a case of twelve-and-a-half-ounce cans of tuna, lapped up a couple gallons of mountain red burgundy and shards of glass and left a bloody trail that wound off through the ponderosa pines like a pink ribbon. Not then. No, she'd seen him under more intimate circumstances—in her own bedroom, in fact. She'd been asleep in the rear bedroom with her eight-year-old son Adrian (they slept in the same room to conserve heat, shutting down the thermostat and tossing a handful of coal into the stove in the corner) when suddenly the back window went to pieces. The air came in at them like a spearthrust, there was the dull booming thump of the bear's big body against the outer wall, and an explosion of bottles, cans and whatnot as he tore into the garbage on the back porch. She and Adrian had jolted awake in time to see the bear's puzzled shaggy face appear in the empty windowframe, and then they were up like Goldilocks and out the front door, where they locked themselves in the car. They came to me in their pajamas, trembling like refugees. By the time I got there with my Weatherby, the bear was gone.

"I've seen him," Jill said. "He broke the damn window out of my back bedroom and now I've got it all boarded up." Josh, the younger guy, seemed to find this funny, and he began a low snickering suck and blow of air like an old dog with something caught in his throat.

"Hell," Jill said, lighting up, centerstage, "I was in my nightie and barefoot too and I didn't hesitate a second — zoom, I grabbed my son by the hand and out the door we went."

"Your nightie, huh?" Boo said, a big appreciative grin transforming his face so that for a minute, in the dim light, he could have been a leering, hairy-hocked satyr come in from the cold.

"Maybe it wasn't just the leftovers he wanted," I offered, and everyone cracked up. Just then Marshall stepped through the door, arms laden, stamping the snow from his boots. I got up to help him, and when he began fumbling in his breast pocket, I felt a surge of relief; he'd remembered my check. I was on my way out the door to help with the supplies when I heard Boo's rumbling bass like distant thunder: "Don't you worry, pretty lady," he was saying, "we'll get him."

Regina showed up three days later. For the past few years she'd rented a room up here over the holidays, ostensibly for her health, the cross-country skiing and the change of scene, but actually so she could display her backend in stretch pants to the sex-crazed hermits who lived year-round amidst the big pines and sequoias. She was from Los Angeles, where she worked as a dental hygienist. Her teeth were perfect, she smiled nonstop and with the serenity of the Mona Lisa, and she wore the kind of bra that was popular in the fifties — the kind that thrust the breasts out of her ski sweater like nuclear warheads. She'd been known to give the tumble to the occasional tourist or one of the lucky locals when the mood took her, but she really had it for Marshall. For two weeks every Christmas and another week at Easter, she became a fixture at the bar, as much a part of the decor as the moosehead or the stuffed bear, perched on a barstool in Norwegian sweater, red ski pants and mukluks, sipping a champagne cocktail and waiting for him to get off work. Sometimes she couldn't hold out and someone else would walk off with her while Marshall scowled from behind the grill, but usually she just waited there for him like a flower about to drop its petals.

She came into the white world that afternoon like a foretaste of the good times to come — city women, weekend cowboys, grandmas, children, dogs and lawyers were on their way, trees and decorations going up, the big festival of the goose-eating Christians about to commence — rolling into the snowbound parking lot in her Honda with the neat little chain-wrapped tires that always remind me of Tonka toys. It was about four p.m., the sky was a sorrowful gray, and a loose flurry was dusting the huge logs piled up on the veranda. In she came, stamping and shaking, the knit cap pulled down to her eyebrows, already on the lookout for Marshall.

I was sitting in my usual place, working on my fifth beer, a third of the way through the check Marshall had brought me three days previous and calculating gloomily that I'd be out of money by Christmas at this rate. Scooter was bartending, and his daughter-in-law Mae-Mae, who happened to be a widow, was hunched morosely over a Tom Collins three stools up from me. Mae-Mae had lost her husband to the mountain two years earlier (or rather to the tortuous road that connected us to civilization and snaked up 7,300 feet from the floor of the San Joaquin Valley in a mere twenty-six miles, treacherous as a goat trail in the Himalayas) and hadn't spoken or smiled since. She was a Thai. Scooter's son, a Vietnam hero, had brought her back from Southeast Asia with him. When Jill was off, or the holiday crowd bearing down on the place, Scooter would drive up the mountain from his cabin at Little Creek, elevation 5,500 feet, hang his ski parka on a hook in back, and shake, stir and blend cocktails. He brought Mae-Mae with him to get her out of the house.

Scooter and I had been discussing some of the finer points of the prevent defense with respect to the coming pro football playoffs when Regina's Honda had rolled into the lot, and now we gave it up to gape at her as she shook herself like a go-go dancer, opened her jacket to expose the jutting armaments of her breasts, and slid onto a barstool. Scooter slicked back his white hair and gave her a big grin. "Well," he said, fumbling for her name, "um, uh, good to see you again."

She flashed him her fluoridated smile, glanced past the absorbed Mae-Mae to where I sat grinning like an overworked dog, then turned back to him. "Marshall around?"

Scooter informed her that Marshall had gone down the mountain on a supply run and should be back by dinnertime. And what would she like?

She sighed, crossed her legs, lit a cigarette. The hat she was wearing was part of a set—hand-knit, imported from Scandinavia, woven from rams' whiskers by the trolls themselves, two hundred bucks at I. Magnin. Or something like that. It was gray, like her eyes. She swept it from her head with a flourish, fluffed out her short black hair and ordered a champagne cocktail. I looked at my watch.

I'd read somewhere that nine out of ten adults in Alaska had a drinking problem. I could believe it. Snow, ice, sleet, wind, the dark night of the soul: what else were you supposed to do? It was the same way up on the mountain. Big Timber was a collection of maybe a hundred widely scattered cabins atop a broad-beamed peak in the western Sierras. The cabins belonged to summer people from L.A. and San Diego, to cross-country skiers, gynecologists, talent agents, ad men, drunks and nature lovers, for the most part, and to twenty-seven hard-core anti-social types who called the place home year-round. I was one of this latter group. So was Jill. Of the remaining twenty-five xenophobes and rustics, three were women, and two of them were married and post-menopausal to boot. The sole remaining female was an alcoholic poet with a walleye who lived in her parents' cabin on the outer verge of the development and hated men. TV reception was spotty, radio nonexistent and the nearest library a one-room affair at the base of the mountain that boasted three copies of *The Thorn Birds* and the complete works of Irving Wallace.

And so we drank.

Social life, such as it was, revolved around Marshall's lodge, which dispensed all the amenities in a single huge room, from burgers and chili omelets to antacid pills, cold remedies, cans of pickled beets and toilet paper, as well as spirits, human fraternity and a chance to fight off alien invaders at the controls of the video game in the corner. Marshall organized his Friday-night family dinners, did a turkey thing on Thanksgiving and Christmas, threw a New Year's party, and kept the bar open on weekends through the long solitary winter, thinking not so much of profit, but of our sanity. The lodge also boasted eight woodsy hotel rooms, usually empty, but now—with the arrival of Boo and his fellow hit men, Regina and a couple other tourists—beginning to fill up.

On the day Regina rolled in, Jill had taken advantage of the break in the weather to schuss down the mountain in her station wagon and do some Christmas shopping. I was supposed to have gone with her, but we'd had a fight. Over Boo. I'd come in the night before from my late-afternoon stroll to see Jill half spread across the bar with a blank bovine look on her face while Boo mumbled his baritone blandishments into her eyes about six inches away. I saw that, and then I saw that she'd locked fingers with him, as if they'd been arm wrestling or something. Marshall was out in the kitchen, Josh was sticking it to the video game, and Scott must have been up in his room. "Hey," Boo said, casually turning his head, "what's happening?" Jill gave me a defiant look before extricating herself and turning her back to fool around with the cash register. I stood there in the doorway, saying nothing. *Bishzz, bishzz*, went the video game, *zoot-zoot-zoot*. Marshall dropped something out in the kitchen. "Buy this man a drink, honey," Boo said. I turned and walked out the door.

"Christ, I can't believe you," Jill had said when I came round to pick her up after work. "It's my job, you know? What am I supposed to do, hang a sign around my neck that says 'Property of M. Koerner?'"

I told her I thought that was a pretty good idea.

"Forget the ride," she said. "I'm walking."

"And what about the bear?" I said, knowing how the specter of it terrified her, knowing that she dreaded walking those dark snowlit roads for fear of chancing across him — knowing it and wanting for her to admit it, to tell me she needed me.

But all she said was "Screw the bear," and then she was gone.

Now I ordered another beer, sauntered along the bar and sat down one stool up from Regina. "Hi," I said, "remember me? Michael Koerner? I live up back of Malloy's place?"

She narrowed her eyes and gave me a smile I could feel all the way down in the remotest nodes of my reproductive tract. She no more knew me than she would have known a Chinese peasant plucked at random from the faceless hordes. "Sure," she said.

We made small talk. How slippery the roads were — worse than last year. A renegade bear? Really? Marshall grew a beard?

I'd bought her two champagne cocktails and was working on yet another beer when Jill catapulted through the door, arms festooned with foil-wrapped packages and eyes ablaze with goodwill and holiday cheer; Adrian tagged along at her side, looking as if he'd just sprung down from the back of a flying reindeer. If Jill felt put out by the spectacle of Regina — or more particularly by my proximity to and involvement in that spectacle — she didn't miss a beat. The packages hit the bar with a thump, Scooter and Mae-Mae were treated to joyous salutatory squeals, Regina was embraced, and I was ignored. Adrian went straight for the video game, pausing only to scoop up the six quarters I held out to him like an offering. Jill ordered herself a cocktail and started in on Regina, bantering away about hairstyles, nails, shoes, blouses and the like as if she were glad to see her. "I just love that hat!" she shouted at one point, reaching out to finger the material. I swung round on my stool and stared out the window.

It was then that Boo came into sight. Distant, snow-softened, trudging across the barren white expanse of the lot as if in a dream. He was wearing his white parka, hood up, a rifle was slung over his shoulder and he was dragging something behind him. Something heavy and dark, a long low-slung form that raveled out from his heels like a shadow. When he paused to straighten up and catch his streaming breath, I saw with a shock that the carcass of an animal lay at his feet, red and raw like a gash in the snow. "Hey!" I shouted, "Boo got the bear!" and the next minute we were all out in the wind-blown parking lot, hemmed in by the forbidding ranks of the trees and the belly of the gray deflated sky, as Boo looked up puzzled from the carcass of a gutted deer. "What happened, the bar catch fire?" he said, his sharp blue eyes parrying briefly with mine, swooping past Scooter, Adrian and Mae-Mae to pause a moment over Jill and finally lock on Regina's wide-eyed stare. He was grinning.

The deer's black lip was pulled back from ratty yellowed teeth, its eyes were opaque in death. Boo had slit it from chest to crotch, and a half-frozen bulb of grayish intestine poked from the lower end of the ragged incision. I felt foolish.

"Bait," Boo said in explanation, his eyes roving over us again. "I'm leaving a blood smear you could follow with your eyes closed and your nose stopped up. Then I'm going to hang the meat up a tree and wait for Mr. Bear."

Jill turned away, a bit theatrically I thought, and made small noises of protest and disgust on the order of "the poor animal," then took Adrian by the hand and pulled him back in the direction of the lodge. Mae-Mae stared through us all, this carnage like that other that had claimed her husband's life, end-over-end in the bubble of their car, blood on the slope. Regina looked at Boo. He stood over the fallen buck, grinning like a troglodyte with his prey, then bent to catch the thing by its antlers and drag it off across the lot as if it were an old rug for the church rummage sale.

That night the lodge was hopping. Tourists had begun to trickle in and there were ten or twelve fresh faces at the bar. I ate a chicken pot pie and a can of cold beets in the solitude of my cabin, wrapped a tacky black and gold scarf round my neck and ambled through the dark featureless forest to the lodge. As I stepped through the door I smelled perfume, sweet drinks, body heat, and caught the sensuous click of the poolballs as they punctuated the swell of riotous voices churning up around me. Holiday cheer, oh yes indeed.

Jill was tending bar. Everyone in the development was there, including the old wives and the walleyed poetess. An array of roaring strangers and those I recognized vaguely from previous seasons stood, slouched and stamped round the bar or huddled over steaks in the booths to the rear. Marshall was behind the grill. I eased up to the bar between a bearded stranger in a gray felt cowboy hat and a familiar-looking character who shot me a glance of mortal dislike and then turned away. I was absently wondering what I could possibly have done to offend this guy (winter people—I could hardly remember what I'd said and done last week, let alone last year) when I spotted Regina. And Boo. They were sitting at a booth, the table before them littered with empty glasses and beer bottles. Good, I thought to myself, an insidious little smile of satisfaction creeping across my lips, and I glanced toward Jill.

I could see that she was watching them out of the corner of her eye, though an impartial observer might have guessed she was giving her full attention to Alf Cornwall, the old gasbag who sat across the bar from her and toyed with a glass of peppermint schnapps while he went on ad nauseum about the only subject dear to him—i.e., the lamentable state of his health. "Jill," I barked with malicious joy, "how about some service down here?"

She gave me a look that would have corroded metal, then heaved back from the bar as if she had a piano strapped to her back and poured me a long slow shot of Wild Turkey and an even slower glass of beer. I winked at her as she set the drinks down and scraped my money from the bar. "Not tonight, Michael," she said, "I don't feel up to it," and her tone was so dragged down and lugubrious she could have been a professional mourner. It was then that I began to realize just how much Boo had affected her (and by extension, how little I had), and I glanced over my shoulder to focus a quick look of jealous hatred on him. When Jill set down my change I grabbed her wrist. "What the hell do you mean 'not tonight,'" I hissed. "Now I can't even talk to you, or what?"

She looked at me like a martyr, like a twenty-eight-year-old woman deserted by her husband in the backend of nowhere and saddled with an unhappy kid and a deadbeat sometime beau to whom the prospect of marriage was about as appealing as a lobotomy, she looked at me like a woman who's given up on romance. Then she jerked her arm away and slouched off to hear all the fascinating circumstances attending Alf Cornwall's most recent bowel movement.

The crowd began to thin out about eleven, and Marshall came out from behind the grill to saunter up to the bar for a Remy Martin. He too seemed preternaturally interested in Alf Cornwall's digestive tract, and sniffed meditatively at his cognac for five minutes or so before he picked up the glass and strolled over to join Boo and Regina. He slid in next to Regina, nodding and smiling, but he didn't look too pleased.

Like Boo, Marshall was big. Big-headed, big-bellied, with grizzled hair and a beard flecked with white. He was in his mid forties, twice-divorced, and he had a casual folksy way about him that women found appealing, or unique — or whatever. Women who came up the mountain, that is. Jill had had a thing with him the year before I moved in, he was one of the chief reasons the walleyed poetess hated men, and any number of cross-country ski bunnies, doctors' wives and day trippers had taken some extracurricular exercise in the oak-framed waterbed that dominated his room in the back of the lodge. Boo didn't stand a chance. Ten minutes after Marshall had sat down Boo was back up at the bar, a little unsteady from all he'd had to drink, and looking Jill up and down like he had one thing on his mind.

I was on my third shot and fifth beer, the lights were low, the fire going strong and the twenty-foot Christmas tree lit up like a satellite. Alf Cornwall had taken his bullshit home with him, the poetess, the wives and two-thirds of the new people had cleared out. I was discussing beach erosion with the guy in the cowboy hat, who as it turned out was from San Diego, and keeping an eye on Boo and Jill at the far end of the bar. "Well, Christ," San Diego roared as if I was half a mile away, "you put up them godforsaken useless damn seawalls and what have you got, I ask you? Huh?"

I wasn't listening. Boo was stroking Jill's hand like a glove salesman, Marshall and Regina were grappling in the booth, and I was feeling sore and hurt and left out. A log burned through and tumbled into the coals with a thud, Marshall got up to poke it, and all of a sudden I was seething. Turning my back on San Diego, I pushed off of my stool and strode to the end of the bar.

Jill saw the look on my face and drew back. I put my hand on Boo's shoulder and watched him turn to me in slow motion, his face huge, the scar glistening over his eyebrow. "You can't do that," I said.

He just looked at me.

"Michael," Jill said.

"Huh?" he said. "Do what?" Then he turned his head to look at Jill, and when he swung back round he knew.

I shoved him, hard, as he was coming up off the barstool, and he went down on one knee before he caught himself and lunged at me. He would have destroyed me if Marshall hadn't caught hold of him, but I didn't care. As it was, he gave me one terrific shot to the breastbone that flattened me against the bar and sent a couple of glasses flying. Bang, bang, they shattered on the flagstone floor like lightbulbs dropped from a ladder.

"Goddamit," Marshall was roaring, "that's about enough." His face was red to the roots of his whiskers. "Michael," he said — or blared, I should say — and then he waved his hand in disgust. Boo stood behind him, giving me a bad look. "I think you've had enough, Michael," Marshall said. "Go on home."

I wanted to throw it right back in his face, wanted to shout obscenities, take them both on, break up the furniture and set the tree afire, but I didn't. I wasn't sixteen: I was thirty-one and I was reasonable. The lodge was the only bar in twenty-six miles and I'd be mighty thirsty and mighty lonely both if I was banished for good. "All right," I said. "All right." And then, as I shrugged into my jacket: "Sorry."

Boo was grinning, Jill looked like she had the night the bear broke in, Regina was studying me with either interest or amusement — I couldn't tell which — Scooter looked like he had to go to the bathroom, and San Diego just stepped aside. I pulled the door closed behind me. Softly.

Outside, it was snowing. Big, warm, healing flakes. It was the kind of snow my father used to hold his hands out to, murmuring *God must be up there plucking chickens.* I wrapped the scarf round my throat and was about to start off across the lot when I saw something moving through the blur of falling flakes. The first thing I thought of was some late arrival from down below, some part-timer come to claim his cabin. The second thing I thought of was the bear.

I was wrong on both counts. The snow drove down against the dark branchless pillars of the treetrunks, chalk strokes on a blackboard, I counted off three breaths, and then Mae-Mae emerged from the gloom. "Michael?" she said, coming up to me.

I could see her face in the yellow light that seeped through the windows of the lodge and lay like a fungus on the surface of the snow. She gave me a rare smile, and then her face changed as she touched a finger to the corner of my mouth. "What happen you?" she said, and her finger glistened with blood.

I licked my lip. "Nothing. Bit my lip, I guess." The snow caught like confetti in the feathery puff of her hair and her eyes tugged at me from the darkness. "Hey," I said, surprised by inspiration, "you want to maybe come up to my place for a drink?"

Next day, at dusk, I was out in the woods with my axe. The temperature was about ten degrees above zero, I had a pint of Presidente to keep me warm, and I was looking for a nice round-bottomed silver fir about five feet tall. I listened to the snow groan under my boots, watched my breath hang in the air; I looked around me and saw ten thousand little green trees beneath the canopy of the giants, none of them right. By the time I found what I was looking for, the snow had drunk up the light and the trees had become shadows.

As I bent to clear the snow from the base of the tree I'd selected, something made me glance over my shoulder. Failing light, logs under the snow, branches, hummocks. At first I couldn't make him out, but I knew he was there. Sixth sense. But then, before the shaggy silhouette separated itself from the gloom, a more prosaic sense took over: I could smell him. Shit, piss, sweat and hair, dead meat, bad breath, the primal stink. There he was, a shadow among shadows, big around as a fallen tree, the bear, watching me.

Nothing happened. I didn't grin him down, fling the axe at him or climb a tree, and he didn't lumber off in a panic, throw himself on me with a bloody roar or climb a tree either. Frozen like an ice sculpture, not even daring to come out of my crouch for fear of shattering the moment, I watched the bear. Communed with him. He was a renegade, a solitary, airlifted in a groggy stupor from Yellowstone where he'd become too familiar with people. Now he was familiar with me. I wondered if he'd studied my tracks as I'd studied his, wondered what he was doing out in the harsh snowbound woods instead of curled cozily in his den. Ten minutes passed. Fifteen. The woods went dark. I stood up. He was gone.

Christmas was a pretty sad affair. Talk of post-holiday depression, I had it before, during and after. I was broke, Jill and I were on the outs, I'd begun to loathe the sight of three-hundred-foot trees and snow-capped mountains, and I liked the rest of humanity about as much as Gulliver liked the Yahoos. I did stop by Jill's place around six to share a miserable, tight-lipped meal with her and Adrian and exchange presents. I gave Adrian a two-foot-high neon-orange plastic dragon from Taiwan that spewed up puddles of reddish stuff that looked like vomit, and I gave Jill a cheap knit hat with a pink pompon on top. She gave me a pair of gloves. I didn't stay for coffee.

New Year's was different.

I gave a party for one thing. For another, I'd passed from simple misanthropy to nihilism, death of the spirit and beyond. It was two a.m., everybody in the lodge was wearing party hats, I'd kissed half the women in the place — including a reluctant Jill, pliant Regina and sour-breathed poetess — and I felt empty and full, giddy, expansive, hopeful, despondent, drunk. "Party at my place," I shouted as Marshall announced last call and turned up the lights. "Everybody's invited."

Thirty bon vivants tramped through the snowy streets, blowing party horns and flicking paper ticklers at one another, fired up snowmobiles, Jeeps and pickups, carried open bottles out of the bar and hooted at the stars. They filled my little place like fish in a net, squirming against one another, grinning and shouting, making out in the loft, vomiting in the toilet, sniggering around the fireplace. Boo was there, water under the bridge. Jill too. Marshall, Regina, Scooter, Mae-Mae, Josh and Scott, the poetess, San Diego and anybody else who happened to be standing under the moosehead in a glossy duncecap when I made my announcement. Somebody put on a reggae album that sent seismic shudders through the floor, and people began to dance.

I was out in the kitchen fumbling with the ice cube tray when Regina banged through the door with a bar glass in her hand. She gave me a crooked smile and held it out to me. "What're you drinking?" she asked.

"Pink Boys," I said. "Vodka, crushed ice and pink lemonade, slushed in the blender."

"Pink Boys," Regina said, or tried to say. She was wearing her knit hat and matching sweater, the hat pulled down to her eyebrows, the sweater unbuttoned halfway to her navel. I took the glass from her and she moved into me, caught hold of my biceps and stuck her tongue in my mouth. A minute later I had her pinned up against the stove, exploring her exemplary dentition with the tip of my own tongue and dipping my hands into that fabulous sweater as if into the mother lode itself.

I had no problems with any of this. I gave no thought to motives, mores, fidelity or tomorrow: I was a creature of nature, responding to natural needs. Besides which, Jill was locked in an embrace with Marshall in the front room, the old satyr and king of the mountain reestablishing a prior claim, Boo was hunched over the fire with Mae-Mae, giving her the full flash of his eyes and murmuring about bear scat in a voice so deep it would have made Johnny Cash turn pale, and Josh and the poetess were joyfully deflating Edna St. Vincent Millay while swaying their bodies awkwardly to Bob Marley's voodoo backbeat. New Year's Eve. It was like something out of *La Ronde*.

By three-thirty, I'd been rejected by Regina, who'd obviously been using me as a decoy, Marshall and Jill had disappeared and rematerialized twice, Regina had tried unsuccessfully to lure Boo away from Mae-Mae (who was now secreted with him in the bedroom), San Diego had fallen and smashed my coffee table to splinters, one half-gallon of vodka was gone and we were well into the second, and Josh and the poetess had exchanged addresses. Auld lang syne, I thought, surveying the wreckage and moodily crunching taco chips while a drunken San Diego raved in my ear about dune buggies, outboard engines and tuna rigs. Marshall and Jill were holding hands. Regina sat across the room, looking dangerous. She'd had four or five Pink Boys, on top of what she'd consumed at the lodge, but who was counting? Suddenly she stood — or rather jumped to her feet like a marine assaulting a beachhead — and began to gather her things.

What happened next still isn't clear. Somehow her hat had disappeared — that was the start of it. At first she just bustled round the place, overturning piles of scarves and down jackets, poking under the furniture, scooting people from the couch and easy chair, but then she turned frantic. The hat was a keepsake, an heirloom. Brought over from Flekkefjord by her great-grandmother who'd knitted it as a memento of Olaf the Third's coronation, or something like that. Anyway, it was irreplaceable. More precious than the Magna Carta, the Shroud of Turin and the Hope Diamond combined. She grew shrill.

Someone cut the stereo. People began to shuffle their feet. One clown—a total stranger—made a show of looking behind the framed photograph of Dry Gulch, Wyoming, that hangs beside the fireplace. "It'll turn up," I said.

Regina had scattered a heap of newspapers over the floor and was frantically riffling through the box of kindling in the corner. She turned on me with a savage look. "The hell it will," she snarled. "Somebody stole it."

"Stole it?" I echoed.

"That's right," she said, the words coming fast now. She was looking at Jill. "Some bitch. Some fat-assed jealous bitch that just can't stand the idea of somebody showing her up. Some, some—"

She didn't get a chance to finish. Jill was up off the couch like something coming out of the gate at Pamplona and suddenly the two of them were locked in combat, pulling hair and raking at one another like Harpies. Regina was cursing and screeching at the same time; Jill went for the vitals. I didn't know what to do. San Diego made the mistake of trying to separate them and got his cheek raked for the effort. Finally, when they careened into the pole lamp and sent it crashing to the floor with a climactic shriek of broken glass, Marshall took hold of Regina from behind and wrestled her out the door, while I did my best to restrain Jill.

The door slammed. Jill shrugged loose, heaving for breath, and turned her back on me. There were twenty pale astonished faces strung round the room like Japanese lanterns. A few of the men looked sheepish, as if they'd stolen a glimpse of something they shouldn't have. No one said a word. Just then Boo emerged from the bedroom, Mae-Mae in tow. "What's all the commotion?" he said.

I glanced round the room. All of a sudden I felt indescribably weary. "Party's over," I said.

I woke at noon with a hangover. I drank from the tap, threw some water in my face and shambled down to the lodge for breakfast. Marshall was there, behind the grill, looking as if he was made of mashed potatoes. He barely noticed as I shuffled in and took a window seat among a throng of chipper, alert and well-fed tourists.

I was leafing through the *Chronicle* and puffing away at my third cup of coffee when I saw Regina's car sail past the window, negotiate the turn at the end of the lot and swing onto the road that led down the mountain. I couldn't be sure — it was a gloomy day, the sky like smoke — but as near as I could tell she was hatless. No more queen of the mountain for her, I thought. No more champagne cocktails and the tight thrilling clasp of spandex across the bottom — from here on out it was stinking mouths and receding gums. I turned back to the newspaper.

When I looked up again, Boo, Josh and Scott were stepping out of a Jeep Cherokee, a knot of gawkers and Sunday skiers gathered round them. Draped over the hood, still red at the edges with raw meat and blood, was a bearskin, head intact. The fur was reddish, almost cinnamon-colored, and one ear was folded down. I watched as Boo ambled up to the door, stepped aside for a pair of sixteen-year-old ski bunnies with layered hair, and then pushed his way into the lodge.

He took off his shades and stood there a moment in the doorway, carefully wiping them on his parka before slipping them into his breast pocket. Then he started toward the cash register, already easing back to reach for his wallet. "Hey," he said when he saw me, and he stopped to lean over the table for a moment. "We got him," he said, scraping bottom with his baritone and indicating the truck beyond the window with a jerk of his head. There was a discoloration across the breast of his white parka, a brownish spatter. I swiveled my head to glance out the window, then turned back to him, feeling as if I'd had the wind punched out of me. "Yeah," I said.

There was a silence. He looked at me, I looked at him. "Well," he said after a moment, "you take care," and then he strode up to the cash register to pay his bill and check out.

Jill came in about one. She was wearing shades too, and when she slipped behind the bar and removed them, I saw the black-and-blue crescent under her right eye. As for Marshall, she didn't even give him a glance. Later, after I'd been through the paper twice and figured it was time for a Bloody Mary or two and some Bowl games, I took a seat at the bar. "Hi, Michael," she said, "what'll you have?" and her tone was so soft, so contrite, so sweet and friendly and conciliatory, that I could actually feel the great big heaving plates of the world shifting back into alignment beneath my feet.

Oh yes, the hat. A week later, when the soot and dust and wood-chips around the cabin got too much for me, I dragged out the vacuum cleaner for my semiannual sweep around the place. I scooted over the rug, raked the drapes and got the cobwebs in the corners. When I turned over the cushions on the couch, the wand still probing, I found the hat. There was a label inside. *J. C. Penney*, it read, *$7.95*. For a long moment I just stood there, turning the hat over in my hand. Then I tossed it in the fire.

James Purdy

In the Hollow of His Hand

Bess Lytle suspicioned something might happen. She taught the seventh grade in Yellow Brook, a town of 5,000, and was the teacher of the later "disappeared" boy, Chad, only son of Mr. Lewis Coultas.

Bess knew Decatur from when he had gone to school to her, but in actual fact she had known him since he was a small boy. Nowadays he often prowled about the town, but for some days now he had begun to station himself under the biggest of the elms and look over at the schoolhouse. The war had been over in Europe for some months, perhaps years, and back came Decatur from his service overseas, wearing his medals some days.

Then from standing under the elm staring at the schoolhouse, one day he opened the door of the same classroom where she had taught him some fourteen years before. Without saying good morning, how do you do, or even clearing his throat, he went to the back of her classroom and sat down in a vacant seat.

Bess Lytle had the yardstick in her right hand pointing to a map (for they were having a geography lesson), but for the first time in all her teaching career she was speechless, the yardstick held against the map, a surprise or confusion on her face as if the yardstick had turned to dust in her hand.

She turned from the map and stared at Decatur. He was a full-blooded Ojibwa Indian. When he felt like it, as today, he let his hair fall to his shoulders, and his eyes, usually half-closed, made most people look away—they felt, they said, his eyes made them think of the northern lights in winter, or a far-off explosion from a city refinery. His skin appeared to get darker each year. He had lied to the recruiting sergeant about his age and had joined the Army when he was only fifteen, in 1912.

One evening a few days after his first visit to her classroom Decatur returned late in the day when she was straightening up the room, washing the blackboard, picking up some of the gum and candy wrappers dropped on the floor.

"Which is Chad Coultas' seat?" he inquired almost before she was aware he had entered the room.

"Decatur!" She stared at him. He looked like a man enveloped in smoke.

"Which is his seat?"

Before she could collect herself she pointed to the third row, fifth seat.

Decatur went over to it and touched it quickly. Then he put the full weight of his right palm on the seat, and withdrew his hand quickly.

"What do you want to know for?" Her voice followed him going toward the door.

He turned sideways and stopped.

"Ah, I forget." Then he wheeled about after saying this, and his mouth opened showing the teeth which one dentist told him rich folks would give a half million dollars to possess, and look at you, the doctor said, not a penny in your pants pocket.

That was not quite true now, however. Decatur, with his mustering-out pay, had been buying up property, old houses deserted by very old people who had died without heirs. He would stay in one of the houses he had purchased for a few days, then tired of it, he would move on to another house he had recently taken possession of. He also bought several used but luxury cars. But in the end, no matter how many houses or cars he had, he always went up the small mountain near Yellow Brook and disappeared — into a tepee, people joked. But others said it was a house containing twenty-five rooms which he had built by hand, beginning with the foundation, and only recently the massive roof. He himself called it a tepee.

Bess was turning out the overhead light and beginning to gather up her keys when she thought all of a sudden back to the disgrace at Chad Coultas' maternal great-grandma's funeral. The old woman, who was over ninety, had died while opening a box of choice arrowheads she had taken down from the attic. While the elaborate funeral was in progress in her home, a fearful-looking and very old Indian man, clothed in a blanket and wearing a kind of headdress of deeply red feathers, had tried to gain admittance to the ceremony. He was turned away by an usher, but pushing past him, the terrible old man went directly up to Eva Coultas, Chad's mother, and said to her in a loud voice that the old woman lying in her coffin had Indian blood, and he could not therefore be denied admission. Lewis Coultas, seeing his wife being harangued by the Indian, lost his temper and struck the man, whereupon the Indian drew a knife, but only holding it, said, Your punishment will come, is already in preparation — both of you!

He disappeared as quickly as he had come. The old man was Decatur's grandfather, and had reared him on the death of the boy's parents in Canada.

Bess Lytle felt a cold dread come over her. In her troubled state, she forgot to lock the classroom door. And that night she slept hardly more than a few troubled minutes, for she kept hearing Decatur's voice: "Which is his seat?"

Bess Lytle was about forty, but her extreme thinness approaching emaciation made her often appear much younger. She lived in a fourteen-room house inherited from her grandmother, and next door in an even larger house lived her brother Todd. He had been gassed in the war, and for a time could not do any work at all, but then a dairy farmer finally hired him to distribute milk on a horse-drawn truck, and after a few years Todd came to own both the horse and wagon. He began to get his health back, and, not being married, he slept as a matter of fact most of his free time under Bess' roof. But he liked to think he had his own house to go back to. The townspeople criticized both Bess and her brother for keeping such big houses and permitting so many rooms to lie vacant. People felt they were putting on airs and trying to be gentry, when Bess was only a poorly paid public school teacher and her brother a delivery boy for a dairy. But neither of them would give up their property.

It is the year 1925.

"Decatur." Her brother Todd repeated the name as Bess told him the day's events. And he would shake his head like a very old man. In fact almost everybody in Yellow Brook pronounced the name the way Todd did tonight. The way people say *cyclone* or *syphilis* or *murder*. Nothing could be done about Decatur. He was the town Indian. They expected bad things of him, but not too bad. He always wore his Army medals to remind people he was a hero.

As he ate the Brunswick stew Bess had prepared for him that evening, Todd began to give an abbreviated version of a story that went the rounds in the illegal drinking places in town.

Bess held up her right hand to indicate she did not want to hear about something time should have buried.

"But time don't ever bury anything, Bess." Todd felt hurt she forbade him to tell the story.

But then Decatur's visits did not stop. He waited now outside the schoolhouse in his car, which he had cleaned and polished carefully so that it looked brand new. For a while nothing happened. Decatur would wait in the car, and then when all the children had gone home he would drive away.

Then one Friday when she let the children go home a bit early owing to a threatening sky, she saw it happen. Decatur as usual was sitting in one of his cars, this one a Stutz. And before she could rush out of the building to prevent it, she saw Chad Coultas go up to the car, talk to Decatur, and then get inside, and Decatur, like a racing man, stepped on the accelerator and they drove off at a breakneck speed.

She stood at the window, almost gasping. But then she remembered after all Chad knew Decatur. At least his mother Eva knew him, she remembered. Decatur had once worked around the big house in years gone past.

Nonetheless she went to the hall telephone and called Mrs. Coultas.

Mrs. Coultas was very queer on the phone.

"Did you hear what I said, ma'am," Bess kept repeating. "He got in the car with Decatur."

But there was no real response from the mother for a time, until finally Bess heard Eva Coultas say, "Thank you for your concern, Miss Lytle." The voice was cold, aristocratic, really cutting, uncivil. "I am sure young Coultas will be all right, Miss Lytle. Your concern is appreciated, but unnecessary."

That Friday evening therefore, smarting from the coldness of Mrs. Coultas, Bess asked her brother to tell her what they said in the saloons of Yellow Brook about Decatur.

Todd looked up from his supper. It was unlike Bess to want to hear gossip. He had not forgotten she had shut him up once before on this subject.

Chewing his beefsteak and lima beans for a time, he finally said, "Well, brace yourself. And I hope you can keep this to yourself," he added quipping, knowing of course how tight-lipped his sister was. "Well, then" — he removed his napkin from under his chin and lay back against the chair—"they say when Lewis Coultas, who was then and is still a real ladies' man, was gone for a spell to Denver, Colorado, Mrs. Coultas was taken very ill. At least she had sick headaches daily. The doctor had given her laudanum. She was barely conscious for two days. . . . It was then that Decatur . . ."

"Oh, no," Bess almost implored him, and laid her own napkin down on the table, but something in her expression told him to go on.

"Decatur was coming up the staircase when she was in very great pain, and she had carelessly left the door open, or left it open on purpose so that she could get to the bathroom more quickly for her nausea. . . . Decatur, who was a frequent visitor in past times, did many of Eva Coultas' errands, was in her trust, saw that open door. . . . And he slipped in, so goes the story, slipped in and out of her bedroom that day. . . . Then less, much less than a year later . . ."

"God in heaven," Bess whispered inaudibly.

"Less than I say a year later, for she had not been able to have any children after her first-born Melissa—young Chad Coultas was born."

"Chad Coultas, who is himself so dark-complexioned," Bess finished the recital.

"And who looks exactly like him," Todd went further now, "now that Decatur has come back and you can compare the two head to head."

"I must keep out of this," Bess spoke as if in prayer to an empty room. "Merciful God, yes, I must not interfere. . . . That voice of Mrs. Coultas. That ice-cold reproachful actually hateful voice! Warning me to keep out! To keep still!"

Forbidden by Mrs. Coultas' voice, Bess did and said no more. She was haunted by Decatur's face. She sometimes recalled during classwork that she had dreamed about him, but what she dreamed escaped her in daylight. It was his hair more than anything else, which he kept unusually tightly tied under one of his many hats, that stayed in her mind dreaming or awake. He always wore a very expensive hat, for the express purpose, she conjectured, of keeping his long hair safely imprisoned in the crown. His hands, too, resembled the paws of an animal, and each nail except that of the middle finger was blackened so that one might have thought someone had beaten his hands with hammers.

Then it began in earnest, the visits. Each afternoon he came, and each afternoon he was almost always in a different auto, waiting outside the school for young Coultas. Sometimes when the boy came to him, they only talked. Chad did not get in the car, though the door was opened waiting. And then the Indian would drive away with great velocity, his tires screaming. Bess noticed that Chad stood watching after Decatur for a long time, sometimes letting one of his schoolbooks drop to the ground and not bothering to pick it up for a long time, his eyes straining after Decatur.

"Oh, I must see Mrs. Coultas," Bess would say each evening to Todd. "Things have gone too far. I must brave her—for him."

"For him?" Todd barked. "You are a fool to see her when she's told you in plain English it's none of your business."

One day in class during an examination there was a loud thump in the room. Something had fallen out of one of the desks.

Bess saw the object lying beside Chad's feet. She waited, however, until the examination was over and she was busy collecting the papers, then quickly she stooped down to pick up what had fallen, but just then Chad grabbed the object as she almost was touching it. They wrestled with it, but as they did so the boy's hand closed more resolutely around the object.

Her rule was that pupils who dropped something on the floor from the desk, carelessly, during recitation or examination would have that object taken away from them and placed in a locked drawer until the year's end.

He would not release the object under any condition, but at last her greater strength allowed her to wrest it from him. She let out a funny sigh as she saw what it was now in her hand.

"Who gave this to you?" she thundered.

He glared at her.

"Who is the donor?" she cried so that all the pupils watched them. "You'll stay after school, Chad Coultas," she fulminated.

The object she held was marked *Bear grease*.

So he was kept after school that day. Seated close together as she scolded and complained and he refused to speak, they watched the car waiting outside with Decatur in it. He wore an enormous new hat.

"I asked you," Bess went on as they both sat watching the waiting car, "I asked you and I expect an answer. Who gave this disgusting salve to you?"

"Disgust—" he spoke as if coming out of a drowse.

"We will sit here all night until you tell me."

Desirous then perhaps of leaving, despite his pride and rage against her, he mumbled, "Him out there in the car—him."

"And who is him?" she wondered almost deliriously in her pique.

"Decatur. He don't have no other name."

Bess stood up, and to her discomfiture the jar of grease fell to her feet. He astonished her by handing it to her.

"What does he come here for all the time, Chad, when you have a father and a mother?" She was almost imploring, beseeching him to explain it. Her hand tightened over the jar of pomade.

"Oh, do I now," Chad replied with a kind of savagery, and all at once he seized the jar of hair oil and, removing its lid, took a whiff of the pomade.

"You are insolent," Bess said without force or conviction. "And you are doing so poorly in your schoolwork. You spell like a small child, and you do not even know at this late date the multiplication table."

Not hearing her, he gazed tenaciously at the waiting car.

"I shall therefore have to see your mother."

"She won't care," Chad replied, his gaze never leaving the car. "Won't care about anything. See her!" he commanded then triumphantly. "I dare you."

"Chad Coultas!"

Wearily, also sleepily, she let him keep the pomade, but reminding him that the rule had always been that any object carelessly dropped belonged to the teacher until the year's end.

"He'd give me another," he whispered.

She gazed at him, then looked out again at the car. "No civilized person wears bear grease on his hair," she said. "No one!"

She gave him a look of dismissal. Then as he hesitated she almost shouted: "Go, go to him, and take the pomade along with you. I don't want it to stay in my classroom. Go, Chad, leave!"

She stood at the window watching the boy race out toward the car. He did not even greet the man at the steering wheel. As soon as the boy was seated and even before he closed the door, the wheels of the auto were moving, and they sped off like bank robbers.

Then looking back she saw that he had not taken the bottle.

She took off the stopper from the bear grease and smelled.

"Bergamot? Honeysuckle?" she wondered. She took a small daub and put it on her hair.

The day came finally when Eva Coultas agreed she would see Bess concerning Chad's poor grades and his general inattention in class, his truancy, his daydreaming, his sullen silence. Bess would even mention the bear grease probably. She would mention everything but Decatur. She had promised Todd she would not bring this up.

The big house of the Coultas family with the turret and the mansard roof had been standing as long as Yellow Brook. Mr. Coultas' family went back a long time, much before the Revolution. Mrs. Coultas herself came from across the river, from an even more slumbering village. Her mother had spoiled her, people said, hoping she would marry someone worthy of her beauty and refinement, her accomplishments as a singer and performer on the piano, and harp, and for a time the flute — she gave up the latter instrument on the grounds it spoiled her good looks. For some years after her marriage the doctor feared she would never be able to have children. After an excruciating delivery, she gave birth to a daughter, Melissa. Then the physician told her she would never have any more children. But after some years, to everyone's considerable astonishment, she gave birth to a boy.

"I have another child, you know," Mrs. Coultas began when Bess entered the front parlor. "Sit over there, why don't you, Miss Lytle, where the light is less glaring on the eyes."

Actually there was almost no light in the room. Mrs. Coultas sat in a small weathered Windsor chair, shading her eyes all the while.

"I suffer miserably from migraine," she reminded Bess. "But as I say, we have another child in the house. Melissa. She is very close to me — she was my first. She has helped raise Chad because I am so often ill. She looks after the poor boy, more than I, but she has not been devoted enough to his schoolwork, I am afraid. She has so many activities of her own. She is studying to be an actress."

Bess knew of course that Mrs. Coultas wanted to talk of nearly anything but Chad. She reminded the schoolteacher now of a beautifully rich plumaged bird which is trying to escape from an airless room into which it has wandered by accident.

"Yes, you are beautiful," Bess almost whispered.

"You couldn't help the boy with his arithmetic — in a special way, Miss Lytle?"

It was Bess' turn now to fidget and feel at a disadvantage.

"I have tried and tried," Bess reviewed her own failure with Chad. "But he so seldom pays any attention when I do give him extra time."

She felt at that moment she could smell the bear grease. "I had to give up helping him."

"Oh, I understand. He pays no attention to anything I say. And his . . . father . . . Lewis Coultas is always away on business matters."

A queer almost terrible look came across Eva Coultas' greenish blue eyes.

"But yes," Eva went back to the boy. "His mind is a thousand miles away."

Both women suddenly gave the other a look of riveting understanding as much as to admit they both knew where his mind was! And that they had known all the time where it was but no power on earth would draw the secret from them!

Mrs. Coultas had promised herself she would not mention Decatur by name as fervently as Bess Lytle had promised her brother not to do so also.

But there it was, the name on her tongue, and clasping and unclasping her beautiful hands adorned today only by one small emerald ring, she heard herself trespassing on territory she had forbidden herself.

She caught herself though in time and blurted out:

"Does he . . . daydream a good deal of the time, Miss Lytle?"

Somehow Bess Lytle was positive she had heard Eva mention the name of Decatur, so that, confused, she cried:

"Who, ma'am?"

Relieved by the seeming stupidity of the teacher's question, having escaped saying the dreaded name by so close a call, Eva said:

"Chad does nothing sometimes but daydream at our evening meal. Barely touches his food."

Bess nodded solemnly.

"But tell me, is he more restive now than before?"

There was such supplication in Eva's voice, as Bess would later report to Todd — such a prayer to have her worst fears either confirmed or extinguished by the teacher.

"Oh, he was restive enough before, Mrs. Coultas! But of course . . ."

Then resigned, steady, knowing she had to come to grips with it, Eva said:

"But he's more restive now that he is visited."

A great hot breath came from Bess' lips, combining relief and strength to go on.

"Yes, he's much worse since they see one another."

"Of course, that stands to reason." Eva pressed a handkerchief soaked in witch hazel against her nostrils.

"And, Miss Lytle," Eva steeled herself. "And these visits, as we call them, occur with frequency?"

Eva's eyes almost looked black at that moment from the increased width of the pupils.

"Oh, but he comes every day — to see him."

Bess gave the impression at that moment that she did not believe her own words, that what she said had been handed to her by a letter from the postman. She had never believed Decatur came every day to see him.

"Every day, I see." Eva's response sounded very far away, and the expression in her voice, if there was any, had no color or emphasis.

"Yes, he comes every day now."

Eva pulled on her ring, raised her hands slightly, and let them fall to her lap.

"It doesn't seem . . . right," the mother spoke too low to be heard, for Bess was going on with:

"In different cars. Each evening a different auto."

The mention of *different* cars somehow brought Eva out of her languor.

"And you allow Chad to go with him!"

"But no, Mrs. Coultas, of course not," the teacher too came out of her own reverie and confusion. "I cannot run after him, can I? I cannot watch him once he's gone out of the schoolhouse. The road is a good ten rods away from where I teach!"

"I am afraid, Miss Lytle, I am like my boy. I don't know how far a rod is."

"Well, it would take me some haste to reach Chad in time. And I could never force him to not go with him, could I?"

"In a different car each evening! And I was not told of this by anyone!"

The mother looked about the room like one expecting assistance from someone.

"I am sorry I have upset you, Mrs. Coultas. But I felt —"

"If Chad's father were only at home more often." Eva was now fully awake, and her eyes were brimming over with her tears. "He is the one who should deal with it! But I do thank you for coming. It was thoughtful, conscientious, deeply considerate of you. I frankly do not know what to do! He is as wild as . . ."

Both women gave each other a look of something like terror. They must have heard the sentence finished for them as if from another room, by an invisible speaker.

Eva rose then with the sentence not finished and shook hands with Bess.

"I do not like to cause anyone pain. But Decatur—" she spoke at last the name and brought to sound the man they had really been speaking of all the time. "Decatur," she repeated as if she had just now learned the name for the first time.

"We can do nothing, Miss Lytle!"

And to the schoolteacher's considerable embarrassment Eva took her in her arms and kissed her.

After the embrace, Eva brought from the table an envelope and pressed it into Bess' hands.

"But, Mrs. Coultas," the teacher protested. "This does not contain money, does it?"

Eva nodded.

"But then I could never accept it!"

"Cannot I give someone a gift if I so choose, Miss Lytle? When we are both in possession of this terrible secret, this terrible man!"

"But I am not allowed to receive emoluments from a pupil's parent. How would it look in any case, allowed or not!"

"But who would know, or if they knew, care, Miss Lytle? And when I am so desperate, you have shared my desperation today! You deserve it all!"

Bess Lytle laid the envelope very gently down on the table from which Eva had taken it.

Eva did not seem to notice her gift had been returned to her.

Forgetting all and any resolutions, the mother went on like one carried away:

"You don't know what the very mention of his name does to me, Miss Lytle!" Taking the teacher again in her arms, she said, "Help me, my dear, if you can. Help my boy, too, as you have in the past. I don't expect the impossible. But I need help and have no one to turn to for it."

Bess felt a kind of fear she had never experienced before. She saw there was something here and in Decatur's visits which she had no clue to.

She longed for Todd at that moment even more keenly than Mrs. Coultas longed for her husband.

Bidding Eva another good-bye, she hurried out of the house and almost ran down the street.

Chad and his mother usually took their supper alone in the big gloomy dining room. Mrs. Coultas did not even bother to have the hired girl remove some of the leaves of the huge table for their repast, and so they sat at a board which could have accommodated twenty persons easily. Mother and son sat, Eva thought, perhaps as many rods from one another as Miss Lytle was distant from the daily abduction of her boy. Chad's sister, Melissa, took her supper upstairs more often than not. She was always in preparation, she said, for a dramatic role in the Little Theater Guild.

Chad had already put his napkin in the silver ring and was about to ask his mother to excuse him when Mrs. Coultas said, "I must speak to you, Chad."

"About what, madam."

She flushed at the term. She knew that Chad and his sister got together upstairs and discussed her, and that the *madam* was like a concentrated drop of poison on his tongue.

"Bess has called today about you . . . I mean Miss Lytle." She corrected ashamedly her own familiarity in calling the teacher by her first name.

"Oh, well, Mother, as you always say, what does an old dried-up maid know about anything!"

Stung by the exact reiteration of her own words in his mouth, Eva for a moment could think of nothing to say.

She was about to give her litany, "If only your father were here," but the visit of the teacher and the rudeness of Chad reduced her to a kind of moody silence.

"Chad," she began, but she had not quite regained mastery of her voice.

"I'm still here, Mother."

When she still said nothing, perhaps a bit concerned, he said:
"Well, what?"

"You have failed in your mathematics again, and you withheld your report card from me."

"You only sign it when you are shown it, Mother. You never look at my marks or ask anything about my schoolwork. And Melissa is always too busy acting to help me with anything."

"You mean to tell me you have signed my own name to your report card, and handed it back unseen by me to Miss Lytle!"

He grinned at her.

"I think they call that forgery in law," she spoke in a low voice, an octave below her usual range.

He stared at her, unmoved.

"You are being escorted home every evening by a dark-complexioned man," she accused him in her low, rather terrible voice.

"An Indian," Chad pretended to be helpful. He noticed his mother color violently.

"This has upset Miss Lytle greatly."

"Oh, so I gathered. She watches me like a whole nest of eagles from the school window."

"I don't know what is to become of you, Chad. I swear I don't!"

She looked about the room in her old helpless manner.

"How did you meet this man, will you tell me!"

"Decatur?" He looked at her very sharply then, his mouth compressing itself into a bitter smile.

"What has he said to you?" Mrs. Coultas whispered, watching that smile.

"He has hardly said ten words to me. I supposed," he went on lethargically, "that my dad sent him to see I got home all right."

"Your dad!" Her anger mounted at this patent prevarication. "Your dad knows no such person."

"What makes you think he don't?" he pressed her.

"What makes me think anything! Have you looked at this person who escorts you home as if you were some young prince. What on earth do you think you are doing riding about with him in state! Chad, listen to me now, I forbid you to see this man. So does Bess, that is Miss Lytle."

"Shouldn't my own dad have some say in all this?" His eyes rolled loftily now as his insolence increased.

"Your dad," she said throatily, "is away." She rose now, not bothering to place her own napkin through the solid silver ring. "I warn you, if you go on seeing this . . . Decatur . . . I caution you, Chad, if you go on seeing him . . ."

He pretended to prompt her by looking sympathetic.

"If you see him again, young man, watch out, do you hear? There will be trouble."

"There's already trouble!"

She had turned her back on him before he said this, and now hearing this statement she wheeled about and faced him, her countenance burning.

"What has he said about me?"

"Who?"

"This swarthy companion of yours of course, who else! What has he said to you to make you dare speak to your own mother in this rude, unconscionable manner! Will you tell me?"

"I told you," he replied brazenly, "he does not say ten words. He probably can only speak Algonquin!" He laughed mischievously, even hatefully.

Mrs. Coultas studied her own son's dark features. Ever since the boy could remember, it had seemed his mother only looked at him sideways—while his dad looked at him straightforwardly. But now she stared holes through him. As a result of such scrutiny he felt his own left hand slowly touch his face.

"You have always told me," he began somewhat appeasedly, "that my dad was the one who made the rules and shot the orders. Until I hear from him about Decatur I will go on seeing him, go on doing as I please. You have no jurisdiction over me." He almost screamed out these last words. "You don't know what you're doing, or saying. So go to bed. Do you hear? Go to bed. I will see who I please until the King returns."

"The King!" she shouted as if he had blasphemed. "You insolent, disrespectful puppy!"

She advanced so quickly he had not time to shield himself. She slapped his face three times resolutely. "You go to bed, do you hear, or I will call for help to put you there!"

"You'll regret this, madam. You will live to be very sorry for all you've said and done today. You mark my words."

He picked up the ring with the napkin and threw it across the table.

But Eva Coultas was not paying heed to what he said or what he threw. She was looking with appalled unbelief at his complexion which under the heat of their quarrel had turned a deep reddish copper.

Eva Coultas' elder child, Melissa, was so different in appearance from her brother, Chad, that no one would take them for even distant relations. There was, however, one similarity, which only a careful observer would take note of. Chad's right eye was the same sky-blue as his mother's and Melissa's, while his left eye was of a deep intense black. If one looked only at that right eye one would perhaps think Melissa and he related.

Melissa spent all of her free time studying to be an actress. She lived in front of the nine-foot mirror in her own room, and spent countless hours looking at herself in the downstairs hall mirrors. In fact, the Coultas house had more mirrors than many a hall of mirrors described in travel guides to European showplaces.

Melissa and her mother had a controlled but intense relationship. Since there was nobody else to confide in, both found themselves driven into the other's confidence.

Eva's only occupation now was sewing. She made beautiful quilts (some had won prizes at the county fairs), and she was always making dresses for her daughter and herself. Her one finger, Melissa once pointed out, was worn to the appearance almost of deformity, despite her always using a gold thimble.

"What am I to do with him?" Eva spoke as soon as Melissa entered the room the evening of her quarrel with Chad.

"Mother dearest, you will turn into a spider from sewing so much!" She leaned down and kissed Eva on the mouth, then glanced at her mother's present task, a petticoat so elegant it would have made Marie Antoinette's eyes sparkle.

"By him of course you mean Chad?" Melissa yawned widely.

Eva looked up at her daughter. Melissa was extremely good-looking, but, her mother could not help observing, she would never be so beautiful as she herself had been in her prime.

"Who else, darling, would I mean?" Eva put down her sewing for a moment. "He insulted me tonight at the dinner table."

"Oh, now, Mother, a stupid little boy like Chad does not know how to insult."

"And Miss Lytle is driving me mad with her complaints about him!" She shuddered, almost spat.

"Raw-boned, freckled, straight as a broomstick—our Miss Lytle."
Melissa quoted her mother's words of some time ago. Melissa had also
gone to school to the old maid.

"It seems," Eva said, picking up her work and then abruptly biting
a thread, "I am told, that is, Chad keeps company with an Indian
now."

"What Indian?" Melissa's voice was very soft, as if coming from an
adjoining room.

"There is only one in Yellow Brook," came her mother's choked
reply.

"One day about three months ago," Melissa began, speaking in a
kind of whisper.

"You may raise your voice, dear. No one is here at this hour."

"A few months ago," she kept her voice low, "Decatur came into
the house."

Mrs. Coultas' hands froze against the petticoat.

"You say into the house?"

"I was on the third floor—in my little theater room, you
know . . . I heard the door open. As Decatur stood immovable at the
foot of the stairs, Chad was coming down. Decatur acted as if he had
seen . . ."

"Yes, what, dear?" Eva's voice was hard and almost mean.

"Well, a ghost then," Melissa's voice rose in volume.

Eva Coultas almost whipped the petticoat across her lap.

"If Decatur could look pale, he would have been very pale at that
moment. But then, after all, he is almost as black as a Negro, isn't he,
Mother?"

"I haven't observed him that near."

An odd smile moved over the daughter's face.

"Well, then what happened? If you've gone this far!"

"Decatur began swearing when he saw Chad at the top of the
stairs. Or maybe he prayed. Anyhow he got out a whole string of
words."

"What words?" Eva sewed with awkward, obtuse fingers now.

"Oh, I don't know if I can remember, but he said, I think, '*It's true
then! Christ Jesus.*' He kept shaking his head, I recall, so that his hair fell
down about his shoulders."

Mrs. Coultas waited a moment, then wondered: "And what did
Chad do?" She looked directly at her daughter, though her own face
was burning.

"He looked queer also." Melissa's whole demeanor had been changing. She seemed to be back upstairs reading some stage part to herself.

"What do you mean queer?"

"Open-mouthed I guess. . . . But I couldn't see Chad too well. He had his back to me."

"I think you saw everything, Melissa. Look here." She put down her work. "That is how it began then. And you never thought to tell me! Melissa, you must talk to Chad about this. I am afraid Miss Lytle will make trouble."

"Miss Lytle?" Melissa spoke almost contemptuously, certainly incredulously.

"Decatur is taking him under her very eyes for drives each evening after school. Who knows if he will not begin coming here. And what would your father think of that?"

"He's Chad's father also, dearest," the daughter reminded her.

Eva flashed an angry glance in Melissa's direction.

In the ensuing quiet, Eva drew out the needle from the cloth and stared at it as if it had wounded her.

"Let's not push one another too far," Eva said after a long pause.

"I will never push you at all, Mother. I think you know that."

"Thank you, Melissa. You're always dependable in the end."

"It's you I love and need, Mama." The girl rose now and went over to her mother. "I'll do anything you ask of me." She tried not to look at the tears streaming down Eva's face.

"Dearest, if you could go to Chad, then," she struggled with her sobs. "If you could ask him, my darling, what he is doing with . . . Decatur! What they find in one another's company! What, in fact, do they *know*!"

"What they *know*?"

"Yes." Eva looked up desperately now at her daughter, her face like that of a spent swimmer. "Something is going on between them. It's not right for a young boy to meet a stranger like that every evening after school. Bess Lytle is right for once. I don't know what they are hatching together!"

"Mother!"

"Yes, Mother. I know you think I'm an hysteric. Very well. I won't sleep any more nonetheless until I know what this is all about."

Oh, you make it sound so sinister, darling."

"Yes, don't I? Well, let me tell you something then. It is sinister.

Oh, Melissa, your father, should he find out everything . . ." She gave Melissa almost a look of terror. "Your father is capable of driving me out of the house!"

"Father loves you, dear." Melissa's words were dry, toneless.

"Oh, Melissa."

"Yes, after all these years, all this time, he is very much in love with you."

"But if he knew everything, Melissa, do you think his love would withstand what we are talking about?"

"Father has his ladies, Mother."

Eva put down her work then.

"But his ladies are not very real, are they, dear? They come and go like the flowers and the little birds, and are gone forever. They don't come back to claim something. They don't come in cars, waiting for something."

"I'll speak to Chad and bring you his answer."

Melissa was too frightened now herself to say more. She took her mother's right hand, the one with the damaged finger, and pressed it, and went out.

"I do wonder at you so, Chad. I do."

Melissa was seated in a dilapidated but costly rocking chair, placed near her brother's study desk. A day had passed since her painful talk with her mother.

"What are you poring over so hard?" Melissa said when her brother did not answer her beginning words. Chad was staring at a book without really concentrating on what was written on its pages.

"Well, I guess I'm trying to do these arithmetic problems for old Bess Lytle," he muttered at last in reply.

They both snickered.

"I'm failing in math, you know."

"Oh, math, Chad. I could never get through plane geometry. The young man teacher finally took pity on me and passed me on to the next grade. . . . But Bess Lytle! To think she's still alive!"

"What have you been up to, Meliss?" Chad closed the arithmetic book and came over to her chair and lazily kissed her on the forehead and then on the mouth. She took his hand and pressed it against her breast.

"I was just about to ask you that, sweetheart. You're the one who's been up to something."

"So you've talked with Mother."

"I'm afraid Bess Lytle has stirred her up." Melissa smoothed down her dress, which had come far up against her legs, and she tightened one of her rings.

"You always look such a princess, Meliss. You ought to live in a castle, not in Yellow Brook."

He saw that something was bothering her, and her troubled face made him uneasy.

"You have nothing to tell me, your best friend?"

For answer he sat down all at once in her lap and threw his arms around her, then buried his face in her breast.

"I don't think I have," he mumbled against the perfume of her blouse.

"But, Chad," she put her hand through his thick black hair. "This man who meets you after school all the time, in different cars. You have nothing to tell me about him?"

"What do you want to know about him?"

"Why does he . . . meet you, Chad?"

"Why, isn't he a friend of Mama's."

"A man . . . who looks like him?" Melissa spoke with her mouth pressed against his hair.

At that moment, as if a bell had sounded to prompt them, they both looked up at the enormous mirror at the far end of the room and caught the reflection of Chad, his ebony-colored hair and coppery complexion against the paleness of his sister. Chad's hair had never looked so long or so black. And though only his left black eye was fully visible, his right blue eye too gave the impression of being also of a black hue.

Chad rose and moved a distance away from his sister. He looked over at the mathematics book, and then turned to half-face Melissa.

"I've grown accustomed to him waiting for me," Chad said at last.

"But perhaps you're not safe with him, Chad dear?"

He sniggered, and shrugged.

"Well, what do you two talk about?" she wondered.

"Oh, nothing," he said with his old sulkiness.

"Chad! You can't go riding around with someone every afternoon and not open your head!"

"I know. But that's what we do, Melissa. We don't say anything to one another except hello and good-bye. . . . But he looks at me a lot, sideways."

"I don't like it. I think you should stop it."

"What else, though, do I have, Melissa? Except you, of course. You know Mama pays no attention to me."

"Oh, Mama!"

They were both silent for a lengthy while.

"I should never have told you that day — you were too little — that Mama has had . . . lovers," she said. "I fear it spoiled your love for her."

"No, I love Mama," he said drowsily. "But she don't give me much in return."

"She's not very well," Melissa whispered.

"And you say nothing to this dark-complexioned man," Melissa summarized their talk. "You wouldn't *story* to me now, would you, darling?"

She went over to him and kissed him on the mouth. "Want me to help you with your math?"

"Owin' to your having done so badly in geometry, I wonder if you could."

They laughed.

"There is a mystery to all this, I suppose. But I don't want to know what it is."

Having said this, she held Chad in her arms for a considerable while. Then she kissed him abruptly and abruptly went out.

There came the afternoon, then, when Decatur did not show up for his appointed meeting with Chad. Bess watched the boy waiting under the biggest of the elm trees. A dowse of rain began falling, then abated to a sprinkling indifferent wetting. A westerly wind blew the stray leaves over the acre or so of school yard where the boys were released for recess.

Bess watched him on and on. Occasionally she would glance at the wall clock, now pointing to five. The factory whistles blew for quitting time. Mechanically she reached for the pile of examination papers she would need to grade that night and walked out of her classroom.

He fidgeted when he saw her coming toward him, and unaccountably put down his satchel on the ground and went over to the tree and touched its wet bark assiduously.

"He's not coming, and you know it!" Bess scolded, waiting near him. Chad hung his head.

"Do you hear what I say? Decatur's not coming this evening."

"You don't know that," he responded without turning away from the tree.

She picked up his satchel for him. "I will drive you to your mother's house."

"No, Miss Lytle, I will wait a bit longer." He was imploring, almost desperate.

She took his face in her hand and brought him before her. He studied the collection of freckles on her partly exposed chest.

"In any case, I can't let you stand here in the rain." She almost pulled him with her toward her car, then as he made no effort to go back to the tree, she went ahead, he lagging behind almost stumbling.

"This is not a good thing," Bess was speaking to him, as she opened the door of her battered Ford. "It is not a thing which can continue."

Turning to face him again, she said, "What does he tell you when you're together? I mean, you're with him every afternoon. What do you talk about?"

He shook his head.

"I mean," she began again when he made no answer, "what would your father say if he knew?"

"My father?" He spoke in a kind of surprise as if he were astonished to think she thought he had a father. Her own hand trembled on the steering wheel.

"If I didn't know Decatur from times past," she went on with her own thoughts, rather than speaking directly to him, "for I was his teacher too, you must remember. I say if I didn't know him from so far back I would be afraid for you. But I will speak to him certainly. It cannot go on, that's all there is to it. These daily rendezvous." The word, coming out unexpected like this, stopped her.

He almost dodged now when the word came out, as he often did in class when she shook or even slapped him for bad deportment or dropping something during an exam.

When she did nothing after she had said the strange word, he stared at her, as he often stared at Eva, with a kind of sullen, contemptuous insolence and hate.

"It is for your own good, Chad, that you don't see him."

They were arrived at the gloomy old Coultas house at last. She opened the car door for him, and he rushed out without a word, carrying his little satchel by one finger. As he reached the last of the twelve steps leading to the front door he turned around and waved to Miss Lytle who went on sitting in the car as if, he thought, she had turned for a moment into Decatur.

Then Chad plunged into the darkness of the great front parlor.

Sam Avery

Pigeons

The first time my husband Ralph disappeared he was trying to convince me to jog.

"Three miles," he said. "Two miles. One and a half. One. A quarter mile, then. Around the block, even," he said.

We were in the kitchen. It was morning. I was watching him bend and stretch and make a fool of himself in general as beginning joggers do.

He was warming up, and because he wasn't paying close attention to me I was watching him fairly intently. I was imagining that I had the eyes of a stranger and that Ralph was not my husband but someone mysterious and unknown that I was seeing for the first time.

If you knew Ralph, believe me, you would know what imagination that took.

For it seemed to me, then, that Ralph was constant and eternal. He was as inspired as the back of your hand. On that morning I would have sworn there was not the slightest bit of mystery to Ralph . . . to me he was and would always be the same person I had met four years ago, during a blackout.

Even in the blackout, I could imagine him instantly. He came up and bumped into me and I knew right then who he was and that he was the man for me.

At 5'8" we are exactly the same height. Looking at Ralph critically on this morning, however, I had to admit that he was balding and that his waist was thick where mine was thin. The T-shirt he wore clung to him and rose up his belly like a distraught cat I'd once had who was constantly chased up trees by a neighbor's dog. I could see where the cotton seemed to grab Ralph under the shoulders as if there were small paws there, digging their way up to his neck.

"Jog," he said.

"Never," I said. "Never, never, never, Ralph."

"You'd feel much better. Much, much better. And it's not hard. I'll show you lots of ways to keep going. Just when you think you're on your last lap, you'll be surprised. I have lots of tricks I can show you."

He shook his bare arm at me, as if to show he had nothing up his sleeve. And that was when it happened. For a moment, the sun was so bright I had trouble focusing. I could see his arm waving in front of me, and then I could not. In the diamond of light in which we were standing, Ralph dissolved before me . . . appearing and disappearing like a mirage.

For months before, although I could not have told you why, I had feared that Ralph might be taken away from me. And then, on this morning, I saw him disappearing—or seeming to disappear—in the morning sun. And suddenly I thought of what life would be like without Ralph . . . the drawn-out sense of loss that would come between me and the world. Instead of my marriage, which was a series of stops and starts and ups and downs, I would be left with a life as interesting as the slow turn of a wheel.

It was then I decided there was nothing I would not do to keep Ralph. Except jog.

"Just forget it," I said. "Run along and jog now, will you? You're making me nervous. I have things to do."

"You'll regret it," he said. "You'll be sorry." And then he was gone, leaving nothing but the slam of the screen door.

At the window, I watched him fade into the distance in his purple satin shorts. Although Ralph had not yet acquired a runner's body, I was sure that he would. And so I pictured his face on the bodies of the men I saw running through the park. Their bodies were like marble in flight. Sometimes the men waved to me, where I sat alone on a bench.

I was just imagining Ralph, or his face on one of those bodies, running toward me in top form and waving, when my mother called. To be polite, I listened to her for a few minutes, and then I began to tell her about the pigeons.

"There are pigeons in the walls. Behind the bedroom walls," I said. "Pigeons?"

"They live there," I whispered. I hadn't yet confessed my fear of the pigeons to Ralph, and talking to my mother on this day I realized for the first time how afraid I was of them.

What I was afraid of, or so I told myself, was not the pigeons themselves but the idea that they might enter the apartment and I would wake to find them strutting across my bed or flapping their dusty wings above me.

Once, on a crowded street, I had been surprised by the sudden arrival of a flock of pigeons a few feet ahead of me. It seemed as if someone had dropped them from above as a sort of practical joke, and despite myself I raised my head. There was nothing there but the flat sky. I had almost expected to see someone I knew, leaning out a window and calling my name.

The pigeons disappeared as suddenly as they had come. To me, it seemed as if they had appeared out of nowhere.

"Pigeons don't live in walls," my mother said.

"These do," I told her. "After all, Mother, they have to live somewhere." This is what Ralph had told me when I first discovered them. Leave them, he had said. They're happy. They have to live somewhere.

"Well, they won't bother you," my mother said. "Is it a family of pigeons?"

"Do pigeons have families?"

"I think so. But I'm not sure. They're true to their mates," she said. "Who cares?"

"I do," I said. I liked them better now that I was able to picture mother and father pigeons, happy husbands and wives bowing over their nests behind the walls.

"Can you hear them cooing?" my mother asked.

"It's almost a warble," I told her. "They don't sound like they do in the street."

"Well," my mother said, "after all, they have a fashionable address. They have to live up to it."

"Uh huh," I said. I could tell she was tired of talking about the pigeons. I don't know what we talked about then. After a while we promised to get together and hung up.

During this time when I was worried about Ralph disappearing, I went to the park every day and watched the men and women jogging. I tried to picture myself jogging along with them . . . one mile, two miles, three . . . until I would be good enough to surprise Ralph one morning by jogging along the river near our home with him.

The morning that Ralph first disappeared I brought a bag of bread crumbs to feed the pigeons. I was trying to convince myself I had a fondness for the things I feared — that was why I was so intent on watching the joggers in the park and feeding the pigeons. I had secretly purchased a paperback book that told me how to conquer all my fears in ninety days.

Slowly become familiar with what you most wish to avoid, it advised me.

While I was trying to catch the pigeons' attention, a middle-aged man in yellow satin shorts approached the bench across from mine and collapsed on it with a sigh. His hair was snow white and seemed to circle his head like a halo.

"You shouldn't just stop like that," I told him. "I don't think. I mean, aren't you supposed to walk around now for a while or something?"

"Who cares," the man said. Then he took something off his head. For a moment I thought it was a halo.

"What's that?" I asked, pointing to it.

"Sony Walkman," he said. "Headphones." He held them up to me. I had never seen such small headphones.

"Do you jog with those?"

"Keeps me going," he said. "I couldn't jog if I didn't wear them. I hate to jog."

"So do I," I said. "My husband jogs. He wants me to jog with him. But I won't."

"Good for you," he said. "Don't know why I said that. You ought to jog. Everyone ought to. Don't you have these?" He held up the headphones. "Everyone has them."

"I don't. May I try them on?"

"Sure," he said. He walked over and put them on my head. His hands were as comforting as a priest's. I felt as if I had been given a blessing.

"Oh," I said. It was all I could think of to say, I was so surprised. "Oh." He had been running to Ravel's *Mother Goose* Suite. "This is beautiful," I said. "I could run to this. No, I couldn't. Well, maybe I could."

"Well," he said, "got to run. Ha ha. You should get these for your husband. Tell him I said so."

"Who are you?" I asked. But he was already gone.

For some reason I had expected him to tell me something else. I had thought that perhaps he would give me a glimpse I would not otherwise have into my life . . . such as the angel Clarence provided Jimmy Stewart with in *It's a Wonderful Life* on the previous night's late movie.

As I sat on the bench I remembered Jimmy Stewart running through a town in which everything he has ever known is different and wrong because the angel has shown him what the world would have been like had he not been born.

All I wanted, all I ever wanted, was for someone to show me that.

The next day, Ralph was so excited by the Walkman I had bought him that he didn't ask me to jog. He had stayed up all night taping music.

"This is great," he said. "Great." He held the Walkman in one hand and did a small tap dance for me across the kitchen floor. "What gave you this idea? Was it expensive?"

"Not at all," I said. But actually, I had overdrawn my checking account and had to find a way to cover it by noon.

"Well," he said. "I'm off."

"Got to run," I said. "Ha ha." For some reason I couldn't get the man in the park off my mind—perhaps because I talked to so few people other than Ralph, my mother, and supermarket clerks.

Since my marriage, I had slowly lost touch with everyone I used to know. Without at first realizing it, I had become an untouchable among my woman friends, simply for marrying. And because of this I had worked all the harder at my marriage, wrapping myself up in it so completely that I had no time for anything else. My mother loved to point this out to me, reminding me that I had been the same way when I was younger . . . always striving to succeed at anything, however unimportant, if I was told I could not or should not do it.

When Ralph was out of sight I reached for the phone, intending to call my mother to see if she had any money I could borrow. Instead, however, I thought of Bob and Bob, friends I sometimes still did see because they lived in the apartment next door. Before I married Ralph, borrowing money from Bob and Bob had been a weekly habit with me. Don't do that, Ralph had said after he moved in. I'll give you money. Don't ask them.

Because I hadn't seen Bob and Bob—or Bobbie as one of them is called—for some time, I felt guilty about asking for a loan. So I decided to visit them under the pretext of finding out whether or not they had heard the family of pigeons.

"It's the stranger," Bob said when he opened the door. "It's the mystery neighbor."

"It hasn't been that long," I said. But I was unconvinced.

"How's Ralph?" they asked in unison. It always amazed me how often they could do this, apparently without signaling to each other. To me, they seemed the perfect couple.

"Pretty good," I said. "Do you *care*? Don't tell me you three are getting along."

"Actually, Ralph isn't so bad," Bobbie said. "Well," he said, "I suppose you need money."

"Me?" I said. "Can't I just come over and visit?" I realized, suddenly, that I didn't want to borrow money from them. I wanted to appear self-sufficient. I decided to call my mother later.

"It's about the pigeons," I said. "There are pigeons in the walls."

"We know," they said. "They're in between your bedroom and our bedroom."

"You *do* need money, don't you?" Bob said.

"I have to cover a check by noon. But it's money I spent on Ralph," I said. I tried to arrange my face into something like a wry smile. I swear I worked harder at justifying my marriage to Ralph than Bob and Bob did at explaining theirs to me. It was for this that I admired them.

"Hey," Bobbie said, "we don't care. We're liberals."

Inevitably, Ralph discovered that I had borrowed the money from "the Bobbies," as he mockingly called them. He insisted that he would go over himself to return it.

The night before he went over I didn't sleep. I was worried that Ralph would create a scene, announce his belief that his manhood was unquestionably greater than theirs.

Whenever Ralph would so much as run into Bob and Bob in the hall he would give a little snort, a disgusted sound, under his breath.

Oh, I knew what Ralph thought of them, all right. I knew what he thought of all men like them. It was hardly a secret.

But still, I loved Ralph. And day after day I worried more and more about losing him. One night, he decided to wear his Walkman while we made love. This solved a continuing problem — Ralph liked a little background music and I did not.

"What are you listening to?" I asked him. But he couldn't hear me. He was above me and it seemed as if the headphones he was wearing were a series of nuts and bolts, keeping him together. He seemed connected to them, as if they were a lifeline holding him to earth.

If the headphones should fall, or if I should reach up and take them off, I imagined that Ralph would dissolve and scatter like ashes. With my eyes shut, I saw this happen. He was there, and then he was not. It was just like in the kitchen, that first morning.

"What are you going to listen to?" I asked him the next day as he was getting ready to jog.

"What?"

"What are you running to? What have you taped?" I said. I brought my hand up to shield my eyes from the morning sun. I was standing at the front door, and Ralph was kneeling outside, lacing his shoes. I kept waiting for him to answer. I waited for the longest time. But when I brought my hand down and looked at him he was already gone. In the distance there was nothing I could see.

One day Ralph called at noon. "I'm going over to the track to jog at lunch," he said. "Got to stay in shape."

"What?" I said. He had never run at any time other than early morning.

"Who knows," he said. "I might enter a marathon is what I might do."

"Oh, sure," I said. "Get all the other electronic gizmo experts at the office to run along with you. It's better exercise than tapping phones or whatever hush-hush things you all get up to over there."

Ralph worked for a government agency. Beyond that I cannot say one word.

I could hear him sigh. For a moment, even across a telephone line, he seemed to slip away from me. When he began to speak, his voice faded in and out until there was only a whisper—a bit of memory—on the other end.

Gently, although I knew he was still speaking, I put the receiver back into its cradle. The phone rang again immediately.

"You hung up," he said.

"I think there was trouble with the line," I said. "I couldn't hear you."

"Why don't you call the phone company?"

"Somehow I don't think this is the phone company's problem," I said. "I don't think they're going to be all that interested. It's the pigeons, maybe," I said. "They make so much noise it's hard to hear anything."

"Well," he said. "Whatever. I'll see you after work, I guess. Have a good lunch, then," he said. "I love you."

At supper that night my ability to see Ralph came and went.

"I wonder if I need glasses," I told him. "You keep fading in and out, in and out." I sighed. Ralph, I knew, probably hadn't heard me. For a moment I wondered if I had actually spoken. "I'm so afraid of losing you," I said, looking down at the roast beef on my plate.

"Great roast beef," he said. He was pushing his knife back and forth across his plate, embarrassed.

The next morning I decided not to say anything, but what I really wanted was for Ralph to ask me to jog. I couldn't remember the last time he had asked.

When he wasn't looking I walked over to his Walkman and tried to see what tape he had in it. He no longer told me what he had taped. But the Walkman was empty. I looked up quickly and pretended to be busy with something else. Then Ralph walked over and picked up the Walkman. He inserted a tape, turning away from me as he did so.

It didn't mean anything, I know. If I had asked him and he had heard me, he would have answered. The tapes weren't secret, I kept telling myself. I had to keep telling myself this. I had started to imagine that he was hiding them from me. I have a good marriage, I said to myself. Ralph is not going to disappear before me.

"I must have cabin fever," I said.

"Get out more," Ralph said.

"I ought to. If I ever found a job I liked I'd go back to work. I'm imagining things."

"Things?" he said. He walked over and sat at the kitchen table with me. We looked at each other for a moment, and then Ralph put his head down next to my palm on the table's edge, pressing his forehead into the cool blue linoleum surface.

"My life, my love, my little pigeon," he said as he patted my hand.

About a week later, just as Ralph and I were getting ready to go on vacation, Bob and Bobbie's water bed broke. Their apartment was a mess.

"Tell them they can stay here," Ralph said. He wouldn't tell them himself.

"Really?"

"Sure," he said. "We'll be gone for a week, why not? You go tell them and I'll straighten up a bit."

It was a small thing, but it gave me a little confidence in Ralph and in our marriage. Don't ask me why.

As a result we had a great vacation. "Think of it," I said one day, "we don't even have to worry about the apartment since someone's in it."

"Do you worry about the apartment usually?" Ralph asked. "I didn't know that."

"Oh, you know. No big deal. One of life's little worries," I said. I was sorry to have spoken. I knew I had been worrying about far too many things and I didn't want Ralph to catch on. So I made a mental note to myself to do something outside the house each day. In this way, I hoped to rid myself of the memory of Ralph appearing and disappearing in the kitchen window's diamond of light.

On Sunday when we got home, Ralph offered to put away the luggage and put new sheets on the bed while I took a bath. When I was through bathing, he was just finishing up, circling the bed to straighten out the corners. He reminded me again of that cat I'd had. There was something curious and fastidious about his movements.

"This is great," I said. "This is nice of you to do this. Do you want me to finish?"

"That's all right," he said. He walked over and picked up his Walkman from the bureau. Nervously, he weighed it, transferring it from one hand to the other.

"You didn't have that all during vacation," I said. I hadn't noticed at the time, but he must have left it behind.

"It was under the bed," he said.

"It was? I didn't see it there. I was sure I packed it, now that I think about it," I said.

"Well," he said, "probably it's just as well you didn't. Might as well give it a rest. You smell so clean," he said, reaching for the switch that turned on the music.

Looking up at him, I had that feeling again that his very existence was somehow connected to his wearing those headphones.

I closed my eyes, imagined Ralph running toward me with nothing on but his purple satin shorts. I pictured his face, smiling, and his arm, waving at me, but placed these on the perfect bodies of the long-distance runners in the park.

And then it happened. Without Ralph realizing it, the headphones slipped from his head. I held my breath, certain that this was the moment when all my fears would come true.

When Ralph didn't dissolve before me, I listened, intent on discovering what music he had surrounded himself with. For a second, it was unlike any tune I knew, almost unlike music at all. In fact, at first I was certain that it was a tape of the pigeons, cooing to each other within the walls.

When I edged my head off the pillow, closer to where the headphones had fallen, the tune made itself clear to me. I knew those sounds, though they were not of my own experience, and they were not the rush of pigeons. What Ralph had managed to tape — what he was listening to while we made love — was Bob and Bob, rapt in passion.

On the ceiling above me, painted the day we moved in, was a map of the heavens. I let my eyes rest on each planet, briefly. I counted the stars. I measured the width of the moons. Finally, I thought about the men jogging in the park. I imagined Ralph's face on the bodies of other men rushing toward me. I thought about Ralph waving and jogging away from me. I looked up at him and saw how he seemed to float above me, the sound of pigeons everywhere around us.

When he caught my eye he was trapped under the heavens. He seemed to hang there, motionless. His face was as open and honest as the moons above us, and when he spoke, in a whisper, it was as loud as a wave and seemed to rush over my whole body.

"I feel as if I've been given something I never knew I could have," he said. "I'm sorry for what I can't be to you."

I just looked at him. I looked and looked until he disappeared completely and there was nothing there. I had been afraid of losing him for so long that it was no trouble at all to imagine he was gone.

Patiently, I stared until there was just a faint outline of Ralph reappearing. Then I let myself imagine him fading in and out, in and out.

"Those men," I said. "The Bobbies . . . you're not like that," I said.

I don't know how long we were in bed like this, the tape spinning at my side, Ralph helpless inside of me.

"I don't think you even wanted me to learn to jog, really," I said.

"You know," he said, "you know, really we're neither of us the people we wanted each other to be."

I looked away from Ralph then. I looked over at the wall. I could see right through it; I could see all the happy little nests . . . the pigeons two by two. For a long time we lay there, just like this . . . my hands on Ralph's shoulders like two small wings. I waited and waited to raise them. I waited for what seemed like forever, until the last possible moment.

Denis Donoghue

The Sublime Blackmur

In 1941 John Crowe Ransom published *The New Criticism*, an account
of certain critical procedures as practised by T. S. Eliot, I. A.
Richards, William Empson, Yvor Winters, and R. P. Blackmur. He
did not present his critics exemplifying a school or a movement: they
seemed, in his account, more different than similar. It was enough for
his purpose that they exhibited loose kinship while each went about his
particular business. Ransom had an interest in showing that a critic
might find his sustenance, and most of his vocabulary, in supposing a
privileged relation between literature and something else, some other
body of preoccupations and lores. Such a body would likely be found
among the social sciences, especially in psychology and history, or
among the stricter concerns of philosophy, such as those of logic. Each
of these critical procedures would be at best a partial affair, and each
would hold out a possibility which it didn't itself fulfill — that of a complete criticism — which Ransom called for in the final chapter. Wanted:
an ontological critic. Or, in the terms common to *The New Criticism* and
an earlier essay, "Criticism, Inc.," Ransom wanted a critic who would
assume that the writing of a poem is a desperate ontological or meta-
physical manoeuvre. The poet "perpetuates in his poem an order of existence which in actual life is constantly crumbling beneath his touch."
In his daily life, a poet has practical interests much the same as anyone
else's: he has to live, he has to use the materials at hand. Only in poetry
is he free to celebrate the natural or human object "which is real, individual, and qualitatively infinite." An ontological critic would respect
the poet for this tenderness and value the poem for being a special form
of discourse and embodying a special kind of attention. Ransom proposed that such a critic would think of a poem as having a logical object
or universal, which might be produced as an imagined scene or story,
and, in addition, "a tissue of irrelevance" from which the object would
not really emerge. The tissue of irrelevance would testify to the plenitude
of sentiment with which the object is suffused.

None of the five critics was sufficiently ontological, by Ransom's exacting standard in that vocabulary. But Blackmur could have protested that his interest in literature did not issue from a prior interest in something else. He was not, like Richards, a psychologist who resorted to literature merely for evidence; or a logician, like Winters, who judged literature upon its capacity to make impeccable statements. Blackmur's approach to literature was technical, it featured a concern for language and form, the adequacy of the arranged words to everything they had to do. Completeness was not, for him, the supreme value it was for Ransom. He never spoke, as Ransom often did, of the companionship of structure and texture.

But I am running ahead of myself. It is enough to say for the moment that *The New Criticism* placed Blackmur's work in company he was happy enough to keep, though in later years he repudiated the orthodoxy generally ascribed to him as a New Critic.

Blackmur's first notable steps in criticism were taken in 1927 when he became one of the editors of *Hound and Horn* and a frequent presence in its analytical pages. He reviewed T. S. Eliot, Santayana, and Wyndham Lewis. In 1929, on the occasion of the presidential election, he wrote an essay—in the form and spirit of *The Education of Henry Adams*—denouncing Herbert Hoover and recommending Al Smith. I have only circumstantial evidence for saying that, with Hoover's victory, Blackmur withdrew from overt comment on political matters and confined himself to literature, an institution he could at least hope to understand. Many years later he enlarged his survey again, pronouncing upon the social and cultural situation and the many forms of trouble-making he saw at large. But in Hoover's America he concentrated on reading literature and thought the best work he could do would be close to the page.

For the time being the only method he used was the one Eliot recommended, that of being very intelligent. High intelligence and exegetical zest amounted to the only credo he acted on.

Over a few years, Blackmur published close work on many writers, mostly modern poets but also a few prosers—Samuel Butler, Henry Adams—who caught his mind for one reason or another. Eliot was never out of his interest for long. Blackmur gradually took up the notion of writing a big book on Adams. After many years, still incomplete, it became a thorn or a burden or a broken promise. He made forays into it, published several essays on Adams, and left it unfinished upon his death; it has now been published in a form adequate to the gist of what he had to say. Henry James was a companionable figure to

Adams—*Hound and Horn*, like the *Little Review* and other journals, brought out a special issue on him, and he remained exemplary to Blackmur for the rest of his life in criticism.

These and other figures inhabited Blackmur's mind, and were always available for reference and provocation. He liked to set them in relation, one to another, as he set James in relation to Adams on the consideration that James's mind was willing to let the pattern of experience emerge as the amassed record of the experience itself, while Adams insisted on having the pattern in advance. "James imagined human reality always through dramatizing the bristling sensual record of the instance—almost any instance that had a story in it—and let the pattern, the type, the *vis a tergo*, take care of itself, which under the stress of the imaginative process it commonly did." The only problem was to know, or to sense, what would make a story, or how the story would stretch all the way from its constituents to the pattern they would, taken together, manage to imply. "Adams, on the other hand, tended in a given case to depend on his feeling for human type and pattern—for history and lines of force—as the source of drama, and hence saw the individual as generalized *first*." To put it another way—and Blackmur liked putting his perceptions in several ways—"Adams's set of intellectual instruments more or less *predicted* what he would discover; James resorted to instruments only to ascertain what his sensibility had *already* discovered."

Blackmur worked such relations for all they seemed to be worth. He wanted to know what would happen in his own mind if he set Eliot in relation to Dante and really worked the relation. Stevens and Pound: Stevens and Eliot: these comparisons were rarely elaborated, Blackmur was content to catch from them a glint, a sharpened insight good for the moment. In *Anni Mirabiles 1921-1925*—lectures he gave at the Library of Congress in January 1956—he nearly turned comparison into a method, and guarded himself against the danger by making most of the instances eccentric. So he compared Faulkner and Proust, Hart Crane and Stevens, Pound and Whitman (a common comparison, this), Cummings and Dryden, Auden and Tennyson, Byron and William Carlos Williams. Sometimes he surrounded a poet with two comparative figures, setting the glints running up and down and all around the town. Hart Crane was beset with Baudelaire and Whitman, Marianne Moore with Keats and D. H. Lawrence, Henry James with Joyce and Proust.

But no procedure amounted to a method or depended upon a

theory. Indeed, it is odd and therefore exhilarating that we are reading Blackmur more ardently than ever in conditions which he would have reproved. He flourished in an Age of Criticism, but he would not have borne in patience an Age of Theory in which literature and criticism are nearly dissolved in favor of the theory of each. In "A Critic's Job of Work" Blackmur compared criticism with walking, how both need a constant intricate shifting and catching of balance, and how neither is done very well. The fact that Blackmur, in his later years, walked little and that little with extreme difficulty makes the comparison the more telling. Most men in our day, he said, prefer "paved walks or some form of rapid transit — some easy theory or outmastering dogma." Not that he would have approved a hard theory; he didn't want a theory near him or pressing upon him any more than he wanted a dogma, though he accepted that some minds think themselves in need of both. Again in "A Critic's Job of Work":

> For most minds, once doctrine is sighted and is held to be the completion of insight, the doctrinal mode of thinking seems the only one possible. When doctrine totters it seems it can fall only into the gulf of bewilderment; few minds risk the fall; most seize the remnants and swear the edifice remains, when doctrine becomes intolerable dogma.

If you hand your mind over to a theory — he seems to say — you have only yourself to rebuke when your theory hardens first into doctrine and then into dogma. Even if it doesn't, you can't do anything with your theory but apply it, forcing it upon your poems as if they could have no other desire than to receive such overbearing attention. No wonder Blackmur thought the best kind of mind the most provisional, and Montaigne the finest exemplar of it, revelling in mobility of perception — "La constance mesme n'est autre chose qu'un branle plus languissant," Montaigne wrote, unruefully. Poetry does not flow from thin air, Blackmur said, "but requires always either a literal faith, an imaginative faith, or, as in Shakespeare, a mind full of many provisional faiths" — the last the best kind of mind, he didn't even consider it necessary to say. When he wrote his early essays on Adams, Blackmur made him seem far more mobile than he was, assimilating him to an idiom he resorted to, with more cause, in describing Montaigne. He described Adams's skeptical intelligence as "restless but attentive, saltatory but serial, provisional in every position yet fixed upon a theme: the theme of thought or imagination conceived as the form of human energy."

It follows that Blackmur's values can be made to coincide with attitude, a preference subjected to the mobility of mood and standing well back from a doctrine. He despised what he called "romantic egoism" and took it as asserting that "whatever I experience is real and final, and whatever I say represents what I experience." He was irritated by poems that proclaimed their spontaneity, and thought it no praise of Whitman and Pound to say that "each remained spontaneous all his life," because that condition, too, was just as congealed as dogma. He was not impressed by minds that offered "an easy vault from casual interpretation to an omnivorous world-view." Like Eliot and perhaps instructed by him, Blackmur thought that ideas as such had no place in a poem, and were a nuisance, killing the feelings they pretended to stand for.

It follows, too, that Blackmur values literature so far as it presents experiences in forms which enable us to know them. "All his life long," he said of James, "and in all but his slightest work, he struggled to use the conventions of society, and to abuse them when necessary, to bring himself directly upon the emotion that lay under the conventions, coiling and recoiling, ready to break through." The tragic character of thought, Blackmur said, is "that it takes a rigid mold too soon" and insists upon a destiny long before it has become necessary to choose one. Hence the value of irony, which postpones destiny and keeps our minds on the stretch, so that even when we succumb to an idea we are not so besotted as to stick to it, Hence, too, the supreme value of imagination, in any of the attributes Blackmur described as rational, dramatic, or symbolic. "In poetry, and largely elsewhere," he said, "imagination is based upon the reality of words and the emotion of their joining." What precedes the words — whether we think of it as obsession, self-delusion, or plain nonsense — doesn't much matter, so long as its presence in the poet's mind is provisional and not dogmatic. Yeats's magic doesn't matter, however seriously he took it and practised it, because it became rational as it reached words and assented to their reality. Dante's imagination "enabled him to dramatize with equal ardor and effect what his doctrine blessed, what it assailed, and what, at heart, it was indifferent to."

But I am merely indicating in Blackmur a broad preference, or a working prejudice, which helped him to get his work done and kept it fresh. Between the prejudice and the sentences of his criticism as they work together in particular essays, we come upon his idiom. Some have found it an obstacle, and wished he had written the kind of prose that cats and dogs can read. He was often as lucid as anyone else. He could even be aphoristic, when he had done whatever he could to wring the perception from its conditions and now, at last, could simply release it; as when he said, having worked through several sentences on Adams's faith, that "he had no faith, but only the need of it." Or when he said of Henry James that "he began at once to cultivate what his father had planted in him, the habit of response across any barrier—the more barrier the more response." Or, again of James and in excessive depreciation of *The Bostonians* and *The Princess Casamassima*, that these novels "have a strangely transformed air of protecting themselves from what they are really about." Or, finally, when he said that there is no sex anywhere in Marianne Moore's poetry—"No poet has been so chaste; but it is not the chastity that rises from an awareness—healthy or morbid—of the flesh, it is a special chastity aside from the flesh—a purity by birth and from the void"—and went on, a page or so later, to hear again the word "aside" and to say that her sensibility "constitutes the perfection of standing aside."

But there is still an obstacle; not, as a general thing, the quirky verbal play which Ransom and other readers of Blackmur have shaken their heads over, but the words and phrases which, because Blackmur uses them with an emphasis designed to be cumulative, amount in the end to his diction. Like any poet's diction, it begins to be recognisable only when its recurrence constitutes a problem. Till then, we take the words as they come.

But they come not in single file but in relations, sometimes specified, often assumed; hence the problem. Perhaps I can dispose them in categories, bringing together the words that are synonymous or nearly so.

There is, to begin with, the set of terms which refer to the "firstness" of experience, the earliest stirrings of sentient life before it knows what it is or why it is stirring. Sometimes Blackmur calls this "emotion," as in the sentence I quoted about James's use and abuse of conventions; sometimes sensation, momentum, intuition, and very often feelings or behavior, the last of which is virtually a technical term in Blackmur. "Behavior is the medium in which our lives take place"; elsewhere "the actual momentum in which the form of life is found." It is our impulse, and it is anarchy unless we want to mitigate the sentence and say, as Blackmur says in "Between the Numen and the Moha," that behavior "may merely want a different sort of order," different, that is, from any of the official sorts on offer. By any name, behavior is the cry of anything that is actual before it reaches the condition of being anything more or other. It is where all the ladders start.

The next stage — next because it has to be represented as coming after our behavior and offering to redeem it or somehow enhance it — marks our aspiration. If the first is behavior, the next is what Blackmur regularly calls manners, or "morals in action." Manners are the ideal insight, so far as it is embodied in society. Ransom associated a code of manners with the formal decency of a poem, and valued the latter as a sign in miniature of the former. Blackmur often settled for a phrase from Croce — "theoretic form" — to represent the sense we make of our feelings. "A theoretic form is a way of seeing: no more." No less, too; and what it sees is our feeling or our behavior so far as we want to make sense of it. Theoretic form is what we do to our behavior when we want to convert the actual into the real; or momentum into performance. "The great drive is in the craving of the actual to become real." We confront our behavior, and thereafter "our great fear is that our behavior may overwhelm us; our great delight is when we have transformed our aspirations into behavior; our fate is that we shall be mainly incarnations of our behavior." But our great delight can't be secured except by an act of the imagination, at once rational, dramatic, and symbolic. In some contexts Blackmur calls this achievement poetry or fiction; or, if he thinks of it in closely linguistic terms, he calls it rhythm, as in what would otherwise be merely the arrangement of syllables. Theoretic form, to try again, is how we construe our behavior when we try to make sense of it by bringing it into relation to different senses already in place: we give it a form and enact it. So in poetry: the poem is always at a remove from the feelings or the behavior that incited it. Steven's success "is due largely to his double adherence to words and experience as existing apart from his private sensibility." His great labor has been "to allow the reality of what he felt personally to pass into the superior impersonal reality of words." What is in its natural condition mostly a torment — behavior — is transformed onto the poem "where it may be rehearsed and understood in permanent form." So too in criticism: its perennial task is that of "bringing the work of art to the condition of performance." In pursuit of the theoretic form of our behavior, we resort to particular skills, which in a novelist are those of his art, and in anyone amount to what Blackmur calls the technical or executive forms.

So much for an ideal conversion of behavior into manners. If it could succeed, all our behaviors would be redeemed, our first steps would arrive, our scribbled first drafts would turn into live poems, the words vivid with the life we've given them. But in frequent practice our imaginations are incomplete or otherwise half-hearted. It would be too cynical to represent this condition as the inevitable third phase; inaccurate, too, because sometimes it doesn't obtrude at all and sometimes it has already obtruded before the act of imagination can properly get started. In a diagram it would be set aslant from the sequence of behavior and manners. But in any event it must be regarded as the perversion of manners, or their degraded form. In Blackmur's terms, the perversion involves the ousting of "morals in action" by "morals prescribed"; the congealment of forms as formulae; repetition and rote instead of performance. Here would come the ossification of feelings in the dreadful form of ideas. Reviewing Blackmur's *Language as Gesture*, Ransom took issue with him on the demeaning of ideas: "he is repudiating the ideas as ideas, and reckoning their usefulness for the poem." In Blackmur's later essays on the novels, especially those now collected in *The Lion and the Honeycomb* and *Eleven Essays on the European Novel*, he felt obliged, in Ransom's view, "to talk directly about those ideas, morals, faiths, which enter into the conduct of life," but the talk seems to me still technical and formal and never addresses itself to ideas as if they had the same substantive value inside the novel as outside. Blackmur never thought of ideas as having, within the poem or novel, the character they have outside. He always repudiated what he regarded as the rigmarole of theory, doctrine, dogma. Or, in a long-established distinction, he could not think of reason as on the same level of value as imagination. Blackmur sometimes spoke well of reason—"Reason is in substance all the living memory of the mind," he said in *Anni Mirabiles*. When he quoted a favorite phrase from Maritain, that "art bitten by poetry longs to be freed from reason," he insisted on saying that reason "is the great reminder of the constant and the grave; what sees the unity, the disparity, the permanent behavior of things." But generally he sided with Adams's prejudice in the *Education*, that "the mind resorts to reason for want of training." And he quoted Elizabeth Sewell's observation in her study of Valéry that "words are the mind's one defence against possession by thought or dreams; even Jacob kept trying to find out the name of the angel he wrestled with." Words, according to that sentiment, are the behavior of mind which thought, given its way, would domesticate. In any of these versions, reason, habit, and formula would suppress the imagination, and prescribe as order what is mere rote.

But Blackmur has a further set of terms. Assuming that the conversion of behavior into morals takes place, or that we can transform our aspirations into behavior, we haven't then come to the end of our possibilities. We have written our poem, perhaps, but there is still poetry itself as more than the sum of poems. We think of Kenneth Burke rather than of Blackmur when we take to the notion of "tracking down the implications" of our vocabularies. Burke, far more determinedly than Blackmur, proposes that we pursue the entelechy of driving our words "to the end of the line." But Blackmur, too, has a sense of ultimacy, though a more occult one than Burke's or Ransom's.

The names we have to invoke to document Blackmur's version of ultimacy are Longinus and, again, Montaigne. Longinus stands for the blow of the sublime, the height of eloquence far beyond any degree of it that could have been predicted. In "Between the Numen and the Moha" Blackmur brings Longinus and Montaigne together, on the strength of a passage which he quotes, in Zeitlin's translation, from Book I, Chapter 37 of Montaigne:

> Here is a wonder: we have far more poets than judges and interpreters of poetry; it is easier to write it than to understand it. At a certain level one may judge it by rules and by art. But the true supreme, and divine poesy is above all rules and reasons. Whoever discerns the beauty of it with assured and steady sight, he does not see it any more than the splendor of a flash of lightning. It does not seduce our judgment; it ravishes and overwhelms it.

Swayed by the last few lines, and sensing in them the tradition of the sublime which Montaigne resumes without having read Longinus, Blackmur posits an ultimacy of insight and eloquence under the auspices of imagination and not of reason. Here, he says, "we see the pride of imagination, which is confronted with reality, in the act of breaking down the pride of reason, which manipulates reality in a merely administrative rather than an understanding sense." The sublime is not the furthest reach of common sense but the ravishing of every sense. In another vocabulary it is epiphany or revelation, and in Shakespeare's vocabulary it is what Ophelia experiences so that she can say "O, to have seen what I have seen, see what I see." Blackmur thought he could at least point in its direction by calling it, in "Notes on

Four Categories in Criticism," symbol, and saying that "symbol stands for nothing previously known, but for what is 'here' made known and what is about to be made known." But the common understanding of symbol is hardly enough to send it into the abyss or wherever it has to go to register the sublime and the authority beyond prediction which is its blow. At least once, Blackmur called such authority God, God "who is reality by definition: the reality yet to be." Sometimes he thought its eloquence such that it must be called silence; and he wrote an essay, "The Language of Silence," not in the hope of annotating it but of testifying to it as a ravishing possibility. Or he called it, in every honorific sense, gibberish, on Stevens's authority who wrote in *Notes toward a Supreme Fiction* of "the poet's gibberish" in its relation to "the gibberish of the vulgate." Once, Blackmur called the sublime power Numen, meaning "that power within us, greater than and other than ourselves, that moves us, sometimes carrying us away, in the end moving us forward unless we drop out, always overwhelming us." Whether the power is in Nature or in us hardly matters. If it is in Nature, we take it to ourselves or supplicate it by magic or superstition or mystery. If it is in ourselves, we recognise it, by preference, in others, and so far as possible reduce its authority in ourselves. Or we are willing to come upon it in paintings and music and literature, or hear it in Myshkin's scream in *The Idiot*—this is one of Blackmur's instances—of which Dostoevski says that in it "everything human seems obliterated and it is impossible, or very difficult, for an observer to realize and admit that it is the man himself screaming: it seems as though it were someone else screaming from within the man."

Blackmur's figure of the sublime is a phrase: to be beside oneself. To be beside oneself is to be in ecstasy, released from one's demeaning contexts—"obsessed, freed, and beside themselves," as Blackmur says of certain animals and men in Marianne Moore's poetry. In "A Burden for Critics" he refers to "those forces that operate in the arts which are greater than ourselves and come from beyond or under ourselves" and, he almost says, drive us beyond ourselves if we attend to them.

How we attend to them is a desperate question. "We have lost," Blackmur believes, "the field of common reference, we have dwindled in our ability to think symbolically, and as we look about us we see all our old unconscious skills at life disappearing without any apparent means of developing new unconscious skills." We have a plethora of new conscious skills, lodged in psychology, anthropology, and sociology, but these are useless for any purpose except that of making trouble for ourselves—they "undermine purpose, blight consciousness, and prevent decision," they promote nothing but "uncertainty, insecurity, anxiety, and incoherence." Besides, so far as they are merely conscious skills, they have no genuine but only mechanical access to the very materials they claim as their own.

Where the old unconscious skills are to be sought is a hard question. With extraordinary daring and tempting effrontery, Blackmur associates them with what he calls bourgeois humanism, but a humanism still in some degree accessible to the sublime. He writes in *Anni Mirabiles*:

> Bourgeois humanism (the treasure of residual reason in live relation to the madness of the senses) is the only conscious art of the mind designed to deal with our megalopolitan mass society: it alone knows what to do with momentum in its new guise; and it alone knows it must be more than itself without losing itself in order to succeed.

If a political program is implied, it must be bourgeois humanism kept alert and uncomplacent by constant recourse to tory anarchy of spirit, so that what it speaks is a live mixture of common sense and the gibberish of the vulgate.

We can now place Blackmur's criticism, taking care never to domesticate it but to bring it into relation to our own concerns and those of his contemporaries. Blackmur's relations to James, Eliot, Ransom, Richards and Burke are well established but not, I think, well enough rehearsed. But it may be more useful to follow Blackmur in considering his relation to a critic with whom indeed he had little in common. Blackmur's review of *The Liberal Imagination*—it is in *The Lion and the Honeycomb*—discloses not only the differences between himself and Trilling but between himself and most of the high criticism written in his time. It is clear from the first paragraphs that Blackmur respects Trilling's criticism but regards it as too willingly taking its bearings from a social understanding of literature and criticism. "We see that he cultivates a mind never entirely his own, a mind always deliberately to some extent what he understands to be the mind of society, and also a mind always deliberately to some extent the mind of the old European society taken as corrective and as prophecy." The sentence is a little excessive; it doesn't say much more than that Trilling too contentedly thinks he is Matthew Arnold. But it leads to a more telling one. Trilling, according to Blackmur, "has always wanted a pattern, whether a set or a current, a pattern of relevant ideas as a vantage from which to take care of his occasional commitments." This begins to sound as if Trilling's mind and needs were akin to Adams's, needing a pattern in advance of any occasion; the unspoken consequence being that Blackmur himself corresponds to James and gains authority by the comparison. Of Blackmur, as of James, it may truly be said that he cultivates a mind entirely his own, or as nearly his own as its subjection to the syntax of prose allows. Blackmur doesn't want a pattern or a set, because he distrusts anything that offers itself as a formula, and he construes predictive capacity as merely setting limits in advance.

He has a further objection, which he merely implies. Literature best serves society by serving it only in the long run. It is under no obligation to endorse its official purposes at any moment or to sustain society's understanding of itself.

"The true business of literature, as of all intellect, critical or creative, is to remind the powers that be, simple and corrupt as they are, of the turbulence they have to control." To which Blackmur appends this admonition: "There is a disorder vital to the individual which is fatal to society. And the other way round is also true."

If we think of Blackmur's insistence on cultivating a mind entirely his own, we find it easy to be patient with his language even when it runs to exorbitance. "It is only the language we use," he says, "which must abbreviate and truncate our full discourse"—which is not much different from Pater's reference, in the Conclusion to *The Renaissance*, to objects "in the solidity with which language invests them." The impression of stability is a compromise worked out between language and our nerves. The abbreviations and truncations of our discourse are a similar compromise worked out between languages and our biological defensiveness. So Blackmur, insisting on a mind of his own, insists equally on working his language hard, forcing it to the twist and torsion which he calls idiom.

Blackmur's meaning for us is far more active when his style is scandalous than when it is ingratiating. We are reading him at a time of rampant illiteracy and rampantly conscious skills—which he regarded as much the same thing. Criticism's recourse to psychology, politics, anthropology, philosophy, and linguistics is rarely seen for the desperate device it is: what are all or any of these but patterns set in advance, or values having as their sole destiny that they are incessantly applicable? Meanwhile our literature remains, in every sense of the word that matters, unread.

Marina Tsvetaeva

Translated from the Russian by Paul Schmidt

Letters to Anatol Steiger

In the winter of 1936, after giving a reading in Paris, the Russian poet Marina Tsvetaeva was introduced to a younger poet, Anatol Steiger. Several months later, when he sent her a copy of his new book of poems, *Ingratitude*, she barely remembered his face. Her reply is lost, but it reached him just before he was to enter a hospital to be operated on for a tubercular lesion, and his response, also lost, must have been a cry from the heart. It was certainly a challenge to every passionate instinct in Tsvetaeva's romantic soul, and she responded with a full flood that joined a tragic sense of longing with a fierce maternal appetite. Steiger answered with a long letter detailing the history of his life, and it is with Tsvetaeva's reply to this that the following selection of letters begins. Of the correspondence that continued over the summer and into the fall, twenty-seven letters of hers and one of his survive. Thirteen of her letters were printed in the journal *Experiments* (*Opyty*) in 1955. The selection below is from those thirteen.

In these letters we can trace the growth of a passion in a poet for whom passion was the purpose of existence. It was a passion, as she wrote, fed not on bread but on fairy tales, and one for which she seems to have been perfectly designed. But the clarity of her mind and her prose have left us a record, these letters: rarely has pure romantic abandon been so meticulously and so relentlessly analyzed.

The forty-four-year-old Tsvetaeva and the twenty-nine-year-old Steiger met only once again, in October 1936, when he presumably told her what she had been unable or unwilling to understand from his biographical letter, and that he, out of whatever hesitation or weakness from his hospitalization, had not been able to make clear to her: that he was gay, and that no relationship beyond that of friendship was possible between them. Their correspondence ceased, and they never saw one another again.

— PAUL SCHMIDT

My first (my only) disenchantment — how can you address me by name-and-patronymic just like everybody else (the un-dear and the sincerely-yourers). Look, my name *beat* in every line of my letter. In my mind I wrote "Call me Marina," and if I did not write that in my letter it was only to avoid being obvious — and vulgar. Often — don't ever forget this — I will pass in silence over what shrieks to be heard. I had no desire in what I said to make my name stick in your throat — in your mouth, I mean, no desire to be stuck between name and mouth, almost *entre la coupe et les lèvres.* I was *sure* you would write Marina.

Your entire confession is the life history of a romantic. Even his hackneyed biography. Your entire life is your soul's history, and it contains but a single *Geschehniss* — your soul. Your *soul* causes and directs events. Your entire life is its purest authorship. And how is one to respond to it all: *all of you*, with your aunt and Fraulein Martha, and that ship's canvas that cut life and soul in two — and your poverty — and such a warlike ancestor — and that blue shirt from Nice and your sanatoried illness (you wear a ring — silver, by its dazzling whiteness — whose? what's on it? in it? behind it?) How can I respond to this *Geschehniss* if not to embrace it? *You entirely* with *all* there is inside you: your infinite heart and your inadequate lungs, for I warn you: to me, everything inside ("someone like you" — that's too cold . . . if I say "inside you" — you won't believe me) inside *us*, then, is totally valuable, and that includes our faults — inadequate lungs no less than a boundless heart.

And if I said *mother* — it was because that word *itself* is accommodating and embraces all, from the vastest to the most minute, and it demands *nothing.* A word before which *all, all* other words are barriers.

And whether you will or no, I have already embraced you here inside, where I take everything I love. I am never successful in making things out, since I *see* everything already *inside*. You are my capture and my catch, like this morning's remnant of the Roman aqueduct, with the dawn gushing through it, which I have immersed within me more truly and eternally than has the river Loing, in which the ruin sees itself eternally reflected.

This is my capture — no other's. In life, perhaps, I will never take your hand, which — I see — will be half-a-yard distant from me, wholly accessible, as accessible as the cigarette holder that's constantly in my mouth. To take hold of something is to admit that it's *outside* of you; with that movement of the hand we do not "admit" but withdraw: we move the object into the ranks of exterior things. All partings begin with that same movement of the hand. But *knowing* that, perhaps I will take it anyway, because how else can I *give*? . . . perhaps only in order to feel.

"I will come and show you." Child, there's no need to show me. And I tell you in advance—no matter what you have been, when you walk through my door I will love you despite everything, because I love you already; because that miracle has happened already, and the question now is only one of the degree of pain. The better you turn out, the worse it will be for me.

For *years*—I think eight already—I have lived in absolute indifference, I mean loving (a great deal!) this one and that one and the next one, doing all I can for all of them, because somebody has got to do something, but without the slightest joy—or pain: they go away to Russia, I see them off; they come to visit, I entertain.

Your letter has cracked open my icy crust, and beneath it instantly appear my own live depths—where, instantly, totally, *you* have been swallowed up.

———

"Do you know what kind of person *I am*?"

No, but I know who *I* am; there's enough for both, I mean for *all* the pain it will require: yours from me, mine from you, ours both, from both ourselves—you may vary it any way you like, the combinations are infinite—there's *enough.*

———

"You see, I demanded the impossible, knowing that I was demanding the impossible. . . ." Don't forget, what seems to us the impossibility of a thing is the first sign of its naturalness, its stands-to-reason-ness, in some other world. Look, we are all *astonished* that no one can walk on water; after all, water exists—and feet exist. But when Christ walks on the water, we feel immediate recognition and we become calm. How immediately, in dreams, we *recognize* the resilience of air (its ability to hold us up). And right now, isn't it natural that I write to you—natural, too, *what* I write? And wouldn't it have been monstrous of me (being *me*) to answer your letter differently? That *would* have been a miracle —an awful one.

Whatever isn't miraculous is monstrous, and if we are predestined to live with that monstrousness, that doesn't mean it's a law, it means only that we are beyond the pale of *our own* law.

———

(Still on the same theme, your "impossibility") . . . We play games, when it's with the wrong people (the right people *do exist*). It's all impatience (the soul has its own periods of time); we leave a present partner and find some other, inspire him to be our beloved. Notice, by the way, how wrong we are with the wrong one, how pitiable: unfamiliar, awkward, some sort of freak . . . Whenever you start turning away from your other (you feel like "turning over a new leaf" or letting yourself go to the bad)—leave him. He has become your poison.

Be only with one who confirms your sense of yourself (Does that mean be alone? Yes, it means be alone. No, it means be with me.) Choose whichever, both answers are simultaneous, and mine *to the utmost*.

I am writing on my last free day. Tomorrow—the 30th—packing, the day after, departure: first to Vanves, from there to that very castle where we were together today—in a dream. You and I, just ourselves, away from everyone else, that was what it was all about. I was fascinated by your brilliant pallor—in the midst of sunburned faces. Your face shone like silver, and by its splendor (I am nearsighted in dreams, too) I felt I recognized you. The castle is in the mountains, so it will be still easier for me to be friends with you (the castle is very dark, all surrounded by evergreens). That's why your face shone so bright.

M. T.

Vanves (Seine) 65, rue J. B. Potin
August 2, 1936, Sunday

Sweetheart! I'm writing you from Vanves, where I'll be until the 7th. If you are in a great hurry—wait a while longer. But if you won't—or can't—hurry, wait for my letter from the castle, where I will be taking you with me on the 7th at 7 in the morning, just as I brought you with me from Moret-sur-Loing on the 31st, just as I will be taking you with me everywhere from now on, right to the moment (though the event is little probable) when I take you to meet yourself. Then I'll introduce you: *Sie-Ihrer mit Sie-meinem, Sie-Sie mit Sie-ich*, and perhaps they will get along. Perhaps you will coincide with yourself, the way faces of criminals coincide when put next to one another, the way biographies of poets coincide. (There's the explanation of the cliché that must have embarrassed you in that letter. I sometimes think that you are me, and I can't explain that. When you become *not-me*—then ask.) But you are, at times, me—to the point of strangeness: you know the game in the rowboat; I have always used it to test myself and the other person as well (no, never!) whom would I throw—we throw—overboard (*always me!*) But there is one thing you still don't know about: the cry of a young woman in the 18th century—*Je sauverai mon mari et me noyerais avec mon amant!*

And nothing remains of her but that cry. And so everything remains. She remains—entirely. Isn't that worth all our poetry?

I speak to no one about my friendship with you.

M. T.

St. Pierre-de-Rumilly, Haute Savoie
Château d'Arcine
August 8, 1936

Sweetheart, this is truly a filial gambit: a complicated operation—a tubercular spot—surgery soon—the knife may kill . . .

If this is deliberate, I mean, to make me hurt, I mean so that I love you more—sweetheart, I hurt already anyway, and don't forget, I am *always* ahead of *everyone* in *everything*. . . . The train that everyone misses (and, what's more important, that every*thing* misses)—I am always on.

But there's another, an animal pain, anxiety for life—I am powerless before that knife, for it is not I who cuts, nor I who am cut; and if you wanted to stick that knife into me . . .

If you wrote this without thinking, then once again you do not fully value my reactions—I cannot consider this a simple (even though very upsetting) piece of news.

But in the final analysis, perhaps it's better you did write. For if you hadn't written until after the operation, then my first thought would have been: they *operated*, and I didn't know — and then would come the ice of estrangement. Better the live meat of closeness.

———

As soon as you're able to, write exactly what is wrong with your lungs — it is your lungs? I know tuberculosis, it is my *hereditary* illness. And what kind of lesion was it? Where? In a word, the whole history of your illness. And write about the operation itself. What did they use to put you to sleep? And what was the last thing you remembered? How did you wake up? What did you feel? Everything, everything.

———

I wait to hear from you when I can, as soon as it's possible — look, if you can't yourself, ask one of your family to write. A few words, that's all: alive, well, safe.

I embrace you, think about you constantly.

M. T.

St. Pierre-de-Rumilly (Haute Savoie)
Château d'Arcine
August 12, 1936, Wednesday

My first reaction to the sight of your letter: a blow to the heart, a lump in the throat, and until I had (carefully) opened the letter, the lump grew, and when I had gotten as far as the sight of your handwriting, my eyes were already clouded over, and when I had forced them — or myself — to wait and then read through, read right to the end, I could no longer see a thing: everything swam before my eyes. And I myself am adrift . . . this moment along with my eyes, and literally.

(I describe it as if it happened on Mars, or even Saturn, but I — for me, this is as *rare* as *never*.)

You know, my own, this was an operation for me too. Opening the letter was opening up my insides, and so I am as exact and as honest in *my* description as you in yours — and I won't write you any more today either, except

I love you

M.

(A postcard with a view of the Lion Bridge in Petersburg)

St. Pierre-de-Rumilly, Haute Savoie
Château d'Arcine

A long letter when you're stronger: a lot of thought in it, still more feeling; most of all, me, *myself, all of me* — and that, I'm told, is a *lot*, even for someone in the best of health. We'll wait. Until then, here's St. Petersburg to keep the correspondence going, and greetings, and assurance of the continuance of my thoughts — and I beg you not to write if it's difficult — and I beg you *to* write, if you *can*: what's your temperature, do you hurt, can you sleep, how is your appetite, are you able to read, everything, everything, but just a word about each, so you don't get tired, because I want to be a delight and a source of strength for you in all things, and never to make you ill or do you harm, and I'm ready not to write for a whole month and even not to think about you (to leave you alone inside me) if that's necessary.

My own, my little boy, right now you must *get well*, and put off all thought until later. Try to feel, please, even just these few days, as if you were in a huge thick cloud (Oh God, how much simpler it would be to come and hold your hand, instead of all these words!) (I spent all day yesterday copying the letter I'm writing you out of my notebook.)

If it will make you happy and won't tire you I will write you just a little bit every day. And the long letter when you say *on your honor* you're able. Are you able to read — books, I mean? I have a wonderful one, not too long.

Do you know Petersburg? Did you stand on this bridge when you were a child? Yesterday, wandering about my castle's enormous attic, I caught sight of some photos. I stopped to look; Tunsk lake — and two young men. And an inscription: photo by S. Steiger. Is that your father? I don't even know his first name.

God keep you! Get well, darling!

M. T.

(From an uninterrupted inward letter mailed from Château d'Arcine on August 18th.)

My castle, August 8, 1936

Don't be amazed at the gigantic strides of my approach toward you: I know no other.

You too are the creature of a single night, of a single look, and of an entire lifetime of longing — *Sehnsucht*, of the expression "here, take me." (Eventually there get to be a lot of those looks. Each one is a knife.)

You too want immediately not-to-live, so there won't be any afterwards, any future. (No continuation.)

How many times by now would we have died, if the gods had heard us!

Your youthful attraction for X, I mean the *pure passion of longing*: it's the leitmotif of your entire life. There can't be any other, for nothing else is ever present in the soul, since the soul itself is nothing more than that: pure passion of longing. The soul (when it is present; it doesn't ever not exist) is born ready — no, not born, it continues on with the entire load of unconscious and unavailing memories. Unconscious the way the hands recognize keys and shoulders, waves. And unavailing — all the mistakes all over again, as if we had never come to grief before. You can trace all that in our, in your own short life: what is it in life you are recovering from? Nothing. What are you learning? Nothing. And for *you*, in this, I am a *perfect* living example.

How many times does this time make? And yet don't I know that everything comes to an end, and don't I believe that *it* (what I have in me that goes toward you) will come to an end some day, some day I'll be let go, I will become empty of you: will become again an empty, cold, vacant house, an abandoned *domaine*?

All it took for you was to give me a sign — as willow trees do, along the edge of a road, through a speeding window — a sign: for I, at that willow-sign, rushed madly on, knowing everything and believing *nothing*.

———

In life there's nothing can be done about this, and you know it. Together, then, let us *not-live*: truly, militantly, victoriously.

———

My ring is entirely even, flat, wide with a center line, a cross on each side, and roses all around. And it will never be mine again.

———

If you could stick your hand into my soul as if it were the sea — *vous retireriez votre main pleine de vous.*

Don't be astonished. If all this were spread out over the years of our *non*-acquaintance (from the moment of your birth, or even from the moment when you first dropped in on one of my readings) it would appear completely *normal*, but now you're getting all of it at once — only don't be afraid, and don't break beneath it and don't *go mad.*

———

. . . All this time (since I got your first letter, and perhaps even since you wrote it) you and I ought to have been living together, never apart from morning to night and from night to morning — after all, it doesn't make any difference what you call that space *in between*!

No one has ever come to you with their entire being as I do now. The way only the sea comes, as itself entire — a floodtide.

———

Your letter (the most recent) is between the pages of the second *Faust*: it sleeps there, wrapped in the embrace of Goethe's eighty years, lulled by the play of those Nereids and Naiads. You are home. You live there. How many homes you have, besides Berne: myself, my notebook, my castle, Goethe's *Faust*. How loved you are, how *safe* you're kept! If you only knew.

———

Since we will never part anyway (I say *we* because otherwise there is *nothing*: I mean, only the usual thing, I and *ein Idol.*) since we won't part anyway, it's unthinkable not to be together.

But I want to be with you *absolutely*, without anyone else, absolutely alone in the enormous womb of this castle — and we would be waited upon by *hands*, like Alenky Tsvetochek in the story. Do you want to? And I know that all the former inhabitants of the castle would gather around us, drawn by the brightness and warmth, all the young women and young men (I will send you their portraits soon: I've stolen them for you). All the grandmothers in caps and the great-grandfathers in dressing gowns, and they would love us, and we would be king and queen of them all, and then at last we would drift off with them, back onto the very *walls*, and when the people came back — they would find no one there.

————

With you I want one thing only, an unreasonable something: not real dreams, but dream dreams, to go off with you into a dream and to live there. Because you too are a captive spirit as I am, and for the spirit (spirituality) *ein Geist: ein Gast.* I knew and understood this at your first call.

————

Still the 9th, Monday

Today, opening the door to my room, which I knew was empty, I stopped a moment on the threshold with a question in my mind: could it be? And before I had time to be surprised (at my own absentminded-ness) I knew: it is so inhabited by you, that if I am not in it, then, of course, you are.

————

August 10, 1936. Tuesday

When I thought today about that room in which you and I might live together, my mind kept trying out and discarding one after another all the rooms I've known, all those I don't know, and I suddenly understood that our room doesn't exist, because it will have to be a *non*-room: the negation, the opposite of a room: a dream-room, precisely, expanding and contracting, rising and falling according to the inevitability of what was going on within it, with a door when necessary, when *un*-necessary, the impossibility of a door. A dream room. (Do you dream?) A room we would recognize at once, and which would resemble, *a little*, in our memories, the rooms we grew up in.

————

I feel now as if I were my own castle, and you lived in it. Deserted, enormous, *protecting*, embracing you all around, but in a spacious em-brace, and you have so much room within it, and you can go anywhere you want, and there are no locked doors, and over it all is an enormous, empty, echoing attic with a corbeled Gothic vault, and above that yet another vault, and on the very top — a tower full of bells. That no one ever has to ring. They ring themselves.

————

Today, August 18, 1936,
Tuesday.

My enormous son (he's 11, almost as big as I) came in with his enormous stride: laconically: "You got a letter from Steiger." I, very businesslike: "Oh, that's nice." And now, officially set free, I am on my way to see a dog who loved me more than everyone put together, and whom I haven't seen in six years (Dogs remember for two years; intelligent ones, four. Dogs who love you remember for X years.) His name is Pojdsem (Czech: it means Come here.) I'll write you a separate letter about him, which will tell you more about me than all you've already read put together.

This one, the long one, I send off unread. It is yours, and I don't read other people's mail.

I embrace you, my *delight* (and my pain).

Château d'Arcine
August 20, 1936, Thursday

This still isn't an answer to your letter; I am almost never alone these days. Today I didn't even dare mail off as much as a postcard to you, because I mail other things, as I write them, by hand: not only do I not trust other people, but I can't even bear the thought of them passing through other hands (the postman doesn't count, he is like *fate*: the course of events out of our hands, like the course of clouds or the passage of armies). Every letter I send I follow with my mind's eye into the mailbox, as if it were a well where a stone could drop for a hundred years. *Nothing* is simple. That's why this isn't an answer to your letter. But you should know that I will never write you "simply" (I haven't any idea if all this is as necessary and important to you as it seems to me to be. But of course everything "seems," to me. And how powerfully!)

I will answer your letter, my darling, without fail, separately, for it's a substantial one: as serious as the outbreak of a war — or of peace, there's something in it that resembles a duel: these are the rules of the game you have set for me. You're completely right: we've played blind enough.

In my next letter I'll write you about one of my friendships — as it relates to you.

And I'll be waiting for a reply to my invitation to come visit me here — or in Annecy — whichever you prefer, although there would be more complicated, because I have no place to go there, and I wouldn't be able to stay overnight with you there. (But there is a marvelous lake there, and houses like dreams, and everything, including ourselves, is as it might have been two hundred years ago.)

It's time to close. But I still want to try to explain to you what I meant by: I'm longing for you. I'm never *without* you. For: to long for bread means to do nothing but think about it. To long without bread means in fact to be empty of it. Never in my life have I ever longed for someone I've been *without*. The first is repletion, the other is emptiness. I will never be empty of you. *I hope.* (It seems to me I have never ever been empty for a single second.)

Well, now it really is time to close.

M. T.

You shall have a little something to delight you, soon.

A reply to your ultimatum.   August 21, 1936, Friday
                                   St. Pierre de Rumilly, Haute Savoie
                                   Château d'Arcine

The unpardonable epigraph to your letter: "for such a short time it isn't worth the effort . . ." That really comes down, doesn't it, to the question — even to the accusation: might not this cloud that envelops you go on after it has dropped its passenger? Friend, clouds have their own laws that derive from nature itself, and a cloud is vapor, and if it is something more than vapor, then that's only because we inflate it — like the sixteen-year-old Lermontov did his *Sail* — with our own life's breath.

My relationship to you is not only a matter of spontaneous feeling, but of the mind, and of fixed memory, and of conscience (wait before you get angry! I know people don't like that word); I am now responsible to someone or other for you, and I have known that from the first word I wrote to you. Love for the time being, be friends for the time being—that's nonsense, what's crucial is not to *stop* loving. My relationship to you—beyond my *relating* to you: that's simply a wave that rolls on and on—is a matter of *decision*.

Otherwise it turns into conventional cream-lapping, a cat's preoccupation, not a human being's. That's why at the very beginning I used the word *Mother*. Which means, *precisely*: for always. My darling, of course the fullness of my maternal outpouring for you is an impossibility, otherwise I would never have been apart from you physically during these days (as now, I swear, I am not apart from you in my mind). *Payer de ma présence*—I am deprived of that happiness (happiness, by the way, is so *difficult* for me) where you are concerned. Deprived even of the blissful outcry of that eighteen-year-old eighteenth-century woman, where you are concerned, because "myself" and "*me noyer*" belongs to my family. But I conclude with the words of the mother of a man I have loved more than anyone, more *my own* than anyone, supremely—she was still young then—the mother of 76-year-old Prince Sergei Volkonsky (my poem-cycle *The Disciple* was written for him, if you remember it: "Oh, to be your bright-haired boy . . .") to the question of her dearly beloved adolescent son (her son, very timidly and respectfully—and probably *passionately*, for despite the stories and appearances he loved only women all his life, from his earliest years, beginning with his mother and ending with me . . .) anyway, her son was very strongly and passionately jealous of her friendship with Vladimir Soloviev: "You love him more than any of us, *more than me . . .*"

"My children, of course it is you I love more than anyone else—but in *the vastness of my soul . . .*"

No, friend, I am an absolutely ancient woman, and not contemporary to myself at all, but to something a hundred years ago—and beyond, as far as is possible. When my children were born (I am speaking of my son, I will tell you about Alya some other time) I was *bound*, as long as he needs me, to prefer him above all else: poetry, you, myself, with all the vastness of my soul. Factually and physically prefer. And it is thus that I purchase (have purchased all my life!) my own intrinsic freedom, my boundless freedom. *For this reason alone are my poems the poems they are.* In this freedom must you and I exist and live. Our kingdom is not of this world. Of course, if I were free, I mean if what is mine (my son) no longer needed me, I would scarcely be apart from you during these days of your life—but I have absolutely no idea to what extent you need me, my living presence. For if you don't need *that*, then I don't need it either. (Then you will learn that I am, simply, *not there.*)

If you have understood all that, then you now know in what area I could prefer someone else to you, or replace you. Only in the area of living life and kinship, and to put it more simply, of my *duty*. Inside me, my friend, in the freedom of dreams, you are now close to me beyond all else; simply, *you hurt more than anything else* (and I don't know any other measure of closeness). That place within me is yours, and is *sacred*.

. . . I don't know you. If you are one of those nightingales that can't live on fairy tales this won't be enough for you (letter after letter, and never anything alive, and another evening alone, etc.). One fine day you'll just fling all my letters and my feelings right in my face (in fireworks displays, it's called the grand finale). But then I am one of those other nightingales, the fairy-tale kind—I don't live by bread, only fairy tales, I've lived that way all my life, and my best love affairs were that kind too—so it's here we have to come to an agreement, for it's here that *der Hund* (of a possible divergence) *liegt begraben*: in the impossibility of my being really with you: of providing life for you. . . .

I don't know you, I judge according to myself. I am very good at doing without *anything at all*, much less good at doing with only a bit. Such interior consistency may not correspond to any practical consistency; still, it's better to be fully aware that it may not correspond to anything at all.

That's where my pain (where you're concerned) derives: not to be able to be for you all that I can and, within me, *am*, already. Because no matter how little I know how to live, I *know how to love* (to care for, to listen to) down to the smallest detail of a button sewn on before it comes off: to relieve another of the very *shadow* of care. Consistently—with my hands—to come to someone's aid. (I could never love a rich man: there'd be nothing I could do for him. No way to spend an entire day writing—or reading—poems to him.) For me, to love means to be doing something. With my hands.

You see. It's really very simple, perhaps even simpler than you wanted. Did you perhaps want to suffer because of me? That's impossible now.

"Then I won't play."

Then you might as well know that in every game I've ever played, *I* was the stake: right down to my soul's immortality. And I always lost: I always lost myself to somebody else, but since *I* was my own immortal soul, that was a lot for somebody else — too much — and the stake often stayed on the table, or was brushed by an elbow beneath it. There's your answer as far as playing is concerned. The only thing you have to fear is the seriousness of my game. A very wise Jew once said to me, talking about my early poems, thoughtless poems that lacked seriousness (I wasn't even twenty), said, very seriously: "You — not serious? In terms of ordinary human lack of seriousness, man's or woman's, you are a hole in the bottom of the sea. People ought to be *afraid* of you."

And he was . . .

M.

Yannis Ritsos

Translated from the Greek by Edmund Keeley

Signals

Later the statues were completely hidden by weeds. We didn't know
if the statues had grown smaller or the weeds taller. Only
a huge bronze arm could be seen above the terebinth
shaping an unseemly, terrible benediction. The woodcutters
went by on the lower road — they didn't turn their heads.
The women didn't lie down with their men. Nights
we would hear the apples falling into the river one by one; and then
the stars quietly sawing through that raised bronze arm.

Philomela

So, even with a severed tongue, Philomela recounted her tribulations,
weaving them one by one into her robe with patience and faith,
with modest colors — violet, ash, white and black — and as is always true
with works of art, the black is left over. All the rest —
Procne, Tereus with his axe, their pursuit in Daulis,
even the cutting out of the tongue — we consider insignificant, things
    we forget.
That robe of hers is enough, secret and precise, and her transformation
at the crucial moment into a nightingale. Still, we say: without all the
    rest,
those things now contemptible, would this brilliant robe and the
    nightingale exist?

Penelope's Despair

It wasn't that she didn't recognize him in the light from the hearth;
    it wasn't
the beggar's rags, the disguise — no. The signs were clear:
the scar on his knee, the pluck, the cunning in his eye. Frightened,
her back against the wall, she searched for an excuse,
a little time, so she wouldn't have to answer,
give herself away. Was it for him, then, that she'd used up twenty years,
twenty years of waiting and dreaming, for this miserable
blood-soaked, white-bearded man? She collapsed voiceless into a chair,
studied the slaughtered suitors on the floor as though seeing
her own desires dead there. And she said "Welcome" to him,
hearing her voice sound foreign, distant. In the corner, her loom
covered the ceiling with a trellis of shadows; and all the birds she'd woven
with bright red thread in green foliage, now,
this night of the return, suddenly turned ashen and black,
flying low on the level sky of her final enduring.

Marpessa's Choice

It wasn't by chance that Marpessa preferred Idas over Apollo,
despite her passion for the god, despite his incomparable beauty—
the kind that made myrtle tremble into blossom as he went by. She
never dared raise her eyes above his knees.
Between his toenails and his knees, what an inexhaustible world,
what exquisite journeys and discoveries between his toenails and his
    knees. Still,
at the ultimate moment of choice, Marpessa lost her nerve: What
    would she do
with a bequest as grand as that? A mortal, she would grow old one day.
She suddenly imagined her comb with a tuft of white hair in it
left on a chair beside the bed where the immortal one would rest
    shimmering,
she thought also of time's fingerprints on her thighs, her fallen breasts
in front of the black metal mirror. Oh no—and she sank as though dead
against Idas' mortal shoulder. And he lifted her up in his arms like a
    flag
and turned his back on Apollo. But as he left, almost arrogantly,
one could hear something like the sound of cloth ripping (a strange
    sound):
a corner of the flag was held back, trapped by the god's foot.

Vacant Lot

It was ground covered with large yellow thorns.
When the wind passed over it, there was noise.
A free void, uninhabited. The scorpion's tooth hidden.
Around dusk the place gave off flames.
Broken syringes and iron sparkled. The spiders
crossed the space from one thorn to another.
Above the thorns were large vessels.
Below the thorns were beaten children,
hatless old men, sullen women
with many miscarriages, slashed eyebrows,
a wooden cross at the throat. The old beggar woman
with the hole in her basket said: Lord, they now take away
even what we don't have. The eggs are white pebbles,
the rusks bricks, and I no longer have any place to hide
my embittered snake punctured by the thorns.

Disfigurement

This woman had a number of beautiful lovers. Now
she's bored; she doesn't dye her hair any more; she doesn't
remove the hairs with tweezers one by one around her mouth.
she stays in the wide bed until twelve noon.
She keeps her false teeth under the pillow. The men
circulate naked between one room and another. They often
go into the bathroom, close the faucets carefully,
by chance set a flower straight on the center table
as they pass through, noiseless, hideous, no stress now,
no impatience or impudence — the stress anyway
most easily discerned in its dying. Their heavy body hair
thins out, withers, turns white. The recumbent woman
closes her eyes so as not to see her toes
full of corns, disfigured — this once lusty woman.
She doesn't even have the strength to shut her eyes as much as
    she'd like,
obese, sunk in her fat, slack,
like poetry a few years after the revolution.

Contributors

SAM AVERY lives in Minneapolis. He is a graduate of the Iowa Writers' Workshop and a recent recipient of a Loft-McKnight grant.

FRANK BIDART's most recent book of poems is *The Sacrifice*, published by Random House.

PAUL BOWLES's autobiography *Without Stopping* will be reissued by The Ecco Press this fall.

T. CORAGHESSAN BOYLE's most recent novel is *Greasy Lake*.

GEORGE BRADLEY has won the Oliker Award and the Academy of American Poets Prize. His poems have appeared in *The Paris Review*, *The New Yorker*, *Poetry*, and elsewhere.

ANDRÉ BRETON was the founder of the Surrealist movement. Gallimard is preparing to issue his complete works.

JOHN & BOGDANA CARPENTER are the translators of Zbigniew Herbert's latest collection, *Report from the Besieged City*. They both teach at the University of Michigan at Ann Arbor.

SAMUEL CHARTERS is currently working on translations for Tomas Tranströmer's *Selected Poems*, edited by Robert Hass, to be published by The Ecco Press in 1986.

DENIS DONOGHUE is the editor of *The Selected Essays of R. P. Blackmur*, forthcoming from The Ecco Press.

STEPHEN DUNN's fifth collection, *Not Dancing*, was recently issued by Carnegie-Mellon. He is currently on a Guggenheim.

JOHN ENGELS's selected poems were recently published by the University of Georgia Press.

LOUISE ERDICH's first novel *Love Medicine* won the 1984 National Book Critics Circle Award for Fiction.

JEFFREY FISKIN, the writer of the film *Cutter's Way*, lives and works in Hollywood.

RICHARD FORD lives in Coahoma, Mississippi. His newest book, *The Sportswriter*, will be published by Vintage Contemporaries in 1986.

ALLISON FUNK's poems have appeared in *The Iowa Review*, *The Georgia Review*, *Poetry Northwest*, and other magazines. She lives in Beverly, Massachusetts.

TESS GALLAGHER's most recent collection of poems is titled *Willingly* and was published by Graywolf Press.

ZULFIKAR GHOSE was born in Pakistan in 1935. In 1969, on being invited to teach at the University of Texas at Austin, he emigrated to the United States. *The Incredible Brazilian* and *A Beautiful Empire* have both been reissued by the Overlook Press.

JORIE GRAHAM's most recent collection of poems is *Erosion*.

MICHAEL S. HARPER's recent book, *Healing Song for the Inner Ear* was published by the University of Illinois Press.

ROBERT HASS won the 1984 National Book Critics Circle Award for Criticism for his collection *Twentieth Century Pleasures*. He is the translator, with the author, of *Unattainable Earth* by Czeslaw Milosz, forthcoming from The Ecco Press.

ZBIGNIEW HERBERT's latest collection is *Report from the Besieged City*, published by The Ecco Press.

EDMUND KEELEY's translations of Yannis Ritsos, *Exile and Return*, will be published by The Ecco Press this fall.

GALWAY KINNELL was awarded the 1982 Pulitzer Prize for his *Selected Poems.*

STANLEY KUNITZ's eightieth birthday will be celebrated this fall in his native city, Worcester, Massachusetts, by a poetry festival in his honor. His forthcoming collection of verse and prose, *Next-to-Last Things*, will be published by Atlantic Monthly Press.

JAMES LAUGHIN's most recent book is *Stolen & Contaminated Poems* (Turkey Press) to be followed in 1986 by *Selected Poems* (City Lights).

DAVID LONG is at work on a short story collection to be published by The Ecco Press.

W. S. MERWIN is on the faculty of Cooper Union. His most recent collections are *From the Spanish Morning* and *Four French Plays.*

CZESLAW MILOSZ's new collection, *Unattainable Earth* will be published in the spring by The Ecco Press.

JOHN MORGAN teaches at the University of Alaska in Fairbanks. His latest collection, *The Arctic Herd*, was published by the University of Alabama Press; he has a chapbook forthcoming from Owl Creek Press.

ROBERT PINSKY's most recent collection, *History of My Heart* won the William Carlos Williams Award from The Poetry Society of America.

STANLEY PLUMLY's most recent collection is *Summer Celestial.*

FRANCINE PROSE's seventh novel, *True Stories*, is forthcoming from Pantheon. She is currently on the faculty of the Warren Wilson College MFA Program for Writers.

SUSAN PROSPERE was awarded the *Nation*/Discovery Award in 1984. Her poems have appeared in *Poetry*, *The New Yorker*, *American Scholar*, and *The Nation.*

JAMES PURDY's most recent novel *On Glory's Course* was nominated for the 1984 PEN Faulkner Prize.

JAMES REISS's most recent book of poetry, *Express*, was published by the University of Pittsburgh Press in 1983. He is finishing a third collection of poems.

YANNIS RITSOS is generally acknowledged to be the most important living poet writing in Greek; he is also one of the most prolific, having published some ninety-five volumes of poetry. His selected poems, *Exile and Return*, will be published by The Ecco Press this fall.

ZACK ROGOW has a new collection of poems, *A Preview of the Dream*, due from Gull Books this year. In collaboration with Bill Zavatsky he has completed a translation of *Earthlight* (*Clair de terre*), the first half of Breton's poetic work.

IRA SADOFF has work forthcoming in *The Nation*, *The New England Review*, and *Poetry Northwest.*

SHEROD SANTOS teaches at the University of Missouri at Columbia. His first book of poems, *Accidental Weather*, was chosen for the National Poetry Series.

PAUL SCHMIDT is currently translating the collected writings of the Russian poet Velimir Khlebnikov, to be published by Harvard University Press.

DENNIS SCHMITZ's latest volume is titled *Singing* and was published by The Ecco Press.

JAROSLAV SEIFERT was born in Prague, Czechoslovakia in 1901. He was awarded the 1984 Nobel Prize for Literature.

TOM SLEIGH recently won an Ingram-Merrill Foundation Grant. His first book, *After One*, was published by Houghton-Mifflin in 1983.

DAVE SMITH has published nine collections of poems, most recently *The Roundhouse Voices: Selected and New Poems*, and has been awarded a Guggenheim Fellowship, two National Endowment for the Arts Fellowships, and a literature Award from the American Academy and Institute for Arts and Letters.

TOMAS TRANSTRÖMER'S *Selected Poems* will be published by The Ecco Press in 1986.

WILLIAM TREVOR'S *Fools of Fortune* was published by The Viking Press.

CHASE TWICHELL'S new collection, *The Odds*, will be published by the University of Pittsburgh Press in 1986.

ERIK VESVILLE was born in Brno, Czechoslovakia. He builds harpsichords in Los Angeles.

DEREK WALCOTT'S most recent book of poems was *Midsummer* in 1984. His forthcoming *Collected Poems: 1948–1984* will be published by Farrar, Straus & Giroux this fall. He lives in Brookline, Massachusetts and in Trinidad.

C. K. WILLIAMS'S most recent collection, *Tar*, was published by Random House.

TOBIAS WOLFF was the winner of the 1984 PEN/Faulkner Prize for his novella *The Barracks Thief* which was published by The Ecco Press.

BILL ZAVATSKY has published *Theories of Rain and Other Poems* and directs the activities of SUN, a literary publishing company.

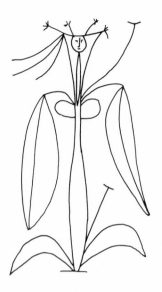

Non-Vicious Circle

TWENTY POEMS OF AIMÉ CÉSAIRE

*Translated,
with an Introduction
and Commentary,
by Gregson Davis*

The black Martinican poet Aimé Césaire, whose first major work was hailed by André Breton as "the greatest lyric monument of our time," has long been regarded in France as one of the leading poets of the 20th century. Moreover, the philosophy of negritude evolved by Césaire and his friend Leopold Senghor is an important bridge between modernism and contemporary Third World nationalist movements. The twenty poems in this book, presented in French with facing English translations, have been chosen to illustrate fundamental aspects of Césaire's thought, imagery, and style as these crystallized into a single, coherent system in the late 1940's and the 1950's. The translator's skillful commentary steers the reader around the pitfalls in Césaire's complex and idiosyncratic use of language, and emphasizes the larger themes and patterns of imagery that link these poems both among themselves and to the rest of Césaire's work. Illustrated with Picasso's etchings for Césaire's *Corps perdu.* $18.50

STANFORD UNIVERSITY PRESS

ANOTHER
REPUBLIC

8.50 PAPER

17 EUROPEAN
& SOUTH AMERICAN WRITERS

EDITED BY

CHARLES SIMIC
&
MARK STRAND

THE ECCO PRESS
18 WEST 30TH ST.
NEW YORK / 10001

RECENT POETRY

Atheneum

JAMES MERRILL
LATE SETTINGS

A new book by a 20th century master. His first since *From the First Nine* and *The Changing Light at Sandover.* Of the former Helen Vendler said "...no reader of this book can depart from it without a sense of a firmly idiosyncratic poet writing at the top of his form...."; of the latter Michael Harrington said "...to say that the future might well regard [it] as major is to make a very large present claim for a powerful and unique poem."   Cloth $12.95; Paper $6.95.

HOWARD MOSS
NEW SELECTED POEMS

An earlier version of Howard Moss's *Selected Poems* won the National Book Award in 1972. This new volume is twice as long, containing a generous selection from the four volumes following it. Reviewing his last volume, *Rules of Sleep*, Peter Stitt wrote, "Howard Moss is a wonder-ful poet; perhaps it is because he works in so quiet a mode that he has never been given the credit he deserves as a writer. But he proves as well as anyone could that it is not necessary to shout to make significant sound."

Cloth $20; Paper $10.95.

PHILIP LEVINE
SWEET WILL

A new book of poems by Philip Levine is always an event. *Sweet Will* is a book of sixteen poems including a long meditation of 500 lines. Philip Levine's last book was his *Selected Poems*, which included work from his first ten books. Of it Edward Hirsch wrote, "Philip Levine's *Selected Poems* is a generous addition to contemporary American poetry that we will be reading and studying for years to come. What I particularly admire about [his] work is its great emotional riskiness, its large, deeply felt commitments."

Cloth $10.95; Paper $5.95.

PETER DAVISON
PRAYING WRONG
New and Selected Poems

"Peter Davison has given us six books previous to this one, and the present volume is a compilation of these, plus a selection of newer poems. It affords us a chance to have a good, long time-sweeping look at the direction the man's life has taken, and how he has chosen to deal with the events of his life in terms of his particular attitude to his craft....Davison will not let things break him. His voice is his; he has earned it and can use it, and as a result is surely one of our better poets."—James Dickey.
Cloth $18.95; Paper $9.95.

DONALD FINKEL
THE DETACHABLE MAN

Donald Finkel's new book is a delight for the discriminating reader of poetry. He once again exhibits the unique sensibility and wit which have informed all his work and made him one of the true originals of his time. A brilliant poem called "The Last Hours of Petronius Arbiter," based on quotations from Tacitus and Petronius is a dazzling piece of work, as is "The Perils of Laughter," based on a passage about cataplexy; it is unthinkable that they could have come from any other poet. Cloth $14.95; Paper $7.95.

ERIC PANKEY
FOR THE NEW YEAR

The Walt Whitman Award winning volume of the Academy of American Poets, chosen by Mark Strand, who says of it, "These poems are beautiful and clear, and seem effortless in their execution. They are highly suggestive without sacrificing concreteness, and intimate without being obscure. The poems compel our interest as well as our admiration. A remarkably poised and accomplished first book of poems." Cloth $12.95; Paper $7.95.

MARVIN BELL
DRAWN BY STONES, BY EARTH, BY THINGS THAT HAVE BEEN IN THE FIRE

"The poems of this book have chosen what Wordsworth called 'the abundant recompense' for primal loss—an increased sympathy for one's fellow humans. To Bell this means coming to terms with the limitations of existence and love, form and tradition. He justifies his poetic vision by saying, 'But I was happy, and my happiness made others happy.' It still does."
—Phoebe Pettingell, *The New Leader*
Cloth $11.95; Paper $6.95.

GEORGE MACBETH
THE LONG DARKNESS

The governing notes of this new collection are feelings of regret and expectation, the grief and joy that spring from a death and precede a birth. These emotions are worked out against the changing seasons of Norfolk, England, where MacBeth now has firm roots. The poems have the sustained power and the true voice of a master craftsman who is willing to subdue all the resources of technique in the service of exactly what he wants to say. Cloth $13.95; Paper $7.95.

Now at your bookstore, or order from Atheneum, Dept. PO, 115 Fifth Avenue, New York, NY 10003
Include $1.50 postage & handling, plus sales tax where applicable.

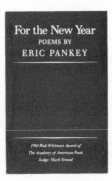

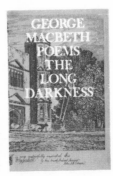

The Poetry Center

CALENDAR OF READINGS, 1985-1986

October

13	Athol Fugard	*Single tickets:	$8
21	Les Murray and Joseph Brodsky		$6
28	Friedrich Dürrenmatt		$8

November

4	Howard Moss and Cynthia Macdonald	$6
11	An evening of war poetry commemorating Veteran's Day with Anthony Hecht, Karl Shapiro, and Jon Stallworthy	$6
	A QUARTET OF COMEDIES	
18	Geraldine Page reads Chaucer's *Wife of Bath's Tale*	$8
25	*The Pleasures of Pope* performed by Richard Howard	$8

December

2	*Satirical Wit & Moral Discrimination:* An Evening of Jane Austen (Reader to be announced)	$8
9	*And Ever the Twain Shall Meet:* Roy Blount Jr. reads Samuel Clemens	$8
16	Two Greek Poets: Andónis Decaválles & Nanos Valaoritis	$6

January

6	Lore Segal & Russell Banks	$6
13	Eugène Ionesco	$10
20	Charles Simic and Rosanna Warren	$6
27	James Tate and Vicki Hearne	$6

February

3	Garrison Keillor	$8
10	Louise Erdrich and Madison Smartt Bell	$6
24	Carolyn Kizer and Al Young	$6

March

3	Peter Shaffer	$8
10	Günter Grass	$10
17	A Celebration of Irish Literature: Plays by W.B. Yeats	$10
24	Marvin Bell and Louis Simpson	$6
31	Gail Godwin and John Irving	$8

April

7	Italo Calvino	$8
14	Robert Bly	$8
21	Adrienne Rich	$8
28	Winners of the 1986 "Discovery"/ *The Nation* Poetry Contest	$6

May

5	Richard Wilbur	$8
12	Alice Walker	$8
19	Robert Penn Warren	$8

Yannis Ritsos

EXILE & RETURN

1967-1974

SELECTED POEMS

translated by

Edmund Keeley

$17.50 cloth

The Ecco Press
18 West 30th Street
New York/10001

hush.

David St. John.

"This is a remarkable first book; for beauty and poise it ranks with James Wright's The Green Wall; for originality it ranks with Ashbery's Some Trees; and for amplitude of feeling it stands alone, beyond any first book I can think of."
—MARK STRAND

David St. John's HUSH is returned to print in a new Johns Hopkins paperback edition. St. John offers "insight into the carnal drift of things" in twenty-five poems that are at once visionary and elegant.

"David St. John's imagination compels us precisely because the emotion has so moved us. His poems have the care of their convictions. They remind us again and again of the power in poetry when skill is equal to its source."—*Stanley Plumly*

"This is a brilliant debut, a crafted work of evocation, nuance, mature and honed response."—*Dick Allen,* POETRY

*Johns Hopkins: Poetry and Fiction**
John T. Irwin, general editor

$6.95 *paperback*

* send for a complete
listing of books in
the series

THE JOHNS HOPKINS
UNIVERSITY PRESS
701 West 40th Street, Baltimore, Maryland 21211

THE TALES OF
Anton Chekhov

Translated by Constance Garnett

Volumes 1-8 currently available

All titles available for $8.50 each or
$70.00 for series subscription.

The Ecco Press
18 West 30th Street
New York / 10001